CHALLENGE TO GENOCIDE

LET IRAQ LIVE

RAMSEY CLARK

PARTICIPANTS IN THE
IRAQ SANCTIONS CHALLENGE
AND OTHERS

International Action Center
New York

Challenge to Genocide:
Let Iraq Live

Copyright © 1998

ISBN 0-9656916-4-0

International Action Center
39 West 14th Street, Suite 206
New York, NY 10011

Phone (212) 633-6646
Fax (212) 633-2889
E-mail iacenter@iacenter.org
Web page http://www.iacenter.org

Library of Congress Cataloging-in-Publication Data

Clark, Ramsey, 1927-
    Challenge to genocide : let Iraq live / Ramsey Clark and others.
        p.   cm.
    ISBN 0-9656916-4-0 (pbk. : alk. paper)
    1.   Economic sanctions, American--Iraq. 2. Persian Gulf War, 1991--Economic aspects.   3. Iraq--Economic conditions.   4. Iraq--Foreign relations--United States.   5. United States--Foreign relations--Iraq. I. Title.
    HF1586.3.C53 1998
    337.567073--dc21

                                    98-14187
                                     CIP

CONTENTS

THE IRAQ SANCTIONS CHALLENGE

The essays in this book include both analysis and narrative re-porting by individuals who traveled to Iraq between 6-13 May 1998 as an act of international civil disobedience. They took $4 million worth of medicine to Iraq without securing a license from the United States government. Thus, they openly risked a possible penalty of twelve years in prison and fines of $1,250,000. The eighty-four-person delegation to Iraq was called the Iraq Sanctions Challenge.

The writers in this book, like the delegation itself, are a remark-able grouping. They represent a broad cross-section of the U.S. pub-lic. By their racial and national diversity, their class composition, and certainly by the values they assert, the Iraq Sanctions Challenge delegates are far more representative of U.S. society than, say, the Congress, the White House, the Supreme Court, or the Joint Chiefs of Staff.

Some names of the Iraq Sanctions Challenge delegates are well known around the world. That is certainly true of Ramsey Clark, the former U.S. Attorney General, Bishop Thomas Gumbleton of the Catholic Diocese in Detroit, and the Rev. Lucius Walker of the Pas-tors for Peace. But almost all the delegates are well known and re-spected activists for justice in their local cities and towns. The age of the delegates ranged from seventeen to eighty-six. They were Mus-lims, Christians, Jews, and atheists.

The Iraq Sanctions Challenge delegation received huge media fanfare throughout the Middle East. The delegates were treated with praise and admiration as they traveled through Jordan, Lebanon, and Syria. In Iraq, of course, their mission was greeted with enthusiasm at all levels of society.

Although they delivered vitally needed medicine to the Iraqi peo-ple, the Iraq Sanctions Challenge was not merely, or even mainly, a humanitarian mission. It was a political protest, by another method, by those who had organized literally hundreds of street demonstra-tions against U.S. aggression toward Iraq. The world might not know it, because the U.S. mainstream media does not report it, but hundreds of thousands of people inside the United States have participated in such demonstrations in the last eight years.

The eighty-four delegates to Iraq could rightfully claim to speak for tens of thousands of people inside the United States. That is how many people actually participated in this Challenge. Donations and medicines were collected in every state. Rallies, meetings, press conferences, and civil disobedience actions were held in support of the challenge. Unions and elected City Councils, in big and small cities, passed resolutions supporting the challenge and decrying U.S./UN sanctions as "an act of genocide."

In addition to being a political protest and pressure tactic, the Iraq Sanctions Challenge functioned as a first-rate fact-finding mission. This book presents piercing eyewitness testimony of the status of Iraqi society after eight years of airtight sanctions. It includes the freshest testimony on Iraq by experts in their field. Doctors, nurses, epidemiologists, water treatment specialists, scientists studying the effects of depleted uranium, and investigators into the causes for a new screwworm fly epidemic in Iraq are all included in this work.

The reader of this volume will find political and historical analysis invaluable for an understanding of the U.S. government's strategy toward Iraq and the entire region. Also included are a few articles and essays by individuals who, while not members of the delegation, have an intimate understanding of Iraq and an historic overview of the struggle against colonialism in the Middle East.

Brian Becker
Sara Flounders

ACKNOWLEDGMENTS

This book and the events it describes were made possible by the thousands of people who raised their voices against sanctions on Iraq and took part in the many activities that gave birth to the Iraq Sanctions Challenge. We cannot acknowledge them all. However, we hope this book, by chronicling the journey of the Iraq Sanctions Challenge, will serve as a lasting tribute to their tireless efforts. For their special role in gathering medicine, we thank American Muslims for Global Peace and Justice, Bruderhof Community, Jim Jennings of Conscience International, and Ann Whitman.

The Iraq Sanctions Challenge delegates who traveled to Iraq and contributed to the book need no further acknowledgment here. However, we would like to thank those individuals who put in long hours behind the scenes assembling, writing, editing, typing, formatting, proofreading, fact checking, indexing, and organizing the many components into a completed volume. Sara Flounders organized the book project. Deirdre Griswold Stapp edited the material in collaboration with a coordination and production team of Paddy Colligan and Sarah Sloan; a research team of Molly Charboneau, Pandy Hopkins, Shubh Mathur, Noel Saltzman, and Deirdre Sinnott; and a proofreading team of Fida Adely, Greg Butterfield, Gregory Dunkel, and Janet Mayes. Lyn Neeley designed the cover and photo section with help from Lal Roohk. Marie Jay coordinated indexing. Kadouri Al-Kaysi, Sharon Ayling, Brian Becker, Richard Becker, Mary Bernier, Pete Dolak, George Goloff, Zoltan Grossman, Sulaifa Habeeb, Carol Holland, Michelle Kimball, Eddie Lamas, Gloria La Riva, Ed Lewinson, Rania Masri, Henri Nereaux, and Tony Murphy provided assistance.

Iraq Sanctions Challenge volunteers helping in the New York office of the International Action Center were Paul Brown, Joe Cavanaugh, Danielle Chynowerth, Juliet Hayes, Tim Scott, Anil Sivakumaran, Marie Tscherne, Carl Vitale, Julie Wokaty, and Maryam Yaqoub.

We want to give special thanks to Fakhri Al Barzinji and the staff of International Graphics for their participation in, consideration and support for this project.

Photo credits for the front and back covers go to Mike Alewitz, Sara Flounders, Kristianna Jo Tho'Mas, and Lilia Velasquez. Other photographs taken on the Iraq Sanctions Challenge trip can be accessed on the International Action Center web site: www.iacenter.org.

Finally, this project would have been impossible without the encouragement and financial assistance of the individuals and organizations whose names follow. In particular, we are tremendously grateful for the generous funding provided by:

Initiators: Dr. Bob Allen and Family; American Muslims for Global Peace and Justice; American Association of Arab Chaldean Businesswomen; Ahmed El-Sherif, American Muslim Council-Midwest; Fisal Hammouda, Save the Children of Iraq; International Relief Association.

Benefactors: Joyce Bacon, Marina Drummer, Moneim Fadali, M.D., Bean Finneran, Rhoda Norman, and Elizabeth Sherif.

Sponsors: Adil Al-Hadithy, Jesse Dorsky and Family, Hossam Fadel, Bob Haynes and Gerri Haynes, Edwin R. Lewinson, Phyllis Lucero, Ethel Sanjines, and Michael A. Zagone.

Donors: Salah Al Askari, M.D., Carl Andre, Mary Ayers and Revis Ayers, Lee Booth and Philip Booth, John Braun and Marie Braun, Don Bustany, Hope Fay Cobb, Ruth Corroon, Bina Donakowski, Ronald C. Force, Cynthia Foster, David Glick, Connie M. Hammond, Houston Coalition Against Sanctions, A Job Is a Right Campaign of Milwaukee, Wis., Tareef Kawaf, Mary Stuart Kellogg, Merle G. Krause, Barbara Lubin, John B. Massen and Minerva Massen, Harvey Parhad, M.D., Yakub Patel and Zubeda Patel, People's Fightback Center of Cleveland, Ohio, Fran Rachel, Phil Runkel, George Salzman, Share-It-Now Foundation, Elizabeth E. Sloan, Al Strasburger, Kutay Ustuner, Evelyn Wolfe and Irving Wolfe, Workers World Party of Buffalo, N.Y.

Endorsers: Yoko Abe, Saladin Ahmed, Lilica Anderson, Edward S. Ardzrooni, Jr., Atlanta All-Peoples Congress, Nouha Azar and Robert Azar, David Bassett and Miyoko Bassett, Frances Boehm, Elden T. Boothe, Jack V. Bournazian, Buff Bradley and Cindy Bradley, Paul Brown, Kim Calhoun, Milton Carpentier, Casa Maria Catholic Worker Community, Christian Brothers of the Midwest Holy Family Community, Dr. Joyce Chumbley, Tona Cornette, Ron Dale and Sigrid Dale, Susan E. Davis, Joe Dowling, Carole Driver and Rod Driver, Beatrice Eisman, Gregory Elich, Lenore Feigenbaum, Irving Fierstein, John Fogarty, Ira Fogel and Susan Fogel, Lorraine Fons, Emily Fox, In Memory Of Thomas Frankland, Garberville CA American Legion Post #494, L.J. Greenfield, Bassam

Habal, Dr. Safei E. Hamed, Patrick Henry, Gene Hibbard and Mary Emma Hibbard, Majid H. Hindi, Tom P. Jabiru, Ray Kell and Vivienne Kell, Kamel T. Khalaf, Ph.D., Dan Kimball and Michelle Kimball, Bob Koenig and Tess Koenig, Mary K. Kral, Andre La Flamme and Carole La Flamme, Michel T. Lama, Sierrocca D'Florencini-Landry, Raymond J. Leszczak, Francis Maria, James Markunas Society, Kay McCann, Mark McGuire, John-Hans Melcher, Constance Metcalf, Maryse Mikhail, John Fredric Maria Millen CF, Joseph Mitchell and Susanne Mitchell, Pax Christi Minnesota, James C. Mosley, Paul O'Hanlon, Donna Panton, Anita Pepper, Ph.D. and Max Pepper, M.D., Tina D. Rhoades, Raj Sahai, Barbara Saint John, Marjorie Schier, Mary Winne Sherwood, David Singer, Frances Steadman, Dr. Ingrid Elizabeth Swenson, Luis Talamantez, William Thomson, Barbara Ulmer and Victor Ulmer, Roselva Ungar, Rae Vogeler, Marlys Weber, James A. Williams, Thomas A. Wood, and Nick Zunich.

CONTRIBUTORS TO THIS BOOK

Sapphire Mann AHMED, M.D., was a community health physician at Harlem Hospital and lived and worked in the Sudan opposing sanctions.

Kadouri AL-KAYSI is an Iraqi American who has traveled to Iraq with Ramsey Clark each year since the Gulf War.

Fatima ALI-KHAN is a graduate student at New York University pursuing a Masters Degree in International Development with a focus on the Middle East.

Christopher ALLEN-DOUÇOT is a founding member of the St. Martin De Porres Catholic Worker community.

Dennis APEL is a Catholic Worker in Guadalupe, Calif. He has served as the director of the St. Camillus Center for Pastoral Care in Los Angeles.

Johann Christoph ARNOLD has been minister of a Christian church community for twenty-six years and Elder of all the Bruderhof communities for the past fifteen years. He is currently working on his fifth book.

Barbara Nimri AZIZ is an anthropologist and journalist specializing in Middle East issues.

Brian BECKER is a coordinator of the Iraq Sanctions Challenge and the International Action Center in New York.

Richard BECKER is the Western Regional Coordinator of the International Action Center and an organizer of the Iraq Sanctions Challenge.

Johanna Marie BERRIGAN has worked as a nurse and physician's assistant and with the Catholic Worker in Los Angeles and Philadelphia.

Walter BLACK has worked with the Baltimore All Peoples Congress, the Congress of Racial Equality, and the United Brotherhood of Carpenters and Joiners.

Lee BOOTH is a Michigan mother of three with a life-long concern for justice who has been socially active since the 1970s.

Philip A. BOOTH practiced pharmacy at the University of Michigan and University Pharmacy while raising a family. He has been active in the movement for peace and justice since the 1970s.

Jack V. BOURNAZIAN works in San Diego as an immigration defense attorney. As a delegate, he lobbied the Humanitarian Law Project at the UN Commission on Human Rights on the issue of the sanctions on Iraq.

Marie BRAUN has been active for peace and justice since the 1960s. She is in Women against Military Madness, Women's Political Alliance, Pax Christi, and the Midwest Institute for Social Transformation.

Patrick CARKIN is with the Maine Council of Veterans for Peace and published a photographic essay on the Iraq Sanctions Challenge on his web page, ProActivist.com.

Sharon Black CECI is a hospice nurse, an active trade unionist, and a community organizer for the Baltimore All-Peoples Congress.

Fredy CHAMPAGNE is a Vietnam veteran who has led return tours to Vietnam through the Vietnam Veterans' Restoration Project and, as we go to press, is organizing a trip of Gulf War veterans to Iraq.

Ramsey CLARK, U.S. Attorney General in the Johnson administration, is an international lawyer and human rights advocate, the founder of the International Action Center, and author of and contributor to many books.

Hillel COHEN is an epidemiologist and delegate in 1199 National Health and Human Services Employees Union/SEIU, AFL-CIO. He represented the national union on the Iraq Sanctions Challenge.

Allan CONNOLLY, M.D., is a Canadian psychiatric physician and member of Physicians for Global Survival, the Canadian affiliate to the International Physicians for Prevention of Nuclear War.

Jenifer DIXON is a free-lance writer based in Washington, D.C., who works with Women's Strike for Peace.

Edith ECKART is with Veterans for Peace and has been an anti-war activist for twenty years.

Ahmed EL-SHERIF of Kansas City is president of the American Muslim Council Midwest and of Shifa International, a humanitarian group.

Sharon EOLIS, R.N., M.S., is a family nurse practitioner and certified emergency nurse in New York City.

Sara FLOUNDERS is a coordinator of the Iraq Sanctions Challenge and International Action Center in New York. She organized the 1992 International War Crimes Tribunal on the U.S. Role in the Gulf War and is an editor of *The Children Are Dying: the Impact of Sanctions on Iraq.*

Ken FREELAND refused to participate in the Vietnam War. He was an organizer for Committee in Solidarity with the People of El Salvador and is a member of the Houston Coalition to End the War Against Iraq.

Manzoor GHORI is a clinical laboratory scientist from India and a member of American Muslims for Global Peace and Justice.

Thomas J. GUMBLETON is Assistant Bishop of the East Region of the Catholic Diocese in Detroit. He was Founding President of Pax Christi, USA, from 1972 to 1991.

Berta JOUBERT, M.D., is a practicing psychiatrist in Philadelphia and community activist with the National Peoples Campaign.

Kathy KELLY has been to the Middle East eight times, including during the Gulf War, as a peace activist with Voices in the Wilderness.

Saad KHADIM is an Iraqi American restaurateur in Harlem and coordinator of the West Harlem Coalition.

Michelle KIMBALL is an Islamic Studies scholar and author of a comprehensive reference book on Muslim women. She is a member of Fellowship of Reconciliation and the Santa Barbara Peace Coalition.

Edwin R. LEWINSON, Professor Emeritus of History at Seton Hall University, has served as president of the Seton Hall chapter of the American Association of University Professors and the Northern New Jersey chapter of the National Federation of the Blind.

Sam MARCY, a Marxist theoretician and organizer, was a regular contributor to *Workers World* newspaper until his death in February 1998.

Rania MASRI is coordinator of the Internet-based Iraq Action Coalition. She is UN representative of the Arab Women's Solidarity Association and a national board member of Peace Action.

Mary Ellen McDONOUGH, B.V.M., is a Sister of Charity of the Blessed Virgin Mary and worked for seven years as a Catholic Worker in inner-city Kansas City.

Nabil MIGALLI, president of the American Arab Anti-Discrimination Committee-New Hampshire chapter, received the Alex Odeh Memorial Award (1990) and Martin Luther King Award for New Hampshire (1997).

Monica MOOREHEAD is a civil rights activist, writer for *Workers World* newspaper, and Workers World Party's 1996 presidential candidate.

Maria MOHAMMED is originally from Poland and has been a public school teacher for the past twenty years.

Sonya OSTROM is president of the Metro New York Council of Peace Action.

P. J. PARK, a high school student at Sidwell Friends School in Washington, D.C., helped organize a school assembly on the Iraq sanctions issue.

George PUMPHREY, a GI organizer during the Vietnam War, worked with the Black Panther Party and went into exile in Europe in 1972. He now lives in Bonn, Germany, where he has published a book on racism and human rights in the U.S. and other works against militarism.

Melysha SARGIS is a representative of Life for Relief and Development in Chicago, a division of the International Relief Association, and a writer and program director at the Arab American Action Network.

Deirdre SINNOTT is an organizer for the International Action Center who visited Iraq in November 1997 with Ramsey Clark and on her return spoke against sanctions on many campuses.

Sarah SLOAN is an intern at the International Action Center.

David SOLE is an analytical chemist and president of UAW Local 2334-Sanitary Chemists and Technicians Association.

Rev. Lucius WALKER of Pastors for Peace/Interreligious Foundation for Community Organization has led many challenges to the blockade of Cuba and Nicaragua and taken Friendshipments to Chiapas, Mexico.

Preston WOOD is a nurse in Los Angeles, an organizer for the National Peoples Campaign, and an activist in the lesbian and gay community.

ESSAYS
ON
WAR
AND
SANCTIONS

FIRE AND ICE

RAMSEY CLARK

> *Some say the world will end in fire,*
> *Some say in ice.*
>
> Robert Frost

I. U.S. Strategy for Domination of the Gulf

The reasons for U.S. actions in the Middle East and Gulf are no mystery. The British withdrawal from the region, beginning fifty years ago, left up for grabs the vast oil resources and strategic area where southwest Asia and northeast Africa front on Europe. The whole region began to be shaken by anti-colonial nationalist movements. U.S. policy makers, as an excuse for intervention, used the argument that it was exposed to Soviet seizure, with Israel unprotected on its eastern flank.

By 1953, the U.S. had placed the young Shah on the Peacock Throne in Iran. For twenty-five years Iran was the U.S. surrogate in the region, and the most powerful military presence, purchasing tens of billions of dollars in advanced U.S. weaponry. It also served as a major regional distribution center for American products. William Colby, former director of the CIA, called this the CIA's proudest achievement, even after the Shah's disastrous demise. It assured U.S. domination of the region for one fourth of the twentieth century.

Shortly after the popular nationalist revolution came to power in Iraq on Bastille Day 1958, the CIA formed a "health alterations committee" to plot the assassination of the new Iraqi leader, Abdel Karim Kassem. At the same time, U.S. generals in Turkey devised a military plan, code-named Cannonbone, for invading northern Iraq and seizing the oil fields there, the same oil fields targeted by the U.S. severance of areas of Iraq it called "Kurdish" in 1991. In 1963, Kassem and thousands of his supporters were massacred in a bloody

CIA-backed coup. Testifying before a Senate committee about the coup, a CIA member quipped, "The target suffered a terminal illness before a firing squad in Baghdad."

When Iraq nationalized its oil industry in 1972, the United States placed it on a list of countries that it claimed supported terrorism. In 1975, Iraq agreed to share control of the disputed Shatt-al-Arab waterway with Iran in a pact reached in Algiers. The United States and the Shah abruptly terminated their support for the Kurdish insurgents in Iraq, whose leadership abandoned the struggle and fled the country. But the fate of the Kurds left behind did not concern the U.S. government. As Henry Kissinger explained to an aide, "Covert operations should not be confused with missionary work."[1]

Over the years, the U.S. has supported Iran, Iraq, and most directly and fatally, Turkey, in assaults on the Kurdish people. In 1991, the U.S. exercised its new-found concern to protect the Kurds from Iraq by excluding the government of Iraq from most of the northwestern part of the country. It then assisted Turkey when the latter sent division-strength ground forces and continuous air assaults to crush the Kurdish people in that region. Yet a major part of the demonization of Saddam Hussein has been based on the false portrayal of Iraqi government policy toward the Kurds.

The one constant in U.S. policy through all the years was the determination to dominate the vast oil resources of this region, not only for their wealth, but for the economic and military advantage this gave over both rich and poor oil-importing countries. Among scores of statements reflecting this policy is a warning in 1977 from Senator Henry Jackson's Energy and Natural Resources Committee of the U.S. Senate: "A U.S. commitment to the defense of oil resources of the Gulf and to political stability in the region constitutes one of the most vital and enduring interests of the United States."

In February 1979 the Shah fled Iran, having killed as many Iranians as he dared, probably forty-five thousand in the previous year alone. The Iranian people had won their long struggle to overthrow U.S. control of their lives. That November the U.S. Embassy in Tehran, after months of protest demonstrations, was overrun by Iranian students, tens of thousands of whom had studied in the U.S. The small remaining U.S. staff was taken hostage.

U.S. policy then took another sharp turn. Adopting a supportive stance toward Iraq, National Security Adviser Zbigniew Brzezinski publicly encouraged Baghdad to attack Iran and take back the Shatt-al-Arab waterway—although just four years earlier Iraq had been pressured by the U.S. to cede control of this strategic route to Iran.[2] Washington expressed no moral outrage at the 1980 Iraqi attack on Iran. The attack served U.S. interests as a means of weakening Iran—where U.S. Embassy personnel were still being held hostage— and the anti-U.S. influence of its Islamic government in the Muslim world. War against the much larger Iran would weaken Iraq as well. Washington did not want either side to win.

"We wanted to avoid victory by both sides," a Reagan administration official told the *New York Times*.[3] Henry Kissinger has been quoted variously as stating, "I hope they kill each other" and "Too bad they both can't lose."[4]

In 1984 the United States increased its support for Iraq, becoming its principal trading partner by increasing purchases of Iraqi oil while encouraging Europe and Japan to do the same. The Reagan administration issued a still top-secret authorization for increased intelligence sharing with Iraq. Leslie Gelb, writing in the *New York Times*, reported that the authorization was interpreted as mandating that the United States "do anything and everything" to help Iraq prevail against Iran.[5] That same year Vice President Bush, the State Department and the CIA began lobbying the Export-Import Bank to begin large-scale financing of U.S. exports to Iraq. And in 1986 the U.S. dispatched a high-level CIA team to Baghdad to advise the Iraqi military. The Pentagon encouraged and helped funnel billions of dollars worth of arms to Iraq through pro-U.S. governments in Saudi Arabia, Kuwait, and elsewhere.

During the Iran-Iraq war, the Reagan administration removed Iraq from the list of countries it charged with supporting terrorism. This allowed U.S. companies to sell directly to Baghdad such "dual-use" equipment as jeeps, helicopters, and Lockheed L-100 transport planes. The Agriculture Department extended $5 billion in credits to Iraq through a program, authorized for agricultural purchases only, that illegally funded many of these sales. Among the items sold to Iraq were forty-five Bell helicopters originally built as troop carriers for the Shah's army.[6]

The eight-year Iran-Iraq war was a clear consequence of U.S. actions in overthrowing Iran's democratic Mossadegh government in the early 1950s and installing the Shah. He radically altered the country by pursuing U.S.-approved plans to make it a major industrialized nation. Then, after the fall of the Shah, Iraq was induced to attack Iran.

Isfahan, the wondrous city of Haji Baba, had been among the world's ten largest cities in 1500 A.D., with half a million people. It remained nearly the same size and culturally pristine into the late 1960s. By 1978 this city in Iran had grown to 1.5 million people, the great majority of them peasants who had abandoned the land and millennia-old irrigation systems to live in squalid slums, hoping for work in Bell Helicopter and British Motors assembly plants.

Nearly a million young men died in the Iran-Iraq war, which radically militarized and divided the entire region.

While supporting Iraq against Iran during the war, the U.S. was planning to intervene militarily in the region as the only way remaining to regain domination after the fall of the Shah. Central to new U.S. intervention strategies was War Plan 1002. It was designed at the beginning of the Reagan administration to implement the earlier Carter Doctrine, which said that any challenge to U.S. access to Middle East oil would be met by military force. In addition, the Pentagon had created the Rapid Deployment Joint Task Force in 1980, which in 1983 became U.S. Central Command (CENTCOM) and began secret construction of a more extensive network of military and surveillance bases in Saudi Arabia. Though U.S. military installations were already present in Saudi Arabia in the late seventies, the new facilities were more sophisticated, and would later provide essential in-place support for the assault on Iraq.

By the end of the Iran-Iraq war, the Soviet Union was withdrawing from Afghanistan and collapsing economically. It now became possible for the U.S. to intervene militarily in the region with little risk of Soviet opposition. Only the weak governments in the region and their Muslim populations remained as obstacles.

With the end of the Iran-Iraq war in 1988, contingency plans for war in the Gulf region identified Iraq as the enemy instead of the USSR. In January 1990, CIA director William Webster testified before the Senate Armed Services Committee on the growing Western dependence on Persian/Arab Gulf oil. In February, General Norman Schwarzkopf told the same committee that the United States should increase its military presence in the region. He described new military plans to intervene in a conflict. With Japan and Western Europe's much greater dependence on Gulf oil, the United States considered control over the region crucial to worldwide geopolitical power for decades to come.

In Schwarzkopf's early 1990 testimony before the Senate, he said that CENTCOM should increase its military presence in the Gulf region through permanently assigned ground forces, combined exercises, and "security assistance," a euphemism for arms sales. In 1989, even before this testimony, CENTCOM's War Plan 1002 was revised and renamed War Plan 1002-90.[7] The last two digits of the war plan, of course, stood for 1990. CENTCOM began devising war games targeting Iraq.

In 1990 at least four war games, some premised on an Iraqi invasion of Kuwait, were conducted before the invasion occurred. One of the first, a computer exercise called Internal Look, was held in January. In June 1990, General Schwarzkopf was conducting sophisticated war games pitting thousands of U.S. troops against armored divisions of the Republican Guard.[8]

In May 1990 the Center for Strategic and International Studies (CSIS), a Washington-based think tank, had completed a study *begun two years earlier* predicting the outcome of a war between the United States and Iraq. This study, according to the CSIS's Major James Blackwell (Retired), was widely circulated among Pentagon officials, members of Congress, and military contractors. Thus, far from being a surprise, Iraq's invasion of Kuwait had actually been the scenario for intense U.S. planning.

The cease-fire between Iran and Iraq took effect on 20 August 1988. Almost immediately the U.S. began a systematic propaganda campaign to demonize Saddam Hussein and prepare for its assault on Iraq. In early September, the U.S. announced that Iraq had used poison gas against the Kurds much earlier in the year. On the same day that Iraqi Foreign Minister Sa'dun Hammadi was scheduled to meet Secretary of State George Shultz in Washington for the first time since the war, State Department spokesperson Charles Redman made a blistering attack on Iraq, charging the U.S. was "convinced" chemical weapons were used against Kurdish guerrillas and calling the act "abhorrent."[9] When Minister Hammadi, unaware of the charges, arrived at the State Department two hours later, he was delivered to the U.S. press. Surprised, he was unable to respond. Within twenty-four hours the U.S. Senate voted unanimously to impose sanctions that would cancel technology and food sales to Iraq.

Just when Iraq was struggling to recover from eight years of war, feeling the effect of unilateral U.S. sanctions and fearing default on its foreign debts, Kuwait began violating quotas on oil production set by the Organization of the Petroleum Exporting Countries (OPEC). This forced oil prices down at the same time that Kuwait was demanding repayment of $30 billion it had provided Iraq during the war. Kuwait also began excessive pumping from the Rumaila oil field, which it shared with Iraq. Kuwait accelerated its provocative and hostile actions toward Iraq through months of crisis up to the day it was invaded.

While this was happening, the U.S. took a number of steps designed to make Iraq believe that Washington did not oppose Iraq's rehabilitation of its battered army. Assistant Secretary of State John Kelly in early 1990 had privately assured Saddam Hussein that the U.S. believed Iraq was a "force for moderation" and that the U.S. wanted to improve relations.[10]

On 25 July—a day after the U.S. announced joint military exercises in the Gulf with the United Arab Emirates, while Iraqi troops were massing on the Kuwaiti border, and as General Schwarzkopf readied CENTCOM for war against Iraq—Saddam Hussein summoned U.S. Ambassador April Glaspie to his office in what seems to have been a final attempt to clarify Washington's position on his dispute with Kuwait. Glaspie assured him: "We have no opinion on Arab-Arab conflicts, like your border disagreement with Kuwait. ... [Secretary of State] James Baker has directed our official spokesmen to emphasize this instruction."[11] She said she was expressing official policy. On 24 July, she had received a cable from the State Department explicitly directing her to reiterate that the United States had "no position" on "Arab-Arab" conflicts.[12]

Iraq then invaded Kuwait on 2 August 1990. The Rubicon was crossed. The U.S. frustrated every effort to negotiate an agreement to resolve the Iraqi-Kuwait disputes and Iraqi withdrawal from Kuwait. The U.S., in confident control of the UN Security Council, imposed complete economic sanctions against Iraq on 6 August—Hiroshima Day—and steadily tightened the noose until the assault began nearly six months later. By 16 January 1991, when the bombings started, 540,000 U.S. troops were positioned against Iraq, the vast majority of all the forces, naval and land, arrayed by the so-called UN coalition.

As early as September of 1990, Air Force Chief of Staff Michael Dugan told reporters that, as far as targets went, the "cutting edge would be downtown Baghdad." The *Washington Post* reported that the list of targets Dugan proposed included Iraqi power grids, roads, railroads, and "perhaps" domestic petroleum production facilities.

Within days of that statement, Dugan was fired. Secretary of Defense Dick Cheney called his statements "inappropriate," but the real reason for his firing was that Dugan jeopardized both domestic and international support for military action against Iraq. President Bush had been insisting that the U.S. military buildup in Saudi Arabia was strictly defensive, but Dugan's statements revealed that Washington was not only planning an offensive, but would target civilians. In late January 1991, after two weeks of bombing, the *London Times* observed that allied attacks were closely following Dugan's description, "with the liberation of Kuwait as only part of the overall plan."[13]

II. The Fire This Time

From earliest times most cultures have speculated about how the end of the earth may come. Until the fate of Hiroshima permeated human consciousness, most who believed the end would come assumed that their God's wrath or some natural calamity would be the cause. Even with the proliferation of omnicidal nuclear weapons systems like the Trident II, which have the capacity to destroy human life on earth, few have thought humanity would terminate itself.

Now, more than two millennia after Athens destroyed Melos and Carthage was burned by Rome, the United States, a technologically advanced superpower, has created weapons systems and executed plans to devastate a small and defenseless country half a world away, first with a direct assault by fire, then with the more deadly ice of enforced isolation, malnutrition, and impoverishment.

On the night of 16-17 January 1991, the stars shone above, little changed since Hammurabi ruled from Babylon on the Euphrates four thousand years earlier. The land remembered Ashurbanipal's great library, with its collection of all existing writing from all known languages at Nineveh on the Tigris, and its fabled Palace Without Rival of three thousand years ago. The dreams of Alexander the Great died with him in Babylon as he strove to conquer the world over two thousand years ago. Kublai Khan's brother Hulegu sacked Baghdad and executed the caliph in 1258; within two generations, the empire of the khans was gone. And still the people tilled the earth, crowded into the cities, and absorbed the shards of the many cultures, races, energies, and imaginations that had populated the place.

The Tigris and Euphrates rivers flowed quietly toward the Gulf in the darkness of the early hours. The same stars silently witnessed another approach of human violence, unprecedented in its nature and intensity. The wind gently stirred the date palm fronds. In darkened cities, towns, and farms, men, women, and children tried to sleep, not knowing what the night held for them. In Kuwait, the remaining population and Iraqi occupying forces, backed up in southern Iraq by hundreds of thousands more, waited for war. To the south, 540,000 U.S troops and 150,000 from other countries were on alert, anxiously wondering what might happen to them. They had been told they would engage a dangerous and powerful enemy in direct combat.

At 2:30 a.m. on 17 January 1991 the bombs began to fall, and for forty-two days U.S. aircraft attacked Iraq on an average of once every thirty seconds. U.S. technology smashed the cradle of civilization, and George Bush called it liberation.

Without setting foot on Iraqi soil, or engaging Iraqi troops, U.S. aircraft and missiles systematically destroyed life and life-support systems in Iraq over a period of six weeks. There were two thousand air strikes in the first twenty-four hours. More than 90 percent of Iraq's electrical capacity was bombed out of service in the first few hours. Within several days, "not an electron was flowing." Multimillion-dollar missiles targeted power plants up to the last days of the war, to leave the country without power as economic sanctions sapped life from the survivors. In less than three weeks the U.S. press reported military calculations that the tonnage of high-explosive bombs already released had exceeded the combined allied air offense of World War II.

By the end of the aerial assault, 110,000 aircraft sorties had dropped 88,500 tons of bombs on Iraq, the equivalent of seven and a half atomic bombs of the size that incinerated Hiroshima. Aircraft flew from distances as great as Barksdale Air Force Base in Louisiana and the island of Diego Garcia in the Indian Ocean, without landing—just to show it could be done. Thousands of missiles were fired from ships, including submarines, in the Indian Ocean, the Gulf, and the Mediterranean. More than 93 percent of all bombs were free falling and many of the bombs and missiles directed by laser systems were misguided. Weapons used included five-ton fuel-air explosive bombs that create pressures approaching those of low-yield nuclear weapons. Cluster bombs containing 250 bomblets capable of spewing 500,000 high-velocity, razor-sharp shrapnel fragments over an acre were used against Basra and on congested highways. Napalm bombs were used against people and to ignite oil-well fires.

Within days there was no running water in Iraq. For many weeks, people in Baghdad—without television, radio, or newspapers to warn them—were getting their drinking water from the Tigris in buckets. The Iraqi News Agency and Baghdad Broadcasting Station lost six wireless broadcast stations, twelve television stations, and five radio stations.

Iraq's telephone system was put out of service in the first few days of the war. The International Telecommunications Union's (ITU) fact-finding trip to Iraq in June-July 1991 reported that 400,000 of Iraq's 900,000 phone lines had been destroyed. Fourteen central exchanges were irreparably damaged, with thirteen more put out of service indefinitely.

Lack of communications frustrated attempts to conduct most organized activity, including caring for the sick and injured. The destruction of transportation links compounded the problem. In a country built around two great rivers, 139 automobile and railway bridges were either damaged or destroyed, including twenty-six in Basra province alone. Major highways and other roads were hit, making travel a nightmare. Road maintenance stations were bombed to prevent repairs. All kinds of civilian cars, trucks, buses, and even taxis were attacked along Iraq's major highways.

Iraq's eight major multipurpose dams were repeatedly hit and heavily damaged. This simultaneously wrecked flood control, municipal and industrial water supply, irrigation, and hydroelectric power. Four of Iraq's seven major water-pumping stations were destroyed. Bombs and missiles hit thirty-one municipal water and sewage facilities. Sewage spilled into the Tigris and out into the streets of Baghdad, adding water-borne disease to the list of killers. In Basra, the sewage system completely collapsed. Water purification plants were incapacitated nationwide.

Iraq's agriculture and food-processing storage and distribution system was attacked directly and systematically. Half of Iraq's agricultural production came from irrigated lands, and all of the irrigation systems serving them—including storage dams, barrages, pumping stations, and drainage projects—were attacked. Farmers lost the ability to flood or drain land, cutting food production in half.

Widespread saltwater intrusion occurred in Basra province. At least three food warehouses in the Baghdad province were hit, seven were struck in Asra province, and all of Iraq's General Company of Foodstuffs warehouses in Al-Qadissiya province were destroyed. Important pesticide storage was destroyed. Three separate facilities of the Iraqi Dates Company were damaged.

Iraq's factory in Abu Ghraib to produce baby milk powder, unique to the region, was attacked on January 20, 21, and 22. Although the Pentagon claimed it was a chemical plant, the attacks were simply part of the deliberate targeting of Iraq's food production. The Al-Ma'mun vegetable oils factory and the sugar factory in Meisan Province were hit. In Al-Taji, a small town near Baghdad, the country's biggest frozen-meat storage and distribution center was destroyed. It was bombed three times in one day—at 8 a.m., 3 p.m., and 8 p.m.

Farm herds were decimated—three and a half million sheep from a total of ten million and two million cattle were lost by summer, primarily from feed shortages. Ninety percent of the country's poultry production was destroyed.

Grain silos across the entire country were hit methodically, and hundreds of farms and farm buildings were attacked. The nation's tractor assembly plant and major fertilizer plant were destroyed in bombing raids that took sixteen lives.

In June 1992, more than a year after Iraq was driven from Kuwait and with sanctions still in place, the United States burned grain and wheat fields with incendiary bombs near Mosul in northern Iraq.

U.S. bombing hit twenty-eight civilian hospitals and fifty-two community health centers. Zubair Hospital in Basra province totally collapsed from bombing. At the Ibn Rashid Mental Hospital, southeast of Baghdad, ceilings collapsed onto patients' beds. At Ulwiyya Maternity Hospital, shrapnel and broken glass hit babies and mothers. The student health clinic and school in Hilla was bombed. Five of Iraq's military medical facilities were also damaged.

Allied bombs damaged 676 schools; thirty-eight were totally destroyed. Eight of those hit were parts of universities. Nor were mosques, other religious buildings, or historic sites immune from U.S. attacks, though the Pentagon insisted that they were not targeted. Iraq reported that twenty-five mosques in Baghdad alone were hit, and thirty-one more were reported damaged around the country. During the first week of February, I saw two mosques in Basra that were totally destroyed, six badly damaged, and three damaged Christian churches. The 900-year-old Church of St. Thomas—in Mosul, more than a thousand miles from Kuwait—was attacked, as was the Mutansiriya school, one of the oldest Islamic schools in Iraq.

Bombers hit civilian government office buildings in Baghdad, including the Ba'ath Party headquarters, City Hall, the Supreme Court, the Ministry of Defense, the Ministry of Justice, the Ministry of Labor, the National Palace, and the Central Post Office. Baghdad's impressive new convention and conference center, built to host the international Non-Aligned Nations meeting in 1989, was extensively damaged.

Many manufacturing plants were hit. Seven textile factories sustained damage, as did five engineering plants, five construction facilities, four car assembly plants, three chlorine plants, a major ammonia export facility, and sixteen chemical, petrochemical, and phosphate plants. A major hypodermic syringe facility in Hilla was destroyed by laser-guided rockets.

All major cement plants were hit. Twelve industrial contracting companies reported extensive damage to their facilities. The Baghdad factories of the Al-Sa'ad Company, the Al-Balsam Cosmetics Company, the Baghdad Razor Company, the Akad clothes factory, and the Muwaffak J. Janna factory were all totally destroyed.

Iraq's oil industry was a priority target. U.S. planes hit eleven oil refineries, five oil pipeline and production facilities, export pipeline facilities, and many oil storage tanks. Three oil tankers were sunk and three others set on fire.

Saddam International Airport and Al-Muthana Airport were attacked, along with parked passenger and cargo planes. Rail stations and yards, transportation hubs, bus stations, and car lots were systematically attacked everywhere.

As the infrastructure and life-support systems were being bombed, Iraqi civilians were killed by the thousands. Attacks on life-support systems assured that many more thousands would perish, even though they might be far from the line of fire.

Dr. Q. M. Ismail, director of Baghdad's Saddam Central Children's Hospital, was on duty the night U.S. bombs began to fall. Forty infants were in incubators, their mothers at their sides. When the electricity went out, the incubators stopped working. With the thunder of war all around them, the desperate mothers grabbed their children and rushed them into the basement.

Six hours later, twenty of the children were dead. "Those forty mothers nearly went crazy," Dr. Ismail recalled. "I will never forget the sight of those women."

On 11 February the U.S. press, following a briefing from General Richard Neal on the bombing of Basra, reported it was "a military town." (Like Norfolk, Oceanside, Omaha, San Antonio, San Diego, Watertown, and scores of other American cities?) During the third week it was "a hellish nightmare of fires and smoke so dense that witnesses say the sun hasn't been clearly visible for several days at a time. ... [The bombing is] leveling some entire city blocks ... [and there are] bomb craters the size of football fields and an untold number of casualties."[14]

Four months before the bombing, the Air Force Chief of Staff said the "cutting edge would be downtown Baghdad." "We're going after hard targets in Baghdad. Therefore, it takes more bombs on each target in order to be successful," Lieutenant General Thomas Kelly told reporters.[15]

The sprawling area of Baghdad was bombed every day. On 12 February journalists in Baghdad reported more than twenty-five explosions in the central part of the city. Six days later, the allies launched a fierce two-hour bombardment that began at 11:00 p.m. A journalist wrote of the raid: "[M]issiles began skimming past the windows of the al-Rashid hotel. Against a background roar of high-flying aircraft, the hum of a cruise missile was heard every ten minutes or so, followed by a terrific explosion that shook the entire hotel."[16]

Among the "hard targets" in Baghdad was the Amariyah bomb shelter, which was hit with two missiles early on 13 February, killing many hundreds of civilians, most women and children.

Two nights before the ceasefire, on 27 February at 1:35 a.m., Iraq announced its pullout from Kuwait. Seemingly in response, Baghdad was subjected to another fierce raid, described by a resident as "a sleepless night of horror."

The assault on the Iraqi military, which was as defenseless as the civilian population, was relentless. More than 40,000 tons of bombs targeted the military, often in proximity to civilian areas. B-52s carpet-bombed military areas from extremely high altitudes. Estimates of the numbers of Iraqi soldiers killed by the end of the bombing ranged from 100,000 to 200,000. On March 22, 1991, the Defense Intelligence Agency placed Iraq's military casualties at 100,000.

Near the end of the bombing, as U.S. troops planned to advance on Kuwait City and Iraq, U.S. General Kelly said of Iraqi forces: "There won't be many of them left." When asked for his assessment of the numbers of Iraqi soldiers and civilians killed, General Colin Powell answered, "It's really not a number I'm interested in." General Schwarzkopf had a strict policy that Iraqi dead were not to be counted. Both violated international law requiring respect for enemy dead, their identification, notification of family, and proper religious burial. Americans know how *they* feel about their MIAs from Vietnam and earlier wars.

The U.S. claims to have destroyed 4,300 tanks and 1,856 armored vehicles. The Pentagon claimed 1,500 tanks were destroyed by F-111s alone, confirmed by video camera. Nearly all these planes employed laser-guided depleted-uranium missiles, leaving 900 tons of radioactive waste spread over much of Iraq with no concern for the consequences to future life.[17] The rate of tumors, cancers, leukemia, and other fatal growths has increased alarmingly in the last few years in Iraq. Doctors believe radiation is a major cause.

At the end of the bombing campaign, tens of thousands of Iraqi soldiers were simply murdered. The European Parliament heard this description in April 1991:

> [H]undreds, possibly thousands, of Iraqi soldiers began walking towards the U.S. position unarmed, with their arms raised in an attempt to surrender. However, the orders for this unit were not to take any prisoners. ...
>
> The commander of the unit began the firing by shooting an anti-tank missile through one of the Iraqi soldiers. This is a missile designed to destroy tanks, but it was used against one man.
>
> At that point, everybody in the unit began shooting. Quite simply, it was a slaughter.[18]

The *Toronto Globe and Mail* carried an early Reuters dispatch on the ground action, entitled "Getting Blown to Bits in the Dark":

> The first high-tech video of ground fighting in the Persian Gulf war shows terrified Iraqi infantrymen shot to pieces in the dark by U.S. attack helicopters.
>
> One by one they were cut down, bewildered by an enemy they could not see.
>
> Some were blown to bits by exploding cannon shells. Others, jarred from sleep, fled their bunkers under a firestorm.

The tape was shot through the night-vision gunsights of the Apache AH-64 attack helicopter, which turn pitch dark into ghostly day.

Reporters and even hardened soldiers held their breath when the first video was shown in a briefing tent of the 18th Airborne Corps, whose chopper crews had begun carrying the war to the Iraqis.

Combat reporters permitted to see the video did not say where or when the engagement took place. No casualty count was given. Reports from the front are subject to U.S. military censorship.

Apaches—equipped with cannons, laser-guided missiles, and infrared optics—have led several lightning strikes behind Iraqi lines in recent days, raiding bunkers and taking prisoners.

The pilots of the 6th Cavalry exult in their prowess.

"I just didn't quite envision going up there and shooting the hell out of everything in the dark and have them not know what the hell hit them," said one Balak of Beemer, Neb.

"A truck blows up to the right, the ground blows up to the left. They had no idea where we were or what was hitting them," he said.

"When I got back I sat there on the wing and I was laughing. I wasn't laughing at the Iraqis. I was thinking of the training, the anticipation. ... I was probably laughing at myself ... sneaking up there, and blowing this up and blowing that up.

"A guy came up to me and we were slapping each other on the back and all that stuff, and he said, 'By God, I thought we had shot into a damn farm. It looked like somebody opened the sheep pen.' "[19]

Reuters thus confirmed not only that Iraqi soldiers were totally unable to see the enemy, or defend themselves, but that U.S. troops quickly realized this. It was like slaughtering animals in a pen. A report from William Branigin in the *Washington Post* described what the 1st Cavalry Division encountered as it moved into Iraq:

By the side of a dirt road in Iraq's south-eastern desert sat a truck belonging to President Saddam Hussein's elite Republican Guard. In and around it lay the bodies of eight Iraqi soldiers. The immediate area was cordoned off with white tape like a police crime scene.

The headless corpse of one of the soldiers was on its back a short distance from the truck. Another body was wedged inside the engine compartment. Two more lay face up in the bed of the truck, their feet sticking grotesquely over the side.

This was the gruesome face of the Persian Gulf War, a facet of the conflict not previously seen by many of the young American soldiers who took part in the allied ground offensive against Iraq this week. After weeks of a high-tech war waged largely from the sky, the horrors on the ground took some of the troops by total surprise.

... Already, units of the Army's 1st Cavalry Division that had suffered no combat casualties in their unopposed drive through southern Iraq have seen several of their number killed or wounded by bombs or mines in the area they are holding. ...

A couple of miles away from the vehicles, a large expanse of desert that apparently had been a Republican Guard training area was devastated by aerial bombardment well before the U.S. armored units swept through. ...

The entire area was littered with pieces of ordnance, including hundreds of unexploded individual yellow cluster bombs sticking into the sand.[20]

Even Iraqi units with operational tanks and the will to resist were helpless. Here is how the *New York Times* reported one slaughter:

The battle, which raged on February 27, the day before a cease-fire went into effect, was a showcase for the superiority of American weapons. But it was also the sort of one-sided victory that some American soldiers who tasted combat for the first time say they will not want to talk about a lot when they get home.

The sky was overcast and it was raining as the Americans approached the ridge around noon.

When the battle began the American tanks generally fired from a safe distance of about 2,500 yards. Unable to find the Americans with their targeting system in the overcast weather, the Iraqis aimed their guns at the muzzle flashes of the guns of the American tanks, and their rounds fell well short.

Other soldiers said the biggest fear was not the Iraqis but the worry that the American tanks might be hit by other allied units in the battle.[21]

The psychological effect on the few American troops who actually witnessed this massacre will be important to monitor. Many will be casualties of the horror, psychological victims of American unfriendly fire power.

Reports by the U.S. press, although censored by the Pentagon and approved by the military, still could not help but reveal the war crimes committed against Iraq's armed forces. *New York Newsday* published a graphic, lengthy summary of the "ground war" on March 31, 1991. It portrayed the attack upon an army that did not want to fight. It described "one-sided carnage," vehicles with white flags of surrender being destroyed, and "dazed and starved front-line Iraqi conscripts happily surrender[ing] by the thousands." It spoke of how U.S. pilots called the assault a "turkey shoot," and carrier crews frantically reloaded attack planes so they could shoot "fish in a barrel."

New York Newsday reported yet another slaughter of Iraqi soldiers that was approved by General Schwarzkopf two days after the ceasefire. According to U.S. military officials, it was the biggest clash of the Gulf War ground campaign, yet no Americans were killed.

The battle occurred March 2 after soldiers from the 7,000-man Iraqi force fired at a patrol of the 24th Mechanized Infantry Division. ...

"We really waxed them," said one American Desert Storm commander who asked not to be identified. ...

Although the number of Iraqi troops killed is still unknown, *New York Newsday* has obtained Army footage of the fight showing scores of Iraqi President Saddam Hussein's elite soldiers apparently wounded or killed as Apache helicopters raked the Republican Guard Hammurabi Division with laser-guided Hellfire missiles.

"Say hello to Allah," one American was recorded as saying moments before a Hellfire obliterated one of the 102 vehicles racked up by the Apaches.

... Although McCaffrey's division was equipped with loudspeakers mounted on helicopters, they were never used to broadcast word of the cease-fire. "There wasn't time to use the helicopters," said Lamar.

Instead, after the 6:30 a.m. Iraqi attack, McCaffrey assembled attack helicopters, tanks, fighting vehicles and artillery for the assault, which began at 8:15 a.m. According to Lamar, the attack ended after noon, with the wreckage strewn over a couple of miles of Route 8, the main Euphrates River valley road to Baghdad.

A senior Desert Storm commander said details about the post-cease-fire attack were withheld at the time even though officials in Riyadh and Washington knew the extent of the damage shortly after the battle ended.

... "We knew exactly [what the damage was] but it didn't look good coming after the cease-fire," the Desert Storm officer said. ...

The combat film of the March 2 attack shows the Apaches destroying vehicles to create a roadblock so that the Hammurabi could not escape on the highway, which is elevated above the nearby Haw al Hammer swamp.

"Yee-HAH," said one voice. At one point, an Iraqi soldier runs in front [of] a tank just as the Hellfire explodes, hurling the soldier and chunks of metal into the air.[22]

The Pentagon has documentary evidence, including hours of videotape, of this deadly assault on a virtually defenseless unit.

Months later, *Newsday* broke perhaps the most horrifying story of all. Thousands of Iraqi troops had been buried alive in the first two days of the ground offensive.

The U.S. Army division that broke through Saddam Hussein's defensive front line used plows mounted on tanks and combat earth movers to bury thousands of Iraqi soldiers—some still alive and firing their weapons—in more than seventy miles of trenches, according to U.S. Army officials.

In the first two days of ground fighting in Operation Desert Storm, three brigades of the 1st Mechanized Infantry Division—"The Big Red One"—used the grisly innovation to destroy trenches and bunkers being defended by more than 8,000 Iraqi soldiers, according to division estimates. While 2,000 surrendered, Iraqi dead and wounded as well as defiant soldiers still firing their weapons were buried beneath tons of sand, according to participants in the carefully planned and rehearsed assault.

"Once we went through there, other than the ones who surrendered, there wasn't anybody left," said Captain Bennie Williams, who was awarded the Silver Star for his role in the assault.

The unprecedented tactic has been hidden from public view. ...

"For all I know, we could have killed thousands," said Col. Anthony Moreno, commander of the 2nd Brigade that led the assault on the heaviest defenses.[23]

The article said that after the first wave of bulldozers incapacitated the Iraqi defenders, a second wave filled the trenches with sand, ensuring that none of the wounded could survive.

Many of those massacred fleeing Kuwait were not Iraqi soldiers at all but Palestinians, Sudanese, Egyptians, Filipinos, and other foreign workers. They were trying to escape to save their lives. As *Newsday* reported of the Highway of Death between Kuwait City and Basra:

> The vast majority of the vehicles photographed were cars, buses, and military and civilian trucks apparently carrying Iraqi soldiers and some civilians, as well as their rifles and large quantities of goods they had looted from Kuwait. Reporters described one section of the highway as a virtually unbroken wall of wrecked and fire-blackened vehicles, piled on top of each other in a jumble of charred, twisted metal; truck cabs crushed, cars flattened underneath buses, other cars flipped upside down, tank guns pointing crazily skyward while the rest of the tank lay on its side.
>
> Less than 10 percent of the vehicles in the one section photographed were tanks, personnel carriers, or artillery. ...[24]

North Carolina GI Mike Ange described what he saw:

> I actually went up close and examined two vehicles that basically looked like refugees maybe trying to get out of the area. You know, you had like a little Toyota pick-up truck that was loaded down with the furniture and the suitcases and rugs and the pet cat and that type of thing, all over the back of this truck, and those trucks were taken out just like the military vehicles.[25]

The bombing of Iraq took more than 150,000 lives outright and left a broken and bleeding nation.

The bombs killed indiscriminately, mostly Iraqis, but others as well. Among the dead were Muslims and Christians, Kurds and Assyrians, young and old, men, women, children, babies.

In 110,000 aerial sorties, the U.S. lost thirty-eight aircraft, probably all from mechanical failure, pilot error, and accident. This is a lower rate than aircraft losses in war games when live ammunition is not used. Not a single B-52 was lost as they carpeted Iraq with 27,500 tons of bombs. Major bombing raids against Germany during World War II cost as high as 25 percent of the planes participating.

Total U.S. war casualties, including thirty-seven acknowledged to have died from "friendly fire," were 148, according to the Pentagon.

The U.S. has continued to attack Iraq with its aircraft, which patrol its skies night and day, and by cruise missiles launched from its enormous military positions in the region, including the largest naval armada since World War II. As the end of President Bush's term approached, attacks increased. On 13 January 1993 more than one hundred U.S. aircraft bombed and strafed southern Iraq. The press interviewed the jubilant pilots, who described how they "honed in with deadly accuracy," delivering bombs containing "two thousand pounds of American anger." On 17 January 1993, the second anniversary of the assault on Iraq and three days before President Bush left office, he ordered an attack across Iraq. Baghdad was hit by fifty cruise missiles. One of the missiles hit the al-Rashid Hotel, killing two employees. An international Islamic conference scheduled there at the time, to be attended by Saddam Hussein, had been moved. Strikes the next two days were heavier. Iraq acknowledged twenty-one deaths on 19 January 1993. The attacks were deliberate criminal violence.

President Bill Clinton showed what he was made of by ordering minor attacks in the first days of his new presidency. On 26 June 1993 he authorized an attack with twenty-three cruise missiles on Baghdad. One hit the home of Layla al-Altar, a renowned artist and director of Iraq's National Center for the Arts, killing her and her husband. Sporadic attacks have continued, the most recent in June 1998.

Continuing to call Iraq dangerous and a threat to peace, the U.S. maintains a nuclear arsenal larger by far than all other nations combined. In fiscal year 1996 it spent $264 billion on its military compared to $47 billion spent by the Russian Federation and $32 billion by the People's Republic of China. Iraq's gross national product, with which it had to meet all the needs of its people, was $11.5 billion—less than 5 percent of U.S. military costs.

With an arrogance to match its violence, the U.S. requested that the UN Security Council investigate war crimes committed by Iraq against U.S. soldiers and Kuwaiti citizens. This presaged later requests by the U.S. for UN prosecution of Serbs, Hutus, Pol Pot and—after his death—surviving leaders of the Khmer Rouge, Saddam Hussein and others, while opposing an independent International Criminal Tribunal capable of equal protection under law.

There was no war. No combat. There was only a deliberate, systematic genocide of a defenseless population while barely setting foot on Iraqi soil. When Dr. Martin Luther King Jr. said in 1967, "the greatest purveyor of violence on earth is my own government," he could not have dreamed in his worst nightmare what the U.S. did to Iraq.

III. The New Ice Age

Those who planned the aerial assault on Iraq intended a harm far greater than the bombs themselves could inflict. Those who conducted the forty-two-day assault and those who observed it on television knew the bombs and missiles would cause a continuing threat to life long after their thunder fell silent and the dust of their explosions settled to earth.

A Pentagon planner later candidly acknowledged the major purpose of the bombing: "People say, 'You didn't recognize that it was going to have an effect on water and sewage.' Well, what were we trying to do with sanctions—help out the Iraqi people? No. What we were doing with the attacks on the infrastructure was to accelerate the effect of sanctions."[26]

As early as 23 June 1991, an article in the *Washington Post,* following extensive research on bombing targets and interviews with top Pentagon planners, reported: "Military planners hoped the bombing would amplify the economic and psychological impact of international sanctions on Iraqi society. ... They deliberately did great harm to Iraq's ability to support itself as an industrial society."

On 12 February 1991, immediately after returning from Iraq and with more than two weeks of heavy bombing yet to come, I wrote UN Secretary-General Perez de Cuellar, President Bush, and others, observing in part:

> The effect of the bombing, if continued, will be the destruction of much of the physical and economic basis for life in Iraq. The purpose of the bombing can only be explained rationally as the destruction of Iraq as a viable state for a generation or more. Must the United Nations be a party to this lawless violence?

My letter noted:

> Dr. Ibrahim Al-Nouri has been head of the Red Crescent and Red Cross of Iraq for ten years. He is a pediatrician by training who interned at Children's Hospital in London, later headed Children's Hospital in Baghdad and served in the Ministry of Health for some years, rising to Deputy Minister. Dr. Nouri estimates that there have been 3,000 infant deaths since 1 November 1990

in excess of the normal rate, attributable solely to the shortage of infant milk formula and medicines. Only 14 tons of baby formula have been received during that period. Prior monthly national consumption was approximately 2,500 tons.

The effect of damage to municipal water systems on health and safety is tremendous. The Minister of Health considered potable water for human consumption the single greatest health need in the country. Tens of thousands are known to suffer diarrhea and stomach disorders. There are believed to be hundreds of thousands of unreported cases. Several thousands are believed to have died.

In the hospitals, there is no heat, no clean water except limited quantities for drinking supplied in bottles, no electric light in wards and hospital rooms, and inadequate medicine, even for pain alleviation, in the face of a great increase in critically and severely injured persons. Doctors we talked with in four hospitals are deeply concerned over the absence or shortage of needed medicines and sanitary supplies. Surgeons and medics treating wounds cannot keep their hands clean or gloved, and work in the cold, in poor light with greatly increased numbers of patients in unrelieved pain. Seven hospitals are reported closed by bomb damage. Many if not most have had windows shattered.[27]

Since the end of the bombing, there has been a constant flow of information from a wide range of sources reporting on the deadly effects of the sanctions. Every UN agency dealing with health, food, agriculture, or children, including the World Health Organization, the Food and Agriculture Organization, the World Food Project, and UNICEF, has reported repeatedly and often graphically about tens of thousands of deaths annually resulting directly from the sanctions. UNICEF reported as of August 1991 that already at least 47,500 children had died as a direct result of sanctions.

Independent medical teams from more than forty nations have investigated and reported on the human horror and death deliberately inflicted on the population of Iraq. It has been recognized from the beginning, as all human experience teaches, that the principal victims of the sanctions are infants, the elderly, small children, pregnant and nursing women, and the chronically ill. These are the very people that every decent society has worked hardest to protect.

Both President Bill Clinton and Hillary Rodham Clinton, known for her work to protect children, were informed of the deadly effects of the sanctions before his inauguration on 20 January 1993, and again in February 1993. The President has received reports regularly ever since. A question posed to Hillary Clinton was how can she profess to love children and not speak out on behalf of the children of Iraq. It was pointed out that if President Clinton failed to reverse U.S. policy, he would share responsibility for its genocidal consequences. Now more Iraqis have died as a result of the U.S.-forced sanctions in the Clinton administration than died in the Bush administration from the bombing and sanctions combined.

I have been to Iraq eight times since sanctions were imposed and reported to the UN Security Council and others on the steady deterioration in the human condition there on each occasion after the first. Typical is the report dated 14 November 1997, which included the following:

> Over these years the general health of the people of Iraq has drastically and steadily deteriorated as a direct result of United States forced sanctions imposed by the United Nations.

Deterioration in Health, Medical Supplies and Increased Death Rates Caused by UN Sanctions

> On this trip I found health and hospital conditions poorer than ever. Rates of illness in every category are at all-time highs. The physical conditions of the hospitals, medical care facilities, pharmaceutical and medical supplies plants continue to decline. Availability of medicines, medical supplies, and working equipment are at the lowest level since 1989. Every doctor reports that patients they could save die every day. Often their patients die in their presence because of shortages of medicine, medical supplies, and operational medical equipment.

> The overall death rate from monitored causes due to the sanctions has increased each year since 1989. For children under age five the increase in deaths exceeds a multiple of eight, from 7,100 in 1989 to 57,000 in 1996. For persons over age five the death rate has increased more than four times, from 20,200 to 83,200. Diseases related to malnutrition continue to increase. Kwashiorkor, virtually unknown in 1989, has increased nearly sixty times to reach 21,000 cases last year, marasmus fifty times to 192,000 cases last year. Other malnutrition-related illnesses have increased eighteen-fold to 1,354,000 cases in 1996.

> Sicknesses related to poor sanitation continue a steady increase. Last year amebic dysentery was up twenty-seven-fold to 243,000 cases. Malaria increased more than seven-fold to 32,000 cases. Typhoid fever increased eight times to 15,000 cases. Scabies has increased from no cases in 1989 to 37,000 in 1996.

Cholera is up from no cases to more than 3,000 in 1997 through September.

Births of infants weighing under two and a half kilograms have increased more than five-fold to include 23.8 percent of all live births in September 1997, a tragedy evidencing the stunted generation the sanctions have caused in Iraq.

Major surgery is down from a monthly average exceeding 15,000 operations in 1989 to 4,100 operations in September 1997.

The total cost in lives directly resulting from UN sanctions is now 1,500,000 deaths over the normal death rate.

These tragic statistics do not convey the human horror of the sanctions.

In two large general hospitals, both serving poor areas, one in Basra and one in Saddam City, Baghdad, I saw among many other children, an eleven-month-old child of a young Bedouin woman, her first child, wasted, bloated and not expected to live for more than a day. In Qadisiya Hospital in Baghdad, a nineteen-month-old girl and a three-year-old boy lay wasted and dying in adjoining beds. Ample food and safe drinking water would have prevented the illnesses of all three. Rehydration tablets could have saved all three. All three are by now dead.

A thirty-five-year-old man was dying in Basra, for the lack of simple catheters to perform a crude method of renal dialysis. Only one of the four machines available was working for lack of spare parts. The man was not expected to last through the night. He could have been saved but for the unavailability of catheters. Before sanctions the unit could treat 175 patients a month.

A seventeen-year-old male who had suffered severe headaches was brought in by taxi. No diagnoses were possible for lack of medical supplies. Intravenous feeding required six pints a day. Only one was available in the hospital. He has almost surely died by now.

There is no operational ambulance for all but a few hospitals and the contract with a French company for ambulances has been intentionally delayed by the sanctions committee.

A beautiful fourteen-year-old girl with leukemia, which is occurring in unprecedented numbers apparently from depleted uranium and chemicals released by U.S. bombing, received no treatment, because of the lack of essential medicines and supplies. There is an enormous increase in cancers, tumors, leukemia, birth defects, and miscarriage, probably from the same cause. These victims suffer extreme pain with little or no relief before they die.

A twenty-three-year-old woman who had suffered polio, TB, and was dying from malnutrition was angry and bitter at the injustice of her fate. Most older patients entering hospitals now have multiple medical problems from the effect of the sanctions over these seven years.

A twenty-seven-year-old TB patient, badly wasted, a twenty-one-year-old woman with severe anemia, two older women with advanced diabetes, foot sores, and infections and a woman with breast cancer lay dying with family around them. There has been no insulin for two months. No chemotherapy is available except on rare occasions. All these human beings, near death, were receiving no medications, even pain killers, because nothing was available.

If you saw the faces of these people, needlessly dying, and the doctors, nurses, and families trying to comfort them, you would never forget them.

In Basra, the surgery department in the Training Hospital performs fewer than one hundred operations a month, compared to 1,000 per month in 1989, because of the lack of anesthesia, antiseptics, gauze, bandages, antibiotics, and other medical supplies. Only emergency surgery is performed. Everything else is delayed often until it is too late. Surgery is performed without x-rays in many cases, because of shortages. There is no clean water to wash the floors, no air conditioning, inadequate heat, poor lighting and none in stairwells, recesses, and most corridors. The electricity is off for hours most days. There are not enough sheets, blankets, towels, and other supplies.

Most areas in the city of Basra and parts of Baghdad have no running water or sewage disposal because of the bombing. The sanctions make replacement impossible. This combination compounded by malnutrition is a major cause of death.

Less than half the contracts entered into under UN supervision have been fulfilled because of harassment. Production of pharmaceuticals in Iraq, once nearly half of national needs, has declined to an insignificant level because of lack of machine parts and raw materials.

In short, there is a human disaster created by the United Nations. A genocide intended to destroy a national, religious, and ethnic group, deliberately inflicting conditions of life calculated to bring about its physical destruction in whole or in part.[28]

The *1997 Britannica Book of the Year* shows the death rate for Iraq at 9.8 per thousand. For poor neighboring Jordan it was 3 per thousand. Rich neighboring Kuwait experienced 2.2 deaths for every thousand people in 1997.

Per capita income in Iraq, from the *1989 Britannica Book of the Year*, was $2,420. By 1996 it was down to $720. By 1997 it had dropped to $540, less than 25 percent of the average individual income in 1989.

In May 1998 we were able to take over four million dollars (U.S. wholesale value) in medicine and medical supplies directly to hospitals in Iraq, from Mosul to Basra. The group of eighty-four persons carried more than 140 large boxes of the most urgently needed medicines and supplies by arduous overland travel from Amman, Damascus, and Beirut. Despite the goodwill of thousands in the U.S. who contributed to purchase and transport the desperately needed medicine, there could be no satisfaction from the effort, because it did not meet even one thousandth of the annual need.

The U.S. used the occasion of our shipment and others— including its own strategically employed AmeriCares flight, which was quickly organized for propaganda purposes—to claim medicines are not as badly needed in Iraq as in many other countries. There are few if any countries with the shortages of medicines and medical supplies that exist in Iraq, and there are none that have experienced such a drastic decline in available medicines when professional medical and health care personnel are ready to beneficially use them. And, of course, no other country experiences such shortages because of international sanctions—"man's inhumanity to man."

Ending the sanctions is the essential first step toward the recovery of Iraq and of America's honor.

When this whole tragic story is examined, the most difficult question will be why the member nations of the Security Council surrendered to U.S. pressure to continue sanctions against Iraq and why the American people let their government do it. The criminal nature of the bombing of Iraq was undeniably obvious. Over a period of more than eight years now, Security Council members have accepted the most cynical, duplicitous, and absurd arguments from the U.S. to continue sanctions. During most of these years the sanctions committee reviewed continuation of the sanctions every two months.

As awareness of the murderously criminal effect of the sanctions spread, the U.S. would come up with the most patently foolish and false excuses to continue the sanctions. Sometimes, appealing to prejudice, it would claim that Saddam Hussein had spent extravagant sums for a yacht on the Euphrates which could have been used to purchase medicines. At other times it would appeal to fear, claiming he was obtaining missiles, or developing nuclear weapons, or manufacturing, deploying, or concealing chemical or biological weapons. These claims would be followed by insistence on further inspections, searching the most intimate places of government, demanding follow-up searches, then claiming Iraq is not cooperating, is lying, is concealing weapons or the evidence of their existence.

Occasionally the U.S. would suggest compliance has improved, then follow with new allegations of discovery, deception, or concealment. Through it all, every Security Council member has known it was a charade. Each member has known the U.S. will not agree to end sanctions unless forced to do so. That the U.S. intends to maintain its major military presence in the Gulf, which it uses the UN to justify, is equally clear. A 1997 *Foreign Affairs* article co-authored by Zbigniew Brzezinski and Brent Scowcroft, national security advisers for presidents Carter and Bush, respectively, stated the obvious quite clearly: "Every president since Richard Nixon has recognized that ensuring Persian Gulf security and stability is a vital U.S. interest.[29] ... It is imperative that all parties understand an important strategic reality: the United States is in the Persian Gulf to stay."[30]

The U.S. has always blamed Saddam Hussein for the condition of the Iraqi people. Madeleine Albright has repeatedly argued that she loves the Iraqi people more than Saddam Hussein does. He is constantly cited for using "weapons of mass destruction" against his own people.

Unbearably terrible, the vicious assault on defenseless Iraq and the slow, tortured genocide by sanctions happened and the American people have known it all along. The facts are inescapable and undeniable. Still, knowing that our own government has devastated Iraq doesn't enrage many, because our media, government, and leading public figures falsely tell us that the U.S., with the approval of the United Nations, has acted courageously and selflessly against a dangerous and evil enemy. And most Americans pay little attention. They are distracted by personal problems and insecurities and absorbed in the many circuses provided by power to consume their conscious time and sedate their pain from conscience—television, movies, professional sports, and celebrity antics. The American culture conditions the people to value their own material well-being more than they love justice. As individuals, Americans feel helpless to affect government action anyway. These factors at least partially explain how some millions of Americans could watch a *60 Minutes* TV program filmed in late 1995—which portrayed and described the deaths of more than 500,000 children in Iraq caused by U.S.-forced sanctions and then showed UN Ambassador Madeleine Albright saying of those deaths, "Yes, the price is worth it"—without smashing their TV sets and taking to the streets.

Finally, the U.S. reluctantly agreed in 1996 to permit inadequate sales of oil by Iraq. But it required that nearly half the proceeds go to pay reparations, support enemies of Iraq, and pay for intrusive, meaningless inspections. The U.S. has since systematically delayed, frustrated, and often rejected Iraqi contracts requiring Security Council approval for medicine, medical equipment, and food. It has attempted to control the delivery of every purchase, a means of physical and economic intervention.

It became so embarrassing and transparent, as the U.S. manufactured a new crisis every two months, that in 1996, just as opposition to sanctions was mounting within the Security Council, the U.S. forced an agreement for biannual reviews. Meanwhile, several hundred people die every day.

There can be no better evidence of the importance of the second reform to the UN Charter—replacement of the Security Council—proposed in Chapter 12 of *The Fire This Time*.[31] Permanent membership for five nations is undemocratic and the veto power a guarantee of both abusive action and immoral inaction. Now the Security Council, largely paralyzed for its first forty-five years by the struggle between the U.S. and USSR, has succumbed to the domination of the U.S., which can dictate even genocide.

All the arguments for continuing sanctions against Iraq fail to acknowledge that no threat, or failure, by the government of Iraq can justify sanctions that kill infants, children, pregnant and nursing women, the chronically ill, and the elderly. No sentient moral being can believe the "price is worth it," as Albright proclaimed. But even in a world so cruel and heartless as the secretary of state would have it, there is no rational justification for such sanctions against a small and exhausted Iraq while the U.S. brandishes its nuclear arms, developing more omnicidal delivery systems, and the UN ignores threats of nuclear war in south Asia that are more dangerous than any since Hiroshima and Nagasaki.

As a person who, despite all evidence to the contrary, still believes law is an essential element in the quest for peace, I hesitate to analyze the positive international laws and the domestic laws of my own country that are violated by the fire and ice imposed on Iraq. It demeans law and life to have to parse out how law is violated by such horrendous acts. Most clearly, the law is worthless, indeed dangerous where needed most, if it fails to make criminal the conduct of the U.S. toward Iraq these past eight years.

The aerial assault on Iraq—the Fire—which took more than 150,000 lives, violates the UN Charter; provisions of the Hague Conventions of 1907; the Geneva Conventions of 1949 and Articles 51-57 of Protocol I, Additional to the Geneva Conventions of 1977; the Nuremberg Charter of 1945, including crimes against peace, war crimes, and crimes against humanity; provisions of numerous international covenants, conventions, and declarations, including the Universal Declaration of Human Rights, the International Covenants on Civil, Political, Economic, Social, and Cultural Rights, and the Genocide Convention; various treaties; customary international law; a large number of U.S. criminal statutes, and the laws of armed conflict cited in several U.S. military service manuals, among others.

The sanctions against Iraq that have taken more than one and a half million lives—the Ice—violate the UN Charter; the Nuremberg Charter of 1945, crimes against humanity; Article 54.1, Protocol I Additional, Geneva Convention of 1977 ("Starvation of civilians as a means of warfare is prohibited"); provisions of numerous international covenants, conventions, declarations, and treaties; customary international law; and other agreements, most explicitly the Covenant Against Genocide, which provides:

> [G]enocide means any of the following acts committed with intent to destroy in whole or in part, a national, ethnical, racial or religious group, as such: ...
> (b) Causing serious bodily or mental harm to members of the group;
> (c) Deliberately inflicting on the group conditions of life calculated to bring about its physical destruction in whole or in part; ...[32]
> Starvation of civilians as a means of warfare is prohibited.[33]

It is clear beyond a reasonable doubt that with the sanctions it forced on Iraq, the United States intended to destroy in whole, or in part, the people of Iraq, largely Arab and Muslim, by causing them serious bodily and mental harm and by inflicting on them conditions of life calculated to bring about their physical destruction in whole, or in part. Sadly, the complicity of the UN cannot be ignored, because in a time of moral crisis threatening the life of a nation, it did nothing to prevent tragedy. Dante described some very hot places in hell reserved for such failure.

The sanctions against Iraq must be ended immediately and unconditionally. Sanctions impacting on poor, weak, helpless, hungry, or sick people must be prohibited in all cases.

Then all must work for essential reforms of the United Nations and the United States based on truth and seeking reconciliation.

---

[1] Gerard Chaliand and Ismet Seriff Vanly, *People Without a Country: The Kurds and Kurdistan* (London: Zed Press, 1980), p. 184. See also Daniel Schorr, "1975: Background to Betrayal," *Washington Post*, 7 April 1991, D3; and Christopher Hitchens, "Minority Report," *The Nation*, 6 May 1991, p. 582.

[2] Christopher Hitchens, "Why We Are Stuck in the Sand—Realpolitik in the Gulf: A Game Gone Tilt," *Harper's Magazine*, January 1991, p. 70.

[3] Seymour Hersh, "U.S. Secretly Gave Aid to Iraq Early in Its War Against Iran," *New York Times*, 26 January 1992, p. 1.

[4] Shahram Chubinl and Charles Trip, *Iran and Iraq at War* (Boulder, CO: Westview Press, 1988), p. 207.

[5] Leslie Gelb, "Bush's Iraqi Blunder," *New York Times*, Op-Ed Page, 4 May 1992.

[6] Francis A. Boyle, "International Crisis and Neutrality: U.S. Foreign Policy Toward the Iraq-Iran War," in *Neutrality: Changing Concepts and Practices* (New Orleans: Institute for Comparative Study of Public Policy, University of New Orleans, 1986).

[7] Major James Blackwell, U.S. Army, Ret., *Thunder in the Desert* (New York: Bantam Books, 1991), pp. 80-85, 86-87.

[8] U.S. News & World Report, *Triumph Without Victory: The Unreported History of the Persian Gulf War* (New York: Time Books, 1991), pp. 28-30, and Chapter 2. See also Tom Mathews, et al., "The Road to War," *Newsweek*, 28 January 1991, pp. 54, 57, 58, 60, 61.

[9] *American Foreign Policy: Current Documents*, Document 260 (Washington, DC: Department of State), p. 458.

[10] John K. Cooley, *Payback: America's Long War in the Middle East* (London: Brassey's, 1991), p. 185.

[11] "The Glaspie Transcript: Saddam Meets the U.S. Ambassador," in *The Gulf War Reader*, Micah Sifry and Christopher Cerf, eds. (New York: Times Books, 1991), p. 130.

[12] Leslie H. Gelb, "Mr. Bush's Fateful Blunder," *New York Times*, 17 July 1991, A21.

[13] "Allied Strategy Follows Disgraced Dugan's Predictions," *London Times*, 29 January 1991, p. 2.

[14] Paul Walker, Director of the Institute for Peace and International Security at MIT, quoted in the *Los Angeles Times*, 5 February 1991.

[15] Rick Atkinson and Ann DeVroy, "Allies Step Up Gulf Air Offensive; Strikes Focus on Iraqis in Kuwait," *New York Times*, 12 February 1991.

[16] Alfonso Rojo, "Bombs Rock Capital as Allies Deliver Terrible Warning," *The Guardian*, 20 February 1991.

[17] Depleted Uranium Education Project, *Metal of Dishonor: Depleted Uranium* (New York: International Action Center, 1997).

[18] Mike Erlich of the Military Counseling Network, Testimony, European Parliament Hearings, March-April 1991.

[19] *Globe and Mail*, 25 February 1991.

[20] *Washington Post*, 3 March 1991.

[21] *New York Times*, 8 April 1991.

[22] Patrick Sloyan, "Buried Alive," *Newsday*, 12 September 1991.

[23] *Newsday*, 12 September 1991.

[24] Knute Royce and Timothy Phelps, "Pullback a Bloody Mismatch," *Newsday*, 31 March 1991.

[25] Bill Moyers, PBS Special Report: After the War, Spring 1991.

[26] Barton Gellman, "U.S. Bombs Missed 70% of the Time," *Washington Post*, 16 March 1991.

[27] Letter from Ramsey Clark to UN Secretary-General Perez de Cuellar, 12 February 1991.

[28] Letter from Ramsey Clark to the UN Security Council, 14 November 1997.

[29] *Foreign Affairs*, May-June 1997, p. 20.

[30] Ibid., p. 30.

[31] Ramsey Clark, *The Fire This Time* (New York: Thunder's Mouth Press, 1992).

[32] Article II, Convention on the Prevention and Punishment of the Crime of Genocide, 78 U.N.T.S. 277.

[33] Article 54.1, Protocol I Additional, Geneva Convention, 1977.

SANCTIONS ARE CRIMINAL

RANIA MASRI

In the fifty years since the inception of the United Nations, there have been ten instances of economic sanctions imposed by its Security Council; eight have been during the 1990s. The fact that this new wave of militarily-enforced sanctions has mainly been a feature of the past ten years has led to a situation where their violation of all legal, humanitarian, and other norms of international behavior is only slowly becoming exposed. Economic sanctions against industrialized and industrializing countries, which include a ban on foreign trade, can be more lethal than limited military assaults. In contrast to the use of bombs and missiles, economic warfare typically does not result in the same level of public outcry over the loss of innocent lives. It becomes, thus, a silent form of killing, one that can be maintained for longer periods of time, causing death and destruction upon a broad spectrum of the population, until the politics behind the policy are satisfied.

By blocking foreign trade to a country that depends on foreign trade for its survival, the very life of civilians is threatened. Sanctions thus punish an entire population, targeting children most of all. According to numerous UN reports, the UN sanctions against the Iraqi people have claimed far more deaths than the deadly Gulf War in 1991. The lack of foodstuffs, medical supplies, and spare parts in Iraq, due to the sanctions and the stringent constraints on humanitarian imports imposed by the UN, have caused untold suffering for the general population. One consequence of sanctions is that Iraq's child mortality has increased by six-fold, causing the estimated death of more than 4,500 children each month over the previous mortality.[1]

The sanctions against the people of Iraq have been the most stringent and destructive in history. From their imposition on 6 August 1990, the sanctions have blatantly disregarded international law and morality. These sanctions were imposed upon the people, via UN

Security Council Resolution 661, to demand that Iraq withdraw all its forces to the points in which they were located on 1 August 1990 and to "restore the authority of the legitimate government of Kuwait." Although the sanctions were established to secure specific and concrete objectives, no reference was made in SCR 661 as to when or how the sanctions would be lifted once the said objectives had been achieved. Subsequent resolutions have escalated the sanctions, transformed their objectives, and broadened their spheres.

Soon after SCR 661, the Security Council introduced a new and dangerous mechanism for the enforcement of the sanctions: authorization for member states to utilize maritime forces "to halt all inward and outward maritime shipping in order to inspect and verify their cargoes" (SCR 665). The most dangerous aspect of Resolution 665 is that by changing the means of enforcement from diplomatic and political means to the arbitrary use of various national navy forces, the Security Council drastically mutated the nature of economic sanctions. The maritime blockade, coupled with the air blockade imposed under SCR 670 in 1990, amounted to an act of war, thereby making the economic sanctions an act of war as well under the law.

The Security Council continued mounting its restrictions on Iraq even after the Iraqi forces withdrew from Kuwait. Resolution 687 in 1991 maintained the embargo on civilian supplies without fixing a time for the lifting of the embargo and without specifying the conditions necessary for its lifting. Given the realization of the specific objectives for which the original sanctions were imposed, no legal ground can be claimed—nor was claimed—for the continuing enforcement of the sanctions. Instead, Resolution 687 called for "the need to be assured of Iraq's peaceful intentions," without specifying how such "intentions" would ever be qualified and met. The Security Council was thus given wide latitude to define, based upon its own arbitrary reasons, when such "intentions" have been met, and the U.S. has veto power to override any assurance that does not meet its fancy.

The resolution further listed an additional ambiguous goal of "restoring peace and stability in the region." How can this objective be achieved through the imposition of sanctions against one country in the region, while the other countries in the same region (some of whom have consistently demonstrated their willingness to invade and attack their neighbors) are not required to accept the "restoration of peace and stability in the region," nor were asked to do so? How can peace and stability be achieved through one party alone? Peace and stability for whom?

The preamble in SCR 687 also called for the "establishment of a nuclear-weapon-free zone" and a "zone free of mass destruction weapons" in the Middle East, and the "achievement of balanced and comprehensive control of armaments in the region." Not only has this segment of the resolution been ignored by the Security Council, but the United States continues to supply Israel, a nuclear power in the region, with military equipment and billions of dollars of annual aid. (Israel is in violation of over seventy United Nations resolutions.)

While the sanctions war continues, year after year, the Security Council—more specifically the UN Special Commission (UNSCOM) and the U.S.—have presented as the case against the Iraqi people the possibility and speculation that Iraq may be harboring chemical or biological weapons. What is not speculation is the immense suffering the people of Iraq have been enduring due to the sanctions. During the past seven years, more than 1.2 million Iraqi civilians, including 750,000 children below the age of five, have died from insufficient food and medicine. According to a 1997 UNICEF report, 32 percent of Iraqi children under the age of five— approximately one million preschoolers, toddlers, and infants—are suffering from severe malnutrition. This is a rise of 72 percent since 1991. Almost one quarter of these children are underweight—twice as high as the levels found in neighboring Jordan or Turkey. If these children survive, they will likely suffer permanent emotional, mental, and physical stunting.

Despite the attempts by numerous governmental officials to deny responsibility, the causality between the UN sanctions and the humanitarian tragedy in Iraq remains undeniable, and is evident in UN reports. One of the clearest official signs of UN awareness of this causality is found in an April 1993 report by UNICEF entitled "Children, War, and Sanctions." It says that "Indeed it may be that one fundamental contradiction remains that politically-motivated sanctions (which are by definition imposed to create hardship) cannot be implemented in a manner which spares the vulnerable."

A 1995 UNICEF document further clarifies this point: "Sanctions are inhibiting the importation of spare parts, chemicals, reagents, and the means of transportation required to provide water and sanitation services to the civilian population of Iraq. What has become increasingly clear is that no significant movement towards food security can be achieved so long as the embargo remains in place. All vital contributors to food availability—agricultural production, importation of foodstuffs, economic stability, and income generation—are dependent on Iraq's ability to purchase and import those items vital to the survival of the civilian population."

Furthermore, the UN's own undersecretary for humanitarian affairs, Yasushi Akashi, after his visit to Iraq in May 1997, stated that the "evidence of prevailing human suffering ... is one of the consequences of economic sanctions." While the sanctions continue, and the number of victims consequently increases, the media persist in phrasing the issue only as a policy question, analyzing the "effectiveness" of the sanctions. "To put effectiveness in the center of the debate necessarily puts the ethical dimension on the side," explains Elias Davidsson, an international human rights activist. "No civilized society uses only effectiveness as criteria to determine policies. By ignoring the 'human cost' of the sanctions, [this question] reflects a criminal approach."[2] The sanctions war against the people of Iraq is exactly that: criminal.

The sanctions against the people of Iraq violate the Purpose and Principles of the UN Charter. The sanctions transgress the recognized human rights and freedoms enshrined in the Universal Declaration of Human Rights (1948) and subsequently reiterated and confirmed by numerous international and regional agreements up to and including the Vienna Declaration on Human Rights (1993). The sanctions, in addition, violate international humanitarian norms as expounded in the Geneva Conventions of 1949 and 1977, and other conventions which outlaw collective punishment and reprisals affecting innocent civilians. They also violate the principles of noninterference in internal affairs, freedom of navigation, freedom of international trade, sovereignty over natural resources, and international norms relating to migrant workers. The sanctions breach the legally binding Charter of Economic Rights and Duties of States, adopted by the UN General Assembly (1974). Furthermore, these sanctions also violate Protocol I of the Geneva Convention, which specifically prohibits the "starvation of civilians as a method of warfare."

That is not all. According to the U.S. Legal Code (Title 18 § 2331), the sanctions against the people of Iraq constitute a crime of international terrorism, since they have been shown to be "acts dangerous to human life ... that would be a criminal violation if committed within the jurisdiction of the United States"; "appear to be intended to coerce [the Iraqi] civilian population"; "appear to be intended to influence the policy of [the Iraqi] government by ... coercion," and they "transcend national boundaries in terms of the means by which they are accomplished." International terrorism has been condemned by the General Assembly of the UN, and is included in the list of international crimes in the UN Law Commission's Draft Code of Crimes Against the Peace and Security of Mankind.

Are the UN Member States obliged to enforce such a criminal UN policy? Legally, UN Member States are obliged to violate the sanctions. The Vienna Convention on the Laws of Treaties specifies that a material breach of a multilateral treaty by any of the parties entitles any party (other than the defaulting State) to suspend the obligation. Thus, more specifically, since the sanctions against the people of Iraq violate the Purposes and Principles of the UN Charter, then the UN decisions can rightfully be considered a breach of the treaty, and thus are grounds for Member States to suspend the sanctions against Iraq. Furthermore, the Principles of the Nuremberg Charter state clearly that it is a duty to disobey patently criminal orders. States are responsible for the consequences of carrying out decisions of the Security Council which turn out to be criminal.

Economic sanctions, as with all other forms of policy, must abide by international law. These sanctions have increasingly become an instrument for the imposition of the foreign policy goals of a small number of big powers rather than an instrument for the peaceful settlement of international disputes. Only the powerful and the rich can enforce sanctions and only the weak and the poor will suffer from them. The struggle will continue until one code of law will be enforced upon us all: the code of justice.

For more information on the legal perspectives of the sanctions war, please refer to the section on law in the Iraq Action Coalition website (http://leb.net/IAC/). Also refer to the "End the Sanctions War on Iraq" resolution at the end of this book. Although this resolution may not always be politically feasible, it is the legal right.

---

[1] "Disastrous Situation of Children in Iraq," UNICEF Report PR/GVA/96/035, 4 October 1996.

[2] Elias Davidsson, "The Economic Sanctions Against the Iraqi People: Consequences and Legal Findings." Davidsson is director of the Center for Policy Research in Reykjavik, Iceland.

WHO IS UNSCOM?

DEIRDRE SINNOTT

It was late October 1997. Tensions had been building as the U.S. threatened Iraq with a sustained bombing campaign. In a week I was to travel to Iraq with a delegation from the International Action Center. Our plane was set to leave on 2 November.

The crisis came after the U.S. tried to push a measure through the UN Security Council barring some of Iraq's officials from traveling outside their country. Iraq reacted by barring U.S. weapons inspectors working with the United Nations Special Commission (UNSCOM) from carrying out any further inspections.

A standoff had developed. It seemed at the time that there might be a new bombing campaign carried out by the United States.

Why would barring a few inspectors from one nation lead to bombings and death? Why is it that UNSCOM, inspectors, and inspections were also at the center of the crisis in February 1998? Who is UNSCOM? What is their real mission in Iraq?

UNSCOM was created by Security Council Resolution 687, passed on 3 April 1991. SCR 687 is a cease-fire agreement that ended the war against Iraq. Paragraphs 7 and 13 laid out the basis for the elimination of weapons of mass destruction and some ballistic missiles, and ongoing monitoring within Iraq. The agreement was accepted by the government of Iraq on 18 April 1991. Iraq had just endured forty-two days of high-tech assault that included nearly 110,000 aerial sorties, 80,000 bombing runs carried out with terrible enthusiasm, and the loss of hundreds of thousands of civilians' and soldiers' lives. Before and during the shooting war, Iraq had been cut off from the world by economic sanctions.

When UNSCOM was set up, the composition of appointed countries was thirteen European, three Asian, one Latin American, one African, one Australian, one Canadian, and one from the United States. There was no representation from the Middle East. The present executive chairperson of UNSCOM is Australian Richard Butler. The executive deputy chairperson is Charles Duelfer from the U.S.

Many people have accused UNSCOM of being under the control of the United States. Russia has proposed broadening its membership. As of this writing in mid-1998, there is one deputy chairperson. Russia has suggested the position be made up of five seats, one for each of the permanent members of the Security Council. Then-U.S. Ambassador to the United Nations Bill Richardson said that Washington would "reject any attempt to politicize the disarmament commission."[1] No additional deputy chairpersons have been added.

The inspection teams themselves are also politically structured. During testimony before the Security Council on 20 November 1997, seven inspectors were allowed to testify. Three of the seven were from the U.S.; the other four were from Europe. One of the most notoriously unbalanced teams was the one sent to Iraq on 11 January 1998. One of the agreements that ended the crisis in November was that UNSCOM inspection teams be more balanced and have more participation from all permanent members of the Security Council. The team that started the January crisis was made up of sixteen people: nine were from the U.S., five from Britain, one from Australia, and one from Russia.

That team was led by William Scott Ritter from the U.S. The Iraqis complained about Ritter's behavior as early as November 1997.[2] He is a former U.S. Marine colonel who participated in the high-tech slaughter known as the Gulf War. Is a former combatant a candidate to be an impartial judge of his former deadly enemy? Ritter has worked for UNSCOM since 1991.[3]

It is U.S. policy to keep the sanctions in place until Saddam Hussein is out of power. Former Secretary of State Warren Christopher reaffirmed this in 1994. It appeared at the time that UNSCOM head Rolf Ekeus's report to the Security Council about the readiness of the monitoring equipment could lead to an end of the sanctions.[4] Christopher blocked any discussion of lifting the sanctions, saying, "We want compliance with all the UN resolutions. And I don't believe he [Saddam Hussein] can do that."[5]

British inspectors on the 11 January team can't be considered neutral either. Britain is the former colonial power that was forcibly thrown out by the Iraqi Revolution of 1958.

The Oil for Food deal is in the news a lot. However, only about 53 percent of the money from the sale of Iraq's oil really goes for food and medicine. Part of the money goes to fund UNSCOM. All of the operations, the inspections, the monitoring systems, the support staff, the offices in New York, Bahrain, and Baghdad are all paid for by Iraq. It comes to about $30 million per year.[6] As of mid-1998, UNSCOM had cost Iraq $210 million.

UNSCOM has carried out 7,800 site inspections since it started its work. It regularly monitors at least 340 locations by sending weapons inspectors on surprise visits. It has over 130 cameras installed in thirty other locations. It also employs air-sampling devices that can record minute traces of chemicals.[7] UNSCOM has accounted for or destroyed 817 of 819 missiles Iraq purchased from Russia.[8] That leaves only two unaccounted for. It has completely destroyed a laboratory called Al-Hakam along with tons of chemicals. Many of the chemicals destroyed were so-called dual-use, meaning they could be employed in either civilian or military applications.

UNSCOM biological warfare expert and University of Maryland professor Raymond Zalinskas was interviewed on National Public Radio. The interviewer asked Zalinskas whether Iraq's weapons were a danger to the U.S. and the world. He replied:

> There is more of a *potential* danger than an actual danger. UNSCOM has destroyed all known chemical weapons facilities and also all known chemical weapons. In the biological weapons area UNSCOM has destroyed the dedicated biological weapons production site Al-Hakam plus other ones that were at other institutes. *So far as we know Iraq has no biological weapons stored up.* There are about eighty research, development, and production facilities in Iraq which are civilian facilities, so even if you eliminate the breweries, dairies, and food production plants there are about twenty or thirty that could be converted to BW [biological weapons] use. You have the work force, the scientists, technicians, and engineers and the potential of converting a bunch of civilian facilities to warfare purposes, but all of this would take a rather long time, about six months, to develop these weapons.[9] [Emphasis added.]

UNSCOM is already monitoring these sites with the sophisticated technology needed to detect such activities.

Zalinskas went on to say:

> There are no weapon sites that we know. I was a biological warfare expert. I visited about sixty facilities at one time or another,

most of them are pretty innocuous, the only one that was really something very significant in this area was Al-Hakam, but that was destroyed in June 1996.[10]

Francis A. Boyle, professor of international law and author of the Biological Weapons Anti-Terrorism Act of 1989, who testified before Congress about biological weapons, disagreed with a 26 February 1998 *New York Times* article, "How Iraq's Biological Weapons Program Came to Light." He called the article "nothing more than a piece of pure propaganda mongering for war against Iraq." Boyle said it showed "the way mainstream news media work in the United States of America, including and especially the *New York Times*, which has been mongering for war against Iraq for quite some time."[11]

One of the arguments in the U.S. media is that Iraq is not in compliance, and that until it is, the sanctions must remain in place. There are those who maintain that Iraq is in compliance. But what does compliance have to do with the sanctions?

According to a 1996 UN Food and Agriculture Organization report, the sanctions are directly responsible for the deaths of 1.5 million children, women, and men. These sanctions are genocidal and are against international laws. So the U.S. argument about compliance is in effect claiming the "right" to commit genocide.

Over the years UNSCOM has become an institution. It has a direct stake in keeping inspections going forever. It employs 120 people in its Baghdad office alone.[12] Inspectors are paid a salary plus a stipend of $100 per day to look and look and look. Even if they don't find anything, they are paid to keep looking. The International Atomic Energy Agency reported that:

> The IAEA and UNSCOM have continued their implementation of a joint program of inspection of Iraqi sites which, in the judgment of IAEA and UNSCOM, are deemed to have *capabilities* suitable for conducting work on some aspect of weapons of mass destruction *notwithstanding the lack of evidence or indication of such work.*"[13] [Emphasis added.]

Part of UNSCOM's job is not only to keep under surveillance at least 340 sites but also to monitor all imports of possible dual-use chemicals and equipment to Iraq once sanctions are lifted. This means that many items Iraq cannot buy under the sanctions—such as chlorine, blood pressure monitors, and headlights for cars—will still be under the strictest import guidelines and monitoring for years to come. An image of UNSCOM inspectors that might come to mind is of white-coat professionals carrying clipboards as they check off lists of places to look at and people to question. But if you ask Iraqis how UNSCOM carries out its job, you will hear of inspectors going through garbage cans and harassing female doctors, even searching their purses to make sure they're not smuggling weapons of mass destruction. Some of these incidents have been documented in the second edition of the book *The Children Are Dying*.[14]

Father G. Simon Harak of Fairfield University did extensive interviews with people who experienced UNSCOM inspections first hand. He reports that nuns at a convent of the Chaldean Church in northern Iraq had their rooms searched, drawer by drawer. The bodies of recently deceased nuns were about to be exhumed to check for chemical weapons when Bishop Emmanuel Delly stepped in and stopped it.

Father Harak also found that UNSCOM had visited the University of Mosul about 250 miles north of Baghdad. Inspectors went into the library there, pulled chemistry books from the shelves, threw them out the windows, then dumped them in a ditch and burned them. Sound familiar? UNSCOM must destroy Iraq's *capability* for producing weapons; therefore it must destroy the knowledge. By the same logic, it would have to eliminate a few scientists who have the knowledge.

Incidents like these caused Iraq to insist—in the UN-Iraq Memorandum of Understanding signed in Iraq on 23 February 1998 by UN Secretary-General Kofi Annan and Saddam Hussein—that diplomats from various countries be included in the teams that inspect the so-called presidential sites. During those inspections diplomats often sided with Iraqis against the UNSCOM inspectors and their tactics.[15]

Exaggeration is one of the tools in UNSCOM's bag of tricks. Richard Butler was quoted in a *New York Times* article in January 1998 as saying that Iraq had enough biological weapons to "blow away Tel Aviv." Both the Chinese and Russian ambassadors demanded an explanation for the statement. Butler had to tone it down a bit after that, but the damage was already done. In the minds of many in the U.S., Iraq was going to use biological weapons on Israel.

The team commissioned by Kofi Annan to map Iraq's "sensitive presidential sites" in February 1998 reported they were "much smaller and vastly different than Washington and the UN Special Commission to disarm Iraq have asserted."[16]

It is the height of hypocrisy for the U.S., the country with by far the most weapons of mass destruction—chemical, biological, conventional, and nuclear—to point to any other country and say that possession or potential possession justifies deadly sanctions. At last count the U.S. possessed 12,000 nuclear weapons.[17] There are nine Army chemical weapons storage depots that contain a total of 28,000 tons of nerve gases, such as sarin and VX, and mustard blister agent.[18] Biological weapons developed in the U.S. have been sold all over the world. The Pentagon brags that it is able to carry on two wars at one time. It is the U.S. government and the Pentagon that are the deadly threat to the entire world.

One of the people I met in Iraq was Zainab Tarq. She was a beautiful fourteen-year-old who sat in the terminal ward of the Saddam Training Hospital in Basra suffering from leukemia. We stood over her and talked about her case. There has been a ten-fold increase in cases of leukemia, said her doctors, especially around Basra. They believe it is probably due to the Pentagon's use of depleted uranium weapons in great numbers in the area.

Zainab was about seven years old during the war against Iraq. She had now become a bright, friendly, lovely young woman who should have had her whole life ahead of her. Zainab had a full head of hair because the hospital had no chemotherapy medication or other cancer treatments available. After I took her picture, her mother chased after me to ask if I could send back a print. Maybe this was the only picture of her that Zainab's mother would ever have. Iraqis are not in the position to buy and develop film these days, even if it could be imported under the sanctions. I agreed to send the picture and a friend took it when he visited his family several months later. During the Iraq Sanctions Challenge, one of the delegates asked the doctors about Zainab for me. She had died.

Zainab is just one of about 250 people a day who die as a direct result of the sanctions. Each day the sanctions are in place people in Iraq pay with their lives for this U.S./UN policy that seeks to dominate Iraq and the entire oil-rich region.

UNSCOM is in Iraq to give the policy the veneer of legitimacy. UNSCOM is a political tool that will be stationed in Iraq for many years to come. It should be dismantled. It, or another formation like it, may be hauled out to dominate and terrorize other countries that, like Iraq, attempt to have a measure of independence in the face of U.S. global domination. The worldwide anti-sanctions movement needs to keep a very close eye on UNSCOM in the years to come, to be able to expose its real goals and methods and to demand its decommissioning.

---

[1] "U.S. says no to Russian UNSCOM deputy," United Press International, 6 March 1998.

[2] Press Briefing by UNSCOM Executive Chairman, 20 November 1997.

[3] Daily Press Briefing of Office of Spokesman for Secretary-General, 16 January 1998.

[4] Phyllis Bennis, *Calling the Shots: How Washington Dominates Today's UN* (New York: Olive Branch Press, 1996).

[5] "MacNeil-Lehrer Newshour," PBS, 16 October 1994.

[6] UNSCOM Mandate, Section 8 Finance, http://www.un.org/Depts/unscom/unscom.htm.

[7] Christopher S. Wren, "An attack would damage UN monitoring, aid efforts," *New York Times*, 22 November 1997.

[8] Letter from UNSCOM Chairperson Richard Butler to the President of the UN Security Council, 22 November 1997.

[9] "Morning Show," National Public Radio, 13 February 1998.

[10] Ibid.

[11] Francis A. Boyle, http://www.library.cornell.edu/colldev/mideast/iraqbio.htm, 26 February 1998.

[12] Wren, "An attack would damage ... ."

[13] Report of the International Atomic Energy Agency to the UN Secretary-General, 7 April 1998.

[14] Ramsey Clark, et al., *The Children Are Dying: Impact of U.S./UN Sanctions on Iraq*, 2d ed. (New York: International Action Center, 1998).

[15] Letter from the Secretary-General Addressed to the President of the Security Council, 15 April 1998, § 15 and 16.

[16] Barbara Crossette, "Experts Find Smaller List of Forbidden Sites in Iraq," *New York Times*, 21 February 1998.

[17] Robert S. Norris and William Arkin, Natural Resources Defense Council, "Nuclear Notebook," *Bulletin of Atomic Scientists*, November/December 1997, http://www.bullatomsci.org/issues/nukenotes/nd97nuke note.html.

[18] Carla Anne Robbins, "Army's Huge Supply of Nerve Gas Poses Unnerving Questions," *Wall Street Journal*, 1 June 1998.

WEAPONS OF MASS DESTRUCTION

RICHARD BECKER

The U.S. government has blocked all attempts to end the sanctions on Iraq, using as a justification the threat purportedly posed by Iraq's weapons programs—chemical, biological, and nuclear. The Iraqi government has responded that whatever such weaponry it may have once possessed (Iraq has never had nuclear weapons) was destroyed under UN supervision in the aftermath of the Gulf War. Since the war, UNSCOM weapons inspectors have combed Iraq, conducting thousands of site visits. Every factory and workplace which has "dual-use technology"—technology which could have military as well as civilian applications—is monitored by 24-hour video cameras.

One would certainly get the impression from reading or watching the corporate media that Washington is really opposed to the development and spread of nuclear, chemical, biological, and other lethal weapons. But in fact, the U.S. is far and away the leader in creating and producing virtually all forms of weaponry.

A June 1998 Brookings Institution report has calculated that since 1940, the U.S. government has spent more than nineteen trillion dollars—$19,000,000,000,000—in the pursuit of military objectives. This mind-boggling figure amounts to more than $70,000 for every person presently living in the United States. Had these wasted resources been utilized to meet people's needs, crises like hunger, homelessness, illiteracy, infant mortality, environmental destruction, poor sanitation, and disease could have been largely eliminated.

Nearly a third of U.S. military spending, $5.8 trillion, has been for nuclear weapons. Today, seven years after the end of the "Cold War" was declared, the Pentagon has more than 16,000 nuclear warheads, more than all other countries combined. These "city-busters," as the military planners like to call them, are deployed around the globe aboard submarines, surface ships, missiles, and planes in many of the 100 countries where U.S. troops are based.

The U.S. is the only country to ever drop nuclear bombs on people—the atomic destruction of Hiroshima and Nagasaki in August 1945. The U.S. is also the only admitted nuclear power that has refused to adopt a no-first-strike policy. And, in clear violation of the Comprehensive Test Ban Treaty which it has signed, U.S. scientists are continuing to develop and test "third generation" nuclear bombs.

In the development and use of chemical and biological weapons, the U.S. is also number one—from the intentional spread of diseases among the Native peoples of North America, to the massive poisoning of Vietnam's environment and population (as well as many U.S. GIs) with Agent Orange/dioxin, to the repeated use of biologic agents to devastate Cuba's agriculture.

Today, the greatest threat from weapons of mass destruction comes not from Iraq or Iran or Libya, but from the same country that makes the most noise about this threat: the United States. The attempts by the U.S. ruling class to limit who can possess such weapons is part of Washington's strategy for maintaining and expanding its global domination. It wants to be able to threaten, or actually use, these horrific weapons without having to fear a comparable response from the targeted country. Their propaganda efforts aside, President Bill Clinton, Secretary of State Madeleine Albright, and the Pentagon generals know full well that Iraq has complied with the demands of the UN Security Council in regard to weapons of mass destruction, demands that are onerous and intrusive of Iraq's sovereignty.

During the February 1998 crisis, when the U.S. and Britain were preparing a new bombing war against Iraq, the Clinton administration engaged in a wild campaign of disinformation—better known as lies—to create a war hysteria in the U.S. The president claimed that a new and massive aerial assault was necessary to "protect our children and grandchildren for generations to come." Standing in front of a large map of the U.S. capital at one press conference, Clinton stated that Iraq had hundreds of presidential sites (diplomatic compounds the Iraqis had declared off-limits to weapons inspectors), "one bigger than the District of Columbia"—which covers over sixty square miles. These sites were alleged to be possible storage areas for chemical or biological weapons by administration spokespersons.

On 20 February UN cartographers and surveyors issued their report on the sites in question. There are eight sites, the report said, comprising a total of 12.2 square miles, of which 3.9 square miles are made up of lakes. Many of the buildings on the sites are guest houses and one is a presidential residence.[1] The following day's *New York Times* carried a lengthy story on possible targets for the anticipated U.S./British air war. Buried in the article were admissions by administration officials that they were well aware of the flagrant dishonesty of their anti-Iraq media campaign. "American air power can also strike the eight presidential sites that President Hussein has put off limits," the *Times* reported. "But American officials say it is unlikely that biological and chemical weapons are housed there."[2] A little later in the same article came the startling admission from an administration official that Iraq's "weapons of mass destruction" were now, "in a strict logical sense," nothing more than "a nuisance."

The day after this story appeared, UN Secretary-General Kofi Annan and Iraq's Deputy Prime Minister Tariq Aziz announced that an agreement had been reached to open all sites in Iraq to UN inspection. U.S. officials were clearly unhappy about the agreement, but were forced to accept it and put their bombing plans on hold because of the strength of world-wide opposition to a new war. Since that time, there have been many UNSCOM inspections with full Iraqi cooperation. No discoveries of any existing weapons have been reported by the inspectors or by the U.S. big business media, which has Iraq under microscopic observation.

Richard Butler, the head of UNSCOM and an Australian national who has worked closely with the U.S., has testified that all but two of the 819 SCUD missiles sold to Iraq by the Soviet Union have been recovered.[3] Iraq is banned from producing any missile with a range of more than one hundred miles. This means that, even if Iraq possessed chemical or biological warheads (which it clearly does not), it would have no way to deliver them. While the UN cease-fire resolution that ended the Gulf War required that Iraq destroy its weapons of mass destruction, the U.S. has unilaterally gone one big step further, demanding that Iraq should no longer have the capacity to produce such weaponry. This demand has very far-reaching implications.

Much of civilian industry is potentially "dual-use," regardless of the country in which it is located. Car assembly lines can be refitted to build military vehicles. A plant that today produces pesticides can tomorrow produce poison gases and other chemical agents for military use. The same applies to the entire petrochemical industry. The most important element in technological development is the acquisition of knowledge and technique, that is, the human element. The U.S. position, therefore, really amounts to a demand for the de-industrialization of Iraq, which fits very well into the overall strategy of returning Iraq to its pre-1958 status as a virtual colony.

---

[1] *New York Times*, 21 February 1998.
[2] Ibid.
[3] Letter from UNSCOM Chairperson Richard Butler to the President of the UN Security Council, 22 November 1997.

TOO LITTLE, TOO LATE: OIL FOR FOOD

SARAH SLOAN

Defenders of the sanctions on Iraq, when not talking about Saddam Hussein and his palaces, often note two things: first, that the sanctions have a humanitarian exemption; second, that the UN implemented the Oil for Food deal to relieve the shortage of humanitarian goods.

That the shortage exists despite the exemption is not because of Saddam Hussein, but because the UN has frozen all of Iraq's foreign assets and because the sanctions prevent the sale of oil. It is oil revenue, along with these assets, that Iraq would use to purchase humanitarian goods. However, because of the sanctions, the Iraqi government has few means by which to do so. The exemption, therefore, is meaningless in any assessment of the Iraqi government's role in the humanitarian situation. The exemption allows only donations by nongovernmental organizations. Iraqi doctors reported to me that these donations are not continuous, not adequate, and not geared to their specific needs.

The UN monitors everything Iraq imports. Many absolutely necessary items are barred under the excuse that they are "dual-use," that is, potentially useful in some military form despite their civilian intention. This is extended to include many humanitarian goods such as medicines, medical supplies, scientific and medical textbooks, chemicals with which to treat water, and agricultural machinery.

Under criticism for the resulting hardships and suffering in Iraq, the orchestrators of the sanctions then came up with a new propaganda tool. In 1995 the UN Security Council adopted Resolution 986, commonly referred to as Oil for Food. SCR 986 allowed the Iraqi government to sell $2 billion worth of oil every six months.

Because of protest at the inadequacy of this deal, the UN Security Council on 20 February 1998, as part of the resolution of a new war crisis, voted to increase the amount Iraq is allowed to sell to $5.2 billion every six months. A number of different UN agencies (UNICEF, WHO, WFP, FAO, UNESCO, UNDP/Department of Economic and Social Affairs) and "observers" control this revenue and monitor all aspects of distribution. Between 5 December 1997 and 15 May 1998, UN agencies conducted a total of 107,772 observations (over 650 per day) in six sectors: food, health, agriculture, electricity, water and sanitation, and education.[1]

However, Iraq's oil industry is unable to produce this increased quota of oil because of the lack of spare parts and supplies.

On 22 May 1998 the *Wall Street Journal* reported that Baghdad had rejected a U.S. proposal to automatically renew the Oil for Food deal. The media slant on this was that it proves the U.S. cares about the humanitarian situation in Iraq, while the government of Iraq does not. But this is not the case. The U.S. government created the humanitarian problem and is using the inadequate Oil for Food deal to assuage protest so that sanctions can be continued. Iraq wishes the focus to remain on the sanctions so that people will realize the effects and agitate for their lifting.

UN Secretary-General Kofi Annan described the deal:

> I should like to reiterate, as I have stated in my previous reports to the Council, the exceptional and unprecedented complexity of the humanitarian program being carried out pursuant to Council Resolution 986 (1995) of 14 April 1995 and that it should not, therefore, be confused with a development program and the requirements of such a program. It is a unique program, established by the Council as a temporary measure to provide for the humanitarian needs of the Iraqi people, which is being implemented within the context of a sanctions regime with all its attendant political, psychological, and commercial dimensions. ...[2]

Here, Annan writes with knowledge of the misconceptions about this program, not only in the general public but within the UN—the audience for this report. By noting the "context of a sanctions regime," he is saying that any "humanitarian" measures taken while sanctions are in place would not negate their painful effects, but would instead be negated by the sanctions. In this same report, he also noted that "this sum is inadequate to prevent further deterioration in humanitarian conditions and cannot effect the improvement in the health and nutritional status of the Iraqi population the Council hoped for when it unanimously adopted the measure."

Annan later reported that the "tendency is to increase the funds used for administering the program, which will unquestionably result in a reduction in the additional resources that should be allocated for the purchase of humanitarian supplies."[3] The division of the oil revenue leaves only 53 percent for humanitarian goods.

This report spells out how the oil revenue is to be divided: $2.17 billion for humanitarian goods purchased by Iraq; $523.9 million for humanitarian goods for three northern governates; $1.31 billion for the UN Compensation Fund for Kuwait; $90.8 million for UN operation and administration of SCR 986; $30.8 million for UNSCOM; $275.9 million for transport of petroleum via Turkey's pipeline, and $41 million to an escrow account for payment of requests made by the Secretary-General for any additional expenses incurred by SCR 986 and UNSCOM.

The Food and Agriculture Organization (FAO) and the World Food Program (WFP)—two UN agencies—reported on the effects of Oil for Food. Their report notes that "There is now concern that emergency assistance to vulnerable groups might be curtailed due to widespread perception amongst donors that malnutrition problems have been solved following the implementation of SCR 986."[4]

They note that the amount provided "does not meet the minimum requirements of the population of Iraq" and that it is "quantitatively and qualitatively inadequate." That is, it is not enough and it lacks essentials: meat, fish, eggs, and dairy products are absent; vitamin A and vitamin C are extremely low; calcium, zinc, riboflavin, and vitamin B6 are very low.[5] "Malnutrition still remains a serious problem throughout the country."[6] The Iraqi Ministry of Health, UNICEF, and the WFP, based on a 16-18 March 1998 survey, reported that "the nutritional situation of children under five remains unchanged since the previous survey, in March 1997."[7]

Even U.S. politicians admit this. A letter from a group of Congress members headed by Rep. John Conyers (D-Mich.), circulating at the time of publication of this book, urged President Clinton to rescind the sanctions. It quoted an FAO report saying that if the economic embargo continued, "even allowing for the amelioration that will occur with SCR 986, the situation will progressively deteriorate with grave consequences to the health and life of the Iraqi people."

This letter also noted the slow pace of the UN in approving contracts submitted by the Iraqi government for the purchase of goods.

The agencies also made notations that transcend the dates of their reports. Though the amount of food increased with the upgrading of the deal, other problems persist. The U.S. bombing campaigns during the 1991 Gulf War destroyed the infrastructure of Iraq—including centers of communication, water purification, electricity, and warehousing. In August 1996 and again on 5 June 1998, UNICEF reported that half the rural population draws water from contaminated sources. The Secretary-General's report stated that "substantial improvements in nutritional status cannot be expected until there is a corresponding improvement in related areas that have an effect on nutrition." Contaminated water causes diarrheal disease, which is "one of the most important contributing factors to malnutrition in children."[8]

The FAO/WFP report of 1997 stated:

> Although the advent of SCR 986 has increased food availability, nutritional problems do and will continue to exist. Of major importance is the severe deterioration of the water and sanitation system in Iraq. It is recommended that high priority be given to comprehensive and sustainable rehabilitation of the water and sanitation system, otherwise water-borne diseases, including nutritional marasmus, will remain a major problem despite improved food availability.[9] ... Such lack of water and sanitation services has a direct link with the prevalence of infantile malnutrition.[10]

Malnourished children under five, hospital in-patients, children in orphanages, people in social institutions, displaced persons, and refugees are "not adequately covered."[11] Even when food availability increases enough to alleviate the current undernutrition, many young adults "may remain undersized due to deprivation in childhood."[12]

These problems are caused by the sanctions, not the Iraqi government. Agencies of the UN itself confirm this. The FAO/WFP 1997 report states that "Before the Gulf war, food availability was quite adequate."[13] "A return to these levels [of food availability before 1990] cannot be expected under existing conditions ... the Mission believes that the population would return to these levels if conditions permitted."[14] WFP observers reported that "over 99.5 percent of the population received equally whatever general ration was available during a given month."[15] The WHO report stated that "United

Nations observers note that handling and processing losses remain within the acceptable limit of 2 percent at all points on the distribution chain."[16] The Iraqi government has done a good job of protecting and conserving what food was available and distributing it equitably among the people.

Before 1990, Iraq imported two to three billion dollars worth of food annually, depending on domestic production.[17] The FAO in 1996 estimated the cost of imports (given the rise in population since 1990) at $3.106 billion per year.[18] This does not include nonedible humanitarian goods such as medicine, medical supplies, spare parts for agricultural machinery, water treatment supplies, and many other goods for which there is a great need.

The Secretary-General, the FAO, the WFP, and the WHO have all been to Iraq to witness the suffering caused by the sanctions. I have been there also, and can add my observations that the desperate situation continues, and will continue until the sanctions are lifted.

---

[1] Report of the Secretary-General Pursuant to Paragraph 7 of Resolution 1143 (1997).

[2] Report of the Secretary-General on the UN Iraq-Kuwait Observation Mission (9-24-97 to 3-23-98), S/1998/477, 5 June 1998.

[3] Ibid., Annex IV, p. 46.

[4] FAO/WFP Food Supply and Nutrition Assessment Mission to Iraq, 3 October 1997, section 1, p. 1.

[5] Ibid., section 5.1, p. 9.

[6] Ibid., section 1, p. 1.

[7] See note 2, § 57, p. 17.

[8] Ibid., § 58.

[9] See note 4, section 5.1, p. 10.

[10] Ibid., section 5, p. 8.

[11] Ibid., section 5.1, p. 10.

[12] Ibid., section 5, p. 8.

[13] Ibid., section 5, p. 7.

[14] Ibid., section 5.1, p. 10.

[15] See note 3, § 47.

[16] Ibid., § 48.

[17] See note 4, section 4, p. 6.

[18] "Iraq still faces shortages despite Oil for Food deal," http://www.fao.org/News/1996/960609-E.HTM.

A WOLF IN SHEEP'S CLOTHING

SARA FLOUNDERS

The strangulation of Iraq through sanctions is a policy shrouded in official lies whose devastating consequences have been ignored by the major corporate media. It is held in place globally through more than ten UN Security Council resolutions and backed up by a U.S. military presence in the Gulf that costs $50 billion a year and deploys aircraft carriers, jet fighters, and satellite reconnaissance. Various pieces of U.S. legislation defining the economic blockade devote hundreds of lines to threats of imprisonment and massive fines. And when all else fails, there are always dirty tricks and cynical media lies.

The NBC-TV news magazine "Dateline" on 29 June 1998 gave people in this country an astounding view of Iraq under sanctions—a view totally different from what I experienced a few weeks earlier as a delegate of the Iraq Sanctions Challenge. Anchor John Hockenberry, whose camera team had accompanied a shipment of medicine to Iraq organized by the group AmeriCares, centered the report on Iraqis dancing the night away in happy abandon at discos, purchasing luxury items, building palaces—"new ones all the time"—and watching pirated copies of *Titanic*.

The message of this television special on the AmeriCares' shipment came through loud and clear: "conditions are not as bad as my imagination led me to expect"; "people figure out how to get around" the sanctions; "the food situation is under control"; it's "not as bad as it could be"; there are "periodic shortages of medicine and anesthesia" but "we're not seeing sick, profoundly ill children." The special ended with reassuring phrases: "They will get by. ... Life goes on."

Why didn't the horror of the sanctions get through? Why was NBC so interested in the AmeriCares trip? Could it have something to do with the fact that NBC is owned and controlled by General Electric, the largest military weapons manufacturer in the world?

Selling U.S. wars and military adventures is the bottom line for GE's major stockholders.

The goal of the Iraq Sanctions Challenge was to rip the veneer off the bland word "sanctions" and expose the full horror of that systematic strangulation of a whole country. The eighty-four participants who went to Iraq with four tons of medicine on 6-13 May 1998, and the thousands of supporters who raised funds and support for the effort, did so as a challenge to the criminal sanctions laws and were willing to risk severe legal consequences.

The other shipment of medical supplies, sponsored by AmeriCares, was taken to Iraq just a few days earlier, on 28 April. On the surface both seemed to be humanitarian efforts to bring desperately needed medical supplies to Iraq. But the two trips provide a classic example of the difference between form and essence.

The AmeriCares shipment was a sophisticated effort to reinforce and prolong the sanctions by blaming the Iraqi government for the resulting starvation and disease. This U.S. group was positioning itself to be a "humanitarian" cover for continuing the sanctions. The publicity at the time of that shipment sought to create the impression that a few tons of supplies, if taken past the Iraqi government and directly to the hospitals, would alleviate the crisis. Later, the "Dateline" show went even further and denied there was a crisis.

A closer look at AmeriCares gives an understanding of how humanitarian assistance can function as an arm of the most brutal forms of U.S. foreign policy.

Since the sanctions were first imposed on Iraq in August 1990, the U.S. State Department's official position has been that food and medicine are not included in the restrictions. But these officials know very well that it takes more than a cup of rice to survive. All of Iraq's billions of dollars in hard currency deposited in banks around the world were frozen, all credits were frozen, and all exports—from oil to dates—that could earn hard currency were restricted. The Iraqi dinar became a worthless currency as inflation soared past 2,000 percent.

Iraq's infrastructure was devastated by 110,000 aerial sorties flown during the forty days of bombing in 1991. It could not be rebuilt as no spare parts have been allowed in. Commerce with the outside world is shut down. Industries are denied materials, putting millions out of work. Food production has plummeted without fertilizers, pesticides, or preservatives.

Meanwhile, the U.S. Department of Justice threatens anyone in the U.S. who dares break the sanctions with twelve years of imprisonment. Even the simplest shipment of food or medicine entails highly restrictive licenses and bureaucratic delays of many months.

Around the world millions of people have sent supplies and confronted the policy of starvation with militant demonstrations. Trade unions, human rights, religious and progressive grassroots organizations in many countries have used their modest resources in a collective expression of solidarity and defiance.

In the U.S. many thousands of people were involved in the grassroots campaign of the Iraq Sanctions Challenge. For the first time since the war a broad coalition was formed that included significant religious organizations—Catholic, Protestant, Muslim—along with political and activist groups. The Iraq Sanctions Challenge involved or was in communication with almost every U.S. group concerned about conditions in Iraq.

Just days before the 6 May departure, as centers around the country were organizing major send-off rallies and press events challenging the sanctions, came news of an unexpected shipment of medical supplies to Iraq from AmeriCares. For over seven years this organization had sent no supplies or even issued a press release on the Iraqi health crisis. Major media publicity about the shipment at first raised expectations and enthusiasm. Was the political climate on the sanctions issue changing? However, its real purpose soon became clear.

The organizers of the AmeriCares shipment announced they were abstaining from any political discussion critical of the U.S. role in the sanctions policy. Their shipment was "strictly humanitarian." However, their criticism of Iraq was highly political and reinforced the U.S. State Department line.

Their public statements condemned Saddam Hussein for "manipulating UN humanitarian programs" and called on Iraq to cooperate with the UN Security Council. They declared the medicine they were taking would be delivered directly to hospitals so it would not be stolen or appropriated by the military.

The shipment's arrival on 28 April evoked wide media coverage in the U.S. Both CBS Evening News and ABC World News Tonight did special reports, describing the aid as "pioneering." ABC's Peter Jennings enthused, "This is the first time since the Gulf War that American aid of any kind has been flown in."

Even though all flights to Iraq had been banned for more than seven years, AmeriCares was given permission to fly its shipment of medicine directly to Baghdad. The flight was arranged in coordination with the Royal Jordanian Air Force. Special permission was granted by the UN Security Council. At the last minute, when the Iraqi government refused to allow any military aircraft to land in Baghdad, AmeriCares was able to quickly charter two other planes to take the supplies. Even though the UN Security Council requires one month's advance notice of the exact coordinates and type of any aircraft applying to fly to Iraq, AmeriCares was able to get the approval for this change in plans in one day.

AmeriCares claims its medicines were all donated by major U.S. pharmaceutical firms. In contrast, pharmaceutical companies that had pledged to contribute to the Iraq Sanctions Challenge were threatened by the U.S. Department of Justice that such a donation would be in violation of U.S. law and that they would face prosecution and fines.

Instead of facing threats of imprisonment like the delegates of the Iraq Sanctions Challenge, the AmeriCares delegation was applauded by the Clinton administration, which released the following statement on 28 April: "The United States Government was pleased to assist AmeriCares in its effort to undertake this mission. ... We remain deeply disturbed by the manipulation of UN humanitarian programs by Saddam Hussein, and again call upon the Iraqi regime to cooperate with UN Security Council Resolution 1153, which authorizes increased humanitarian aid to the people of Iraq."

AmeriCares distributed to the media a letter of support from the National Security Council (NSC). The letter to AmeriCares founder and chair Robert C. Macauley was signed by Eric P. Schwartz, the Special Assistant to the President and the Director for Democracy, Human Rights, and Humanitarian Affairs of the NSC. It said, "On behalf of the Administration allow me to express appreciation to you and the entire AmeriCares organization for your efforts in organizing this important mission."[1]

The White House was genuinely grateful because this mission attempted to upstage the efforts of many thousands of people across the U.S. who had, at great sacrifice and risk, collected several million dollars worth of medical supplies for Iraq in order to demonstrate graphically the conditions of famine and plague artificially created by the sanctions.

The AmeriCares shipment was clearly a cynical, one-shot publicity stunt by an organization that functions as an arm of U.S. foreign policy. A call to the national office of AmeriCares in New Canaan, Conn., two months after their much-publicized shipment confirmed they do not plan to send any additional supplies or assistance to Iraq. This is a group that brags it is the world's largest private relief organization.

AmeriCares is a highly political organization. Barbara Bush, wife of former CIA director and U.S. President George Bush, is its ambassador-at-large. Its sixteenth annual fund-raising party was held this year on the USS Intrepid—an aircraft carrier converted into a military museum and docked on the Hudson River in New York City. The co-chairs of the gala were George and Barbara Bush. George's brother, Prescott Bush Jr., is on AmeriCares' board of directors.

The dinner honored Amoco President William Lowrie and Mayo Foundation President Dr. Robert Waller.[2] Amoco, one of the largest oil companies in the world, is a direct beneficiary of the Gulf War. It has provided over $46 million to AmeriCares Foundation. This is hardly generosity, considering the trillions of dollars in oil wealth that Amoco has stolen from the Arab people.

AmeriCares describes itself at its Internet web site as the "humanitarian arm of Corporate America. ... Overseeing AmeriCares operations is an Advisory Committee composed of some of the leading minds in business, medicine, and government, including support from all of the living Presidents."[3]

The founder and chair of AmeriCares is Robert C. Macauley, president of Virginia Fibre—a multimillion-dollar paper manufacturing company. He went to Yale with George Bush and has been his buddy since childhood.[4] Macauley says the inspiration for AmeriCares came from Pope John Paul II at a 1982 Vatican meeting. Its first mission that same year was an airlift and distribution network in Poland,[5] which had become indebted to Western banks and was reeling from the social and political effects of food price increases demanded by its creditors.

Throughout the 1980s AmeriCares continued to play an active role in Eastern Europe in coordination with the Reagan administration and the Vatican, spreading the influence of its corporate patrons in a region where socialist economic planning was crumbling.

Since then AmeriCares' "mission" has spread to over forty countries world-wide. Its literature describes how, just hours after U.S. troops took over Kuwait City at the end of the Gulf War, an Ameri-Cares' Boeing 707 cargo jet arrived carrying a team of physicians from the White House and the Mayo Clinic.[6]

The timing of the recent planeload of supplies to Iraq is hardly the first controversy over a shipment from AmeriCares. Sandinista officials accused AmeriCares of being a CIA front and part of the secret network of private groups used by Marine Corps Lt. Col. Oliver North to deliver aid to the contras. In 1988 the embattled Sandinista government in Nicaragua rejected an airlift of newsprint donated by AmeriCares to the right-wing opposition daily newspaper, *La Prensa*. It had been timed to arrive just before the elections. The newspapers that supported the Sandinista government were unable to buy newsprint at that time because of a U.S.-imposed embargo on newsprint, but Vice President George Bush's staff called the Nicaraguan Embassy to try to expedite the shipment to *La Prensa*. Two years earlier, AmeriCares had delivered 200 tons of newsprint to *La Prensa* during another crisis created by the U.S.[7]

AmeriCares has also delivered supplies to contra terrorists based in Honduras. AmeriCares' tax returns revealed donations of cash and materials to the brother of contra leader Adolfo Calero.[8] The Nicaraguan Freedom Fund, a front organization of Rev. Sun Myung Moon's Unification Church, channeled $350,000 to AmeriCares.[9]

The AmeriCares website shows that its shipments seem to find their way to wherever the CIA is most active. Special "humanitarian supplies" have been shipped to contra forces in Afghanistan and their rear bases in Pakistan. An airlift was organized for U.S.-supported forces in Eritrea and Tigre during the war in Ethiopia. During the civil war raging in the Balkans, aid was sent to Croatia, Bosnia, and Kosovo.

AmeriCares often acts as an arm of U.S. foreign and domestic policy by reinforcing and supplying the most reactionary organizations. It controls the distribution network to millions of people in desperate need. This strengthens the infrastructure and influence of groups with a political agenda supportive of U.S. corporate goals. Millions of dollars of supplies flooding into a region during a war crisis or famine can exert enormous political influence. As *Forbes*, the magazine that calls itself the "capitalist tool," enthused,

"AmeriCares is a splendid example of what a free-enterprise approach can accomplish in charity."[10]

A look at AmeriCares' advisory board shows links to both the U.S. government and right-wing organizations in the United States. Besides its links to the former CIA director, AmeriCares' board includes his brother Prescott Bush, former U.S. Treasury Secretary William Simon, former U.S. Secretary of State Zbigniew Brzezinski, General Colin Powell, and former U.S. Secretary of State Lawrence Eagleburger. If asked what word best characterized this group of people, would anyone say "humanitarians"?

But the most important link between AmeriCares, the CIA, and ultra-right organizations was the chair of AmeriCares—from its founding in 1982 until his death in 1995—J. Peter Grace Jr., chair of W.R. Grace & Co. Grace is still listed posthumously as chairman of the AmeriCares Advisory Committee on the group's stationery.

J. Peter Grace was the chair of the American Institute for Free Labor Development, the CIA's labor front, and a director of both Kennecott Copper Co. and First National City Bank—now Citibank. His prominent role in the organization of the fascist coup that overthrew the Allende government in Chile is well documented. He is also connected to the Liberty Lobby, a racist think tank and militarist lobbying group based in Washington, DC. He served as chair of Radio Free Europe, Radio Liberty Fund.[11] Grace was the key figure in Project Paperclip, which brought nine hundred Nazi scientists to the U.S. after World War II, many of whom had been found guilty of experimentation on humans.[12]

A thread running through all this is J. Peter Grace Jr.'s position as president of the American Eastern Association of the Sovereign Military Order of Malta, also known as the Knights of Malta.

In an issue of *CovertAction Information Bulletin* devoted to "The Nazis, the Vatican, and the CIA," a well-researched and extensively footnoted article explains many of the early links between the Knights of Malta, fascist and other right-wing organizations, and AmeriCares.[13]

Throughout Latin America, AmeriCares is openly connected to the Knights of Malta. AmeriCares' press releases and its website confirm the Knights of Malta as its official arm for distributing supplies in many countries. In a phone interview, Rachel Granger, manager of AmeriCares' International Programs, praised the international network of the Knights of Malta and explained that it reflects the goals and values of AmeriCares.

The other side of this extremely right-wing Roman Catholic organization is that the Knights of Malta has been frequently linked to the CIA and to death squads throughout Latin America that target trade union organizers, human rights activists, grassroots groups, and religious figures who side with the poor.

The Sovereign Military Order of Malta has a membership that includes wealthy corporate and top government officials of many Western countries linked to neo-Nazi and racist organizations. Over the last sixty years it has been closely tied to such organizations as the World Anti-Communist League, the American Security Council, and the Coalition for Peace Through Strength.

Board members and recipients of awards connect it to an international network of anti-Semitic and racist publications in the U.S., France, Germany, Austria, Italy, Spain, and Latin America, and to lobbying organizations and semi-secret groups linked to the CIA. The Grand Cross of Merit of the Knights of Malta has gone to Robert Gayre, editor of the racist magazine *Mankind Quarterly*, and Roger Pearson, president of the World Anti-Communist League and board member of the French neo-Nazi journal *Nouvelle Ecole*.

The connection between the Vatican, the Knights of Malta, and Nazi organizations dates back to the 1930s. The Knights of Malta were important promoters of General Francisco Franco's fascist army in the Spanish Civil War. They supported Mussolini's Fascist party in Italy and Hitler's Nazi party in Germany. Many commanders in Hitler's notorious SS were decorated members of the Knights of Malta.[14] At the end of World War II the "Rat Lines"—secret networks by which so many top Nazi leaders escaped with their fortunes to South America—were organized through the Vatican and the Knights of Malta.[15]

Another prominent and decorated member of the Knights of Malta was a man known as "Hitler's paymaster"—Herman Abs. Abs was chair of the Deutsche Bank from 1940 to 1945. He was also a board member of the notorious I.G. Farben Co. His role was well known to the Nuremberg Tribunal and every book on the Third Reich discusses his role. Abs was convicted of war crimes in absentia in Yugoslavia. Nevertheless, after the war Abs retained his top banking position and reorganized German finances in the interests of U.S. financial domination.[16]

The connection between top financiers, Cabinet-level Treasury officials, and right-wing, racist organizations didn't begin with William Simon and J. Peter Grace. It reflects the way corporate rule is enforced through the interconnection of government agencies, religious institutions, media outlets, and secret organizations.

It is important for the progressive movement to grasp the significance of AmeriCares' cynical public relations shipment to Iraq. It is connected in a living way to the global struggle that pits those fighting for basic union rights and national self-determination against a handful of extremely wealthy corporate rulers.

AmeriCares' shipment to Iraq during a critical time of growing opposition to the continuing war of aggression shows that the U.S. government is determined to continue the sanctions. It is just one of the many covert ways the corporate-military-political complex manipulates public debate to maintain and justify the murderous policy against Iraq.

The anti-sanctions movement should appreciate how deeply threatened U.S. government officials and corporate rulers are by the growing awareness and resistance of grassroots organizations in the U.S. The Iraq Sanctions Challenge not only brought aid to Iraqi children—it challenged the criminal role of top U.S. government officials. The greatest military power on earth fears the anger of world opposition. A simple act of solidarity is a powerful weapon.

---

[1] AmeriCares website, http://www.americares.org.

[2] "AmeriCares Honors Amoco President, Mayo Foundation," AmeriCares press release, 14 May 1998, #1443.

[3] AmeriCares website.

[4] *Houston Chronicle*, 1 October 1994.

[5] AmeriCares website.

[6] Ibid.

[7] *Washington Post*, 14 April 1988.

[8] *New York Newsday*, 13 April 1988.

[9] *New York Times*, 13 August 1985.

[10] *Forbes*, 29 March 1993.

[11] Francoise Hervet, "Knights of Darkness: The Sovereign Military Order of Malta," *CovertAction Information Bulletin*, No. 25, Winter 1986.

[12] Clarence G. Lasby, *Project Paperclip* (New York: Atheneum, 1975). Also, "Escape from Justice: Nazi War Criminals in America," ABC-TV News Closeup, 16 January 1980.

[13] Francoise Hervet, op. cit.

[14] R. Harris Smith, *OSS, The Secret History of America's First Central Intelligence Agency* (Berkeley: University of California Press, 1972).

[15] Charles Higham, *Trading with the Enemy: An Exploration of the Nazi-American Money Plot, 1933-1949* (New York: Delacorte, 1983). See also R. Harris Smith, op. cit.

[16] National Council of the National Front of Democratic Germany, *Brown Book: War and Nazi Criminals in West Germany* (Berlin: Documentation Center of the State Archives Administration of the German Democratic Republic, n.d. [c. 1966]).

DEMONIZING OPPRESSED NATIONS

MONICA MOOREHEAD

On 18 February 1998 activists at Ohio State University hoisted a banner with the slogan "Stop the Racist War Against Iraq" while protesting at a "town meeting" on Iraq featuring Secretary of State Madeleine Albright and Secretary of Defense William Cohen. I thought to myself that the progressive movement owed these students a huge debt. This multinational delegation, which shouted down Albright and Cohen at every opportunity before a worldwide audience on CNN, showed with their slogan that the Iraqi people have a national identity, and that the U.S. racist power structure was attempting to submit them to its will through the sheer terror of military aggression and the continuous devastation of economic sanctions.

More of this kind of anti-imperialist solidarity needed to be shown towards the Vietnamese people by the U.S. anti-war movement during the 1960s and 1970s.

As an African American woman born and raised in the Jim Crow South, I along with millions of other people of color have developed a close affinity with the Iraqi people as they continue to exhibit a defiant fortitude in defending their sovereignty and independence from imperialist bullying. One of the main reasons I decided to be a part of the Iraq Sanctions Challenge delegation was to show solidarity with the Iraqi people as a representative of one nationally oppressed nation to another, thousands of miles away.

Our historical and cultural backgrounds may be different, but the common thread that runs through all our struggles is fighting back against racist and colonial oppression.

The U.S. says it is imposing sanctions on Iraq in order to get Saddam Hussein to "respect human rights." This would be a joke if it weren't so disgusting. It reminds me of that U.S. general who was asked by a CBS reporter why the Air Force had just set a whole Vietnamese village on fire with napalm. He responded, "We had to do it to save them from the Communists."

The Iraq Sanctions Challenge was an act of international civil disobedience against a racist war targeting an oppressed people. This war, which includes the devastation of sanctions, is being perpetuated mainly by the U.S., the most powerful imperialist country in the world, against a country with only twenty-three million people. Racism is the most formidable divide-and-conquer tactic, and U.S. governments have depended upon it many times in history to consolidate the predominant world position enjoyed by U.S. imperialism today.

The U.S. government is trying to push racist buttons when it demonizes a leader like Saddam Hussein, labeling him a "new Hitler" or a "tyrant." Of course, he isn't the first to get this treatment. Back in 1989, the U.S. portrayed President Manuel Noriega of Panama in similar terms. It was the pretext for invading Panama in order to reassert perpetual U.S. control of the Panama Canal. A similar pattern can be seen in the demonization of presidents Qaddafi of Libya, Kim Il Sung of north Korea, or Fidel Castro of Cuba. Once the leader has been made out to be a monster, any "punishment" meted out to the country—and its people—is seen as justified.

In 1991, the U.S. used Iraq's invasion of Kuwait as a pretext to bomb Baghdad and other cities. The world was supposed to believe that the U.S. leaders had suddenly developed a great concern for smaller nations invaded by larger countries. But what about the U.S. invasion of Grenada in 1983, or its totally lopsided wars against Vietnam and Korea?

A brief look at U.S. history exposes this blatant hypocrisy about respect for self-determination.

Would the U.S. have become the dominant imperialist power it is today without the racist, genocidal extermination of whole nations of Native peoples? They were massacred so their lands could be stolen and capitalism could expand into the West. The U.S. also carried out a long and bloody war with Mexico that resulted in the theft of two-thirds of that country—all of what is now known as the Southwest.

What about the enslavement of millions of African people? And the crushing of the struggle for Black democratic rights after the Civil War? What about the brutal wage exploitation of Chinese immigrant workers who built the railroads? All this systematic oppression, genocide, and slavery could not have been possible without racism, both in theory and practice. The racist war against Iraq also has antecedents in the Spanish-American war, through which the U.S.

conquered Puerto Rico, the Philippines, and Cuba and turned them into private plantations and corporate empires.

No one today would dispute the racist character of European colonialism in Africa, the Middle East, and Asia. But when U.S. companies moved into Europe's former colonies after World War II, their objective was the same: to make as much profit as possible by paying as little for labor and resources as they could get away with. In the Middle East, the main prize was and is oil.

In defying the sanctions, we were carrying on the tradition of the civil rights movement when it refused to abide by the unjust and illegal Jim Crow laws some forty years ago. The sanctions law and the Trading with the Enemies Act are immoral. Moreover, the sanctions are in violation of international law, including the UN Convention against Genocide, to which the U.S. is a signatory. Genocide is defined as the destruction or elimination of a people or nation, in whole or in part.

Another reason I went on this trip was to show the people of the U.S. who are suffering injustice that they have more in common with the Iraqi people than with the U.S. capitalist establishment. This becomes crystal clear when you compare U.S. government treatment of the people of Iraq with its treatment of the most disenfranchised sectors here, especially those of color.

For example, let's take bombing. The U.S. military dropped more explosive power on Iraq within a span of a few weeks in 1991 than it did in all of Europe during World War II. But in Philadelphia, on 13 May 1985, the police and FBI, acting independently of the Black mayor, Wilson Goode, dropped incendiary bombs on a home in a Black neighborhood and destroyed sixty houses. The attack was aimed at the environmental communal group called MOVE, which had also been demonized in the press beforehand.

No official was ever charged, much less convicted, with killing the eleven MOVE members, including children, who were incinerated that day. Nor has any U.S. official been charged with the genocide in Iraq. Should it therefore be surprising that an abomination could take place like the lynching of James Byrd in Jasper, Texas, on 7 June 1998, or that the sheriff two weeks later allowed the Ku Klux Klan to march there?

It has been well documented by the United Nations that at least 1.5 million Iraqi people, the majority of them children and the elderly, have perished since the sanctions were put into place. How many poor children in the U.S. have died needlessly since losing health care benefits in the so-called welfare reform bill signed by President Clinton in 1996?

According to the Children's Defense Fund, in 1996, 11.3 million children up to the age of eighteen had no health insurance—the highest number ever recorded by the Census Bureau. More than 1.3 million families have lost welfare benefits since 1993—reducing the rolls by 27 percent. This translates into a growing number of impoverished children dying from preventable diseases because of rising health care costs, an increase in birth defects, and the closing of hospitals and clinics in poor areas, all in the name of streamlining health care. One out of two African American babies is born into poverty.

It is important to make these links. Protest against political and economic sanctions at home and abroad will plant the seeds of international solidarity between the peoples of the U.S. and the Gulf region.

The real goal of the sanctions against Iraq is to grind down the people and weaken the whole country so that the U.S. can ultimately go in there and put in place a puppet government. The oil companies want a client regime just like in the "good old days" before the 1958 Iraqi revolution overthrew the old feudal monarchy.

The real goal is to denationalize Iraq's oil so that Gulf, Exxon, Mobil, Citibank, and Chase Manhattan can take over again. Both Clinton and Bush before him fundamentally serve the interests of these big capitalists. All the talk about human rights, democracy, and the rights of small nations is just so much window dressing designed to conceal their real aims.

ARAB AMERICANS IN THE U.S.

AHMED EL-SHERIF

As an Arab American living in the heart of America—Kansas City—I see bias in U.S. foreign policy. The Oklahoma City bombing brought home to me some harsh reality. In spite of the fact that we Arab Americans contribute as much as any other Americans, we face serious threats and discrimination. This is due to the continuous media stereotyping and the racist foreign policy that continues to target Arabs and Middle Eastern countries.

I regret both the loss of innocent lives in the Oklahoma bombing, especially children, and the way the media immediately jumped to conclusions. They automatically assumed it was an act by someone of Middle Eastern descent. I held my breath, along with my American wife and three children, worrying about the future of my family, my friends, and my Arab American community. There were many bomb threats to our schools, our mosques, and businesses, locally and across the U.S. It was a relief when it turned out to be not by an Arab American or someone with a Middle Eastern background.

Our foreign-policy decisions are based on racist ideas. Look at U.S. history. We destroyed the Native American communities, putting them on reservations. We captured and enslaved Africans. We invaded Vietnam and other countries.

I was invited to talk recently to the Kansas City branch of the "Great Decision Participants." The topic was: "Should religion be a factor in American foreign policy?" This refers to the Religious Persecution Bill, which, if enacted, would allow our country to impose economic sanctions against countries where human rights have been violated. Immediately, the thought came to mind, what about the minorities in our own country who have been discriminated against? Isn't it better to clean our own house before we attempt to be the moral guardians of the world? "People who live in glass houses should not throw stones."

I see plainly that this proposed law would most likely be elastic enough for the government to pick and choose, thus carrying out a racist foreign policy in what might seem a legal and moral way. One of the biggest problems with our foreign policy is its inconsistency toward races, nations, and religions. For example, in one region you find a small country committing all kinds of human rights violations. The parliament of that nation is discussing who is a Jew and who is not, thereby discriminating against their own faith. They bulldoze the homes of innocent civilians in occupied territories to pave the way for their own settlements—similar to what happened to Native Americans here. Yet the only attention this gets from our policy makers or the media is accommodation and excuses. Meanwhile, a country in the same region that bends over backward to accommodate to our biased foreign policies is under severe economic sanctions.

Another dimension of our inconsistent foreign policy is the shift of one hundred eighty degrees from supporting a certain government for many years in spite of "human rights violations," then all of a sudden turning against that same nation and same leadership, this time waving the banner of "human rights violations."

This racist foreign policy makes Arab Americans vulnerable to random acts of violence. As an Arab American who cares about my own country, the United States of America, I would like to help our foreign policy makers see the results of their inconsistencies. We gain very little, and what little we gain is short lived. We lose very much in the long term. How do we look in the eyes of our allies and friends? Can we be trusted? We lose respect and trust from the world community simply because we are inconsistent. We accuse other nations of killing civilians, yet sanctions are nothing but that. Our nation looks cruel in the eyes of the world. That does not serve our interests.

Visiting Iraq in May 1998 with eighty-four American delegates, led by former attorney general and humanitarian Ramsey Clark, was an experience I cannot forget, nor can I keep silent about it. I visited a nation that has been debilitated by seven and a half years of economic sanctions—a nation that used to have everything. In fact, their surplus used to be donated to other countries. Now this nation is literally in a state of starvation.

The Tigris and Euphrates rivers have allowed agriculture to flourish in this fertile crescent for millennia; now they bring unsanitary conditions. This is due to the destruction of the sewage system, water treatment plants, and power plants throughout the whole country during the Gulf War. The sanctions prevent them from buying sufficient chlorine or medicines, so illnesses that are preventable and treatable are leading to death. We visited hospitals that lack almost everything. One doctor said there has been no improvement since 1990 and no replacements for whatever is broken. I saw long lines of children in one of the hospitals waiting for treatment they cannot get.

In the last seven and one-half years of economic sanctions, Iraq has lost about 1.5 million innocent lives. Four thousand to five thousand civilians die every month due to the lack of food, medicine, and sanitation—a condition imposed on them by the United Nations and the United States. I wonder, are we approaching the 21st Century or the Dark Ages? In fact, our television and media do not allow Americans to see the images of the impact of the economic sanctions on Iraq. But I will carry these mental pictures with me forever.

A picture from Vietnam of an eleven-year-old girl burned by napalm, naked, fleeing and screaming in terror, changed American public opinion. There are thousands of such images from Iraq. If one of them were allowed in our biased media, public opinion would change.

On the way to Baghdad, after driving through the desert for about twelve hours, we stopped to gas up, stretch our legs, and get something to eat. The delegation filled three buses. With us was a truck full of medicine, mainly antibiotics. I wondered how we would be received among the Iraqi people.

As we stopped, unannounced, people came to meet us. When they found out we were Americans, they greeted us warmly with their natural hospitality. What a contrast! In spite of what we are doing to them through the economic sanctions, people were friendly and warm. I can feel their pain and see their weak bodies. They have always been generous people, but now they have very little to show except their smiling faces full of pain and their weak, underweight bodies.

Why are we punishing a whole nation of innocent civilians, mothers, fathers, and children? I cannot forget an old man who came to me, knowing we were bringing some medicine, to ask if I had something for rheumatism. His joints hurt him, and there was no medicine.

We spent an evening with a group of intellectuals—a sculptor and his wife, an author, her husband and son. Of course, the discussion was about, "Why are you Americans causing this pain for us?" We listened to sad stories, one after the other, of people who have lost their normal lives. The author told us about a famous writer who is dying of a heart disorder. No airplane can take him anywhere due to the no-fly zone. The author said, "If this were an American writer, you would know how it feels." We heard the story of the Amariyah shelter, where hundreds died as a result of two smart bombs. Whole families were killed, including many children. One woman who left the shelter to wash clothes lost her entire family. As we were talking, the electricity went off. We sat through the night in the front yard, our only light the kerosene lamps and the full moon.

After spending four days in Iraq, where we visited many cities including Mosul, Baghdad, Basra, Karbila, and a few little towns, we came to know that the whole country was rationing electricity and basic food items such as flour and oil. But the calories are not enough to maintain people's weight, especially if they are hit with dysentery—which I had my share of, along with other delegates.

To put a name on this, it is simply genocide in the name of politics.

After a couple of articles reflecting my thoughts and feelings about the trip appeared in the *Kansas City Star*, the newspaper published a letter that said, "Tell Ahmed El-Sherif it's not the U.S. government doing this, it is Saddam Hussein." Obviously, this man doesn't know any better, thanks to the misleading bias of the media. I also had a chance to meet with a congressman who is obsessed with Saddam Hussein. All the children of Iraq are Saddam Hussein to him. I do not understand his politics.

On the other hand, I was received with great sympathy by the office of a congresswoman who was deeply affected by the tragedy. Many Americans in our area from different organizations stood up together in February against the bombing of Iraq. They still hold a vigil every Sunday in a major square in Kansas City Metropolitan, and will until the sanctions are over. Another group is calling for fasting as solidarity with the Iraqi people.

We have an obligation, if we want to sleep with peace of mind. Whether we are politicians, religious leaders, humanitarians, or ordinary people, we need to put an end to this.

FROM VIETNAM TO IRAQ

SHARON BLACK CECI

Soon after returning from Iraq, I spoke at a meeting against sanctions in Washington, D.C. A few days before, CNN had aired an amazing but well-documented special about how the U.S. government used sarin nerve gas on its own troops during the Vietnam War because they had refused to fight in that illegal and unjust war. Immediately, the station came under enormous pressure to retract the charge about nerve gas. That these soldiers were killed by a Special Forces commando unit has not been disputed—only the method.

When they were murdered, they were living in a village in Laos, a country not involved directly in the war but nevertheless being secretly bombed by the Pentagon. I asked the meeting to remember those brave men and women who risked everything, including life, to oppose the Vietnam War.

The government gassed its own people! Isn't this one of the accusations against Iraq that has been used to justify sanctions? The hypocrisy of U.S. propaganda is bottomless. We are put on a war footing, supposedly because Iraq has weapons of mass destruction. Yet the government inciting us against Iraq has more weapons of mass destruction than any in the world, and uses them.

The U.S. government is the only one to ever use nuclear bombs—on the civilian populations of Hiroshima and Nagasaki. Aren't the sanctions themselves a weapon of mass destruction? Over 1.5 million people—one out of every twenty-two Iraqis—have perished slowly and insidiously. The Washington metro area numbers 1.5 million people. It's the equivalent of wiping that entire population off the map.

The truth has been manipulated and obscured by a bought and paid for press—a press that is big business itself—and racism is the biggest weapon in pulling the wool over our eyes. Just before my meeting in D.C., James Byrd, an African American man from Jasper,

Texas, was abducted and viciously murdered by white supremacists. It was not an isolated incident. We live in a society riddled with racism. Because racism is so pervasive, the people of the Middle East can be portrayed in the media here as less than human, thus allowing the crime of sanctions to continue. Arabs and other peoples in the region are presented as bomb-throwing fanatics without human qualities.

But when you stand on the other side of the globe, you begin to cast off some of the distortions so common in this country. You meet workers and poor people in Iraq and Jordan who have many of the same aspirations and hopes we all have.

You begin to look for the real reasons why this government is imposing sanctions. When the U.S. media is far away, you are able to grasp the history of the region with a clearer mind. It becomes obvious why the powers that be in the U.S. and Europe have manipulated and controlled divisions and conflicts. Behind it all are the capitalist banks and powerful oil companies.

The real crime of the people of the Middle East is that they live on top of the world's largest oil deposits! It is not about the good, the bad, or the in-between of Saddam Hussein. It is about oil and who will control that region. It is about the right of the Iraqi people and all the people in that region to determine their own destiny and control their own resources.

Many people today were not yet born at the time of the Vietnam War. But for those who were, especially the youth of that time, the war and the Black liberation movement were the defining events of that period in history. We fought fervently to end the war and we studied, debated, and discussed the causes of racism and militarism.

Several million Vietnamese and over 50,000 GIs lost their lives in that so-called "conflict." Vietnam never recovered, and today has a high rate of birth defects because of Agent Orange and other U.S. chemical weapons. The underlying cause was not to protect democracy but to secure rich mineral and natural resources for U.S. companies and maintain their military domination over Southeast Asia.

Some of the horror of the Vietnam War was televised. Thousands watched as the fertile countryside was carpet bombed. A few reports even showed how the Pentagon executed Vietnamese in cold blood, the same Vietnamese people we were supposedly saving.

U.S. ground troops suffered many more casualties in Vietnam than in Iraq. The thousands of GIs who returned home in body bags to working-class and poor communities everywhere were a catalyst to the anti-war movement and to changing the consciousness of the American people.

It was different during the Iraq war. The Pentagon had learned to manipulate public opinion more effectively. It imposed strict censorship. People watching television saw nothing but missiles striking remote targets—like some kind of video game. The maimed and mutilated children, the targets of the so-called smart bombs, were absent from U.S. television sets and newspapers. Many GIs from this war have also had their lives destroyed—by Gulf War Syndrome and radiation poisoning, which come on more slowly. They are removed from our sight and isolated.

Then came the genocidal sanctions. They have killed many more Iraqis, and they are silent. We must change this. At the meeting, I showed the audience a photo of an Iraqi woman and her malnourished baby at the pediatric hospital in Baghdad. She had asked me to show their picture to the American people and to Clinton. Her story and many others need to be told.

When I returned home from the Sanctions Challenge, I noticed some similarities to Iraq, despite all the differences. The sanctions have brought a feeling of desperation there. School children are desperate for pencils, for scraps of paper, for the barest of necessities. When children fall ill, their families are forced to sell all their belongings to pay for a few medicines. Hyperinflation has created a hell for workers. In Baltimore, where I live, I also sense a feeling of desperation. Neighborhoods are in decay. Youth with no jobs and little hope hang on corners infested with drugs brought in by the CIA. Despite so-called capitalist prosperity, low-wage workers can barely afford to provide for their families.

Baltimore city schools lack books, too. Racism is rampant. In New York, remedial programs that make it possible for working-class youth to attend college are being dismantled. In Washington, the nation's capital, forty percent of all pregnant mothers receive no prenatal medical care. There is a war being waged against the Iraqi people and there is a war being waged against the poor at home.

When we strike a blow against racism here, we begin to dismantle the sanctions. When we end the sanctions, we will win justice right here. The Iraqi people are our friends. Love and justice have no borders.

FAILURE OF MORAL LEADERSHIP

BISHOP THOMAS GUMBLETON

Within five months after the sanctions were first imposed against Iraq—by December of 1990—William Webster, Director of the CIA, testified to the U.S. Congress that the sanctions were working almost one hundred percent. Hundreds of thousands of deaths and indescribable suffering inflicted on the whole nation of Iraq have been the result. Indeed, the United Nations is waging a form of cruel warfare that seems almost unmatched in the history of human wars.

And yet, for some reason, religious leaders in the United States and the United Kingdom—the two nations most responsible for the continuation of the sanctions—have been almost completely silent. This failure in moral leadership is highlighted by the actions of religious leaders in the past couple of years who have come to realize and deplore the failures of the Christian churches fifty years ago during World War II.

In the Catholic community, Japanese bishops have confessed their failure to oppose the aggressive and cruel warfare perpetrated by their nation. German bishops and French bishops have done the same, especially in regard to the Holocaust. Repentance for past failures is admirable and perhaps someday U.S. bishops will repent of our failure to condemn the movement toward "total war"—all-out attacks on noncombatants—that took place during World War II and culminated at Hiroshima and Nagasaki, a "butchery of untold magnitude," in the words of Pope Paul VI.

But moral leadership that waits fifty years to react is still a failure. Real moral leadership cries out and denounces gross evil and violence when it is happening. So far, as a body, U.S. religious leaders have been sinfully silent and have provided no specific moral guidance for the U.S. community and its political leaders.

In November 1997 I made an attempt to put a resolution before the National Conference of Catholic Bishops at their General Meeting. Because my motion to put this on the agenda involved a change of the rules for our meetings, it needed a two-thirds vote of those present, which was 168 votes. The motion received 163. However, merely raising the issue caused some bishops to confront the moral issues surrounding the embargo for the first time.

Since that meeting I have again visited Iraq, and I feel an even stronger need to awaken a moral response to what we are doing to the people of Iraq. This time I visited the southern part of the country where the worst of the bombing and ground war took place. Truly this was a place where "total war" happened. Carpet bombing by B-52s, fuel-air explosives, uranium-tipped missiles, bombing and strafing along "the highway of death"—every high-tech weapon in the U.S. arsenal was used. The result was killing on a scale unmatched for a war of such short duration. Besides those who were killed or wounded in that violence, every one in the area continues to suffer and die because of the almost total destruction of the infrastructure that makes a modern city function: the water purification system, the electrical system, the waste disposal system, the transportation system and so on. Probably the most devastating and frightening result is the radioactive debris spread around the area because of the uranium-tipped missiles.

The results of this brutal war-making especially overwhelmed me during a visit to a hospital in Basra. A group of us from the U.S. were waiting in the lobby of the hospital for the medical director, Dr. Feras Abdul Abbas, to come and greet us. He had not been notified of our visit ahead of time, and probably was not sure of who was waiting to see him.

I spotted him walking down the hall before he saw us. He was moving slowly and looked very tired. His face seemed sad. But as he got closer he looked up and saw us. Immediately his whole face lit up and he broke into a smile. When I moved to greet him and shake his hand he said, "You make me happy. I smile from my heart. You make me strong." Just the fact that we were there and had brought at least token help in the form of medicines obviously gave him encouragement to keep on with his work at the hospital. As we chatted he said to me, "What you see here today will make you very sad. If you stay in Basra for two days it will break your heart."

We didn't stay two days but what I saw did break my heart—even as it provoked in me a deep and abiding anger. The conditions in the hospital were appalling. In a part of the country where temperatures reach 120 degrees Fahrenheit in the summer, there is no longer any air conditioning. Flies are everywhere. Mothers must constantly brush them away from children too weak to do this themselves. Beds are without sheets. Paint is crumbling from the walls. Everything is in a state of disrepair.

Three children are vividly impressed on my memory. A tiny infant, lying naked on the bed, his body severely malnourished, obviously in great distress, but too weak to even cry—and the doctor's words, "He will die this evening or during the night." A mother who cried so easily as she held and comforted her daughter, eight or nine years old, who would die soon. This would be her third child to die. And a twelve-year-old girl who was suffering from kidney failure. I remember her eyes. They showed the pain she felt constantly but most of all they expressed a profound sadness. I found myself unable to maintain eye contact. I had to look away as I wept for her.

Of course, these children, and all the others in the hospital and throughout the country, should not even have been ill. In ordinary circumstances they would have been healthy and carefree, as any child has a right to be. Even if they were somehow afflicted, there would be medicine and medical equipment and good hospital care to restore them to health. Knowing this is what causes me to be angry.

Iraqis previously enjoyed a high standard of living. They had the best health care, education, social security, and public welfare programs in the region. They had an abundance of food, although 70 percent of it was imported. The sanctions have brought hunger, disease, and misery to Iraq because they have caused the economic structure to collapse. Despite survival strategies of working several jobs, selling off possessions, and begging, most Iraqis have suffered a severe decline in their living standards. About 20 percent of the population exists in extreme poverty on a par with the poorest countries in the world. A woman religious from the Dominican Order described the situation: "We are ground down, exhausted by years of death. Since the Gulf War 600,000 have died from malnutrition and lack of medicine. We live with death."

It is surely long past the time for religious leaders to speak out and denounce this barbarous attack against the Iraqi people. In the Roman Catholic Christian tradition there is a clearly developed theology about the use of sanctions. This theology is a special application of the generally accepted theology among Christians for the justified use of lethal violence in war. The U.S. Catholic bishops provided an authoritative presentation of this theology in a pastoral statement promulgated in November of 1993: The Harvest of Justice Is Sown in Peace.

First, we set forth the criteria to be used to morally assess the imposition of economic sanctions:

- Concerns about the limited effectiveness of sanctions and the harm caused to civilian populations require that comprehensive sanctions be considered only in response to aggression or grave and ongoing injustice after less coercive measures have been tried, and with clear and reasonable conditions set for their removal.
- The harm caused by sanctions should be proportionate to the good likely to be achieved; sanctions should avoid grave and irreversible harm to the civilian population. Therefore, sanctions should be targeted as much as possible against those directly responsible for the injustice, distinguishing between the government and the people. ... Embargoes, when employed, must make provisions for the fundamental human needs of the civilian population. The denial of basic needs may not be used as a weapon.
- The consent to sanctions by substantial portions of the affected population is morally relevant.
- Sanctions should always be part of a broader process of diplomacy aimed at finding an effective solution to injustice.

Based on my own experience as well as documented reports from many international groups, including agencies of the UN, I can state unequivocally that the current sanctions violate these criteria and must be condemned.

Furthermore, these sanctions, together with the forty-two days of continuous bombing, clearly constitute cruel and deliberate counter-population warfare. Such warfare has been condemned by the most authoritative teaching body of the Catholic Church, The Second Vatican Council (1962-1965):

> With these truths in mind, this most holy Synod makes its own the condemnations of total war already pronounced by recent Popes and issues the following declaration: Any act of war aimed indiscriminately at the destruction of entire cities or of extensive areas along with their population is a crime against God

and man himself. It merits unequivocal and unhesitating condemnation.[1]

Leaders of the church in Iraq plead with us to end the sanctions. In August 1997 Archbishop Gabriel Kassab of the Southern Region of Iraq stated: "Epidemics rage, taking away infants and sick by the thousands. Those children who survive disease succumb to malnutrition, which stunts their physical and mental development. Our situation is unbearable! ... We appeal to the people of conscience to work to end the blockade of Iraq. ..."

And lest anyone be deceived by the so-called Oil for Food resolution, Archbishop Kassab denounces Resolution 986 as merely serving "to divert world attention from the tragedy, while in some respects aggravating it."

And his judgment on Resolution 986 is supported by Denis Halliday, the UN humanitarian coordinator for Iraq, who stated on 12 January 1998 that Iraq would need in the neighborhood of $30 billion per year to meet its current requirements for food, medicine, and infrastructure. Resolution 986 initially allowed Iraq to sell up to $2.14 billion worth of oil every six months. After allocations are taken out to pay for Gulf War reparations and UN administrative expenses, the amount of money available to the average person in central and southern Iraq is twenty-five cents per person per day.

Currently, the UN is offering to allow Iraq to sell $5.26 billion worth of oil every six months. However, Iraq says that it cannot pump more than $4 billion worth of oil because of the deterioration of oil-field equipment under sanctions. This claim was corroborated by a team of experts working for the United Nations, who stated that "the deplorable state of Iraq's petroleum industry will prevent it from exporting the $5.26 billion worth of oil."[2] In light of damages caused by seven years of comprehensive sanctions coupled with Gulf War bombardment, even the $5.26 billion offer is grossly inadequate to repair Iraq's shattered infrastructure, a medical system near total collapse, and a destroyed economy.

Clearly, whatever the intent of these sanctions, they violate clear moral laws, specifically as articulated in the Catholic Christian tradition. But they also violate the basic human rights of the Iraqi people proclaimed in the UN Universal Declaration of Human Rights because they deprive innocent people of food and medicine, basic requirements for normal life.

Nothing less than prophetic denunciation of those sanctions is the minimum responsibility of anyone who claims to be called to religious leadership.

One religious leader who has been consistent in his denunciation of the Persian Gulf War is Pope John Paul II. In March of 1991 he proclaimed: "I myself, on the occasion of the recent tragic war in the Persian Gulf, repeated the cry, 'Never again war!' No, never again war, which destroys the lives of innocent people, teaches how to kill, throws into upheaval even the lives of those who do the killing and leaves behind a trail of resentment and hatred, thus making it all the more difficult to find a just solution of the very problems which provoked the war."

On 8 June 1998, in a speech in Baghdad, Cardinal Roger Etchegarary, speaking on behalf of the Vatican, stressed that, "it is not enough to say the Church is for peace. ... She must, with every fiber of her daily existence, perform works of peace and justice. And this work must answer the concrete needs of each country." Then he went on to point out that the Church's efforts "go beyond any political or military strategy, denouncing both the mad arms race as well as the *injustice of an economic weapon, when it only ends up wounding innocent people, especially children*" [emphasis added].

Now is the moment for all religious leaders to make this cry our own and demand that the wounding and killing of innocent people, especially children, be stopped. The Church must not fail again.

---

[1] Gaudiam et Spes #80, Second Vatican Council (1962-1965).

[2] Associated Press, 16 April 1998.

AN ACT OF REAL SOLIDARITY

BRIAN BECKER

After the eighty-four delegates of the Iraq Sanctions Challenge arrived in Iraq, we decided to hold a militant demonstration in front of the U.S. Interests Section in downtown Baghdad. This office has served as a de facto U.S. embassy ever since diplomatic ties were severed between the two countries in 1990.

It must have been an unusual sight to the people of Baghdad. Here were citizens and residents of the United States carrying signs denouncing the U.S. government for its mass murder of the Iraqi people.

This was an historic action. It showed a high level of consciousness on the part of the delegates and was a profound act of solidarity with the people of Iraq. It was the clearest way of showing that the Iraq Sanctions Challenge was not an act of charity but a militant protest against imperialism.

The decision to carry out the demonstration was made after a wide-ranging discussion among the delegates. Naturally, in such a large group of people, representing a broad cross-section of U.S. society, the decision did not come without debate. A few delegates initially had doubts. Some worried that the U.S. media would use the demonstration to discredit our delegation as "agents of Iraq." This provoked a wide-ranging assessment of the value of calling a demonstration. The discussion was held in the spirit of mutual respect and was entirely devoid of acrimony. At the conclusion of the discussion, there was near unanimity on proceeding.

This demonstration received top coverage on television and in print media throughout the Middle East. Tens of millions of Arab people saw that a sector of the U.S. population was standing up in a clear and unambiguous way and saying that the U.S. government is not acting on behalf of the people when it carries out genocide against Iraq.

But if the government of the United States doesn't represent the people, who does it serve? Nothing is more avidly drummed into the heads of school kids than that this government is of, by, and for the people. Every day these same children are run through a drill pledging allegiance to an indivisible and united "one nation under god."

Of course, contrary to the patriotic propaganda epitomized in the Pledge of Allegiance, the United States has never been indivisible or united. It was a country divided between slave owners and slaves, between giant industrialists and low-paid workers. For three hundred years settler governments pursued a policy of genocide against Native people who had inhabited this territory for thousands of years. In spite of this history of class strife, racism, and national oppression inside the United States, however, the myth of an indivisible United States holds great merit for the real powers. It obscures the fact that there exists a powerful ruling class representing a tiny clique of bankers and industrialists. To advance "Unites States interests" is clearly understood by this capitalist class as advancing *their* interests. One thing this ruling class has learned in the last one hundred years is that, if it were to put forward truthful political slogans to justify U.S. government policy, it would never win public favor.

Take Iraq, for instance. What if presidents Bush and later Clinton had stated: "On behalf of Exxon, Texaco, Mobil, Citibank, and Chase Manhattan we intend to recolonize Iraq and all of the Middle East. We intend to regain our undiluted control over this oil-rich area and super-exploit the labor of the peoples of this region, from which we derived over 50 percent of all U.S. corporate overseas profits before the anti-colonial Arab revolution swept out our puppet monarchies in the 1950s. When Iraq, Iran, Libya, and the others nationalized our oil companies, this was an act of theft of our property. We intend to use war, embargoes, CIA destabilization campaigns, and all other available methods to recover our position."

No, this message would not be well received. But it is the truth. One percent of the U.S. population owns 40 percent of the wealth of the country. And the richest one percent of that one percent are the dominant powers in the capitalist establishment. This tiny capitalist class dominates the political establishment and owns the media. It may preach the concept of "one indivisible nation," but it is a supremely class-conscious group that understands its interests—the need for super-profits—on a global scale. The drive to destroy the Iraqi government and replace it with a puppet regime is just the latest example of this kind of imperialist class consciousness.

In 1953, the CIA overthrew a democratically elected government in Iran in a bloody coup. It is interesting and instructive for those trying to understand U.S. policy toward Iraq today to see how the capitalist-owned U.S. media covered this act of aggression against Iran.

Before the blood had barely dried, the *New York Times* brazenly editorialized that the events in Iran should serve as a chilling warning to those in the former colonies who wanted to control their own resources: "Underdeveloped countries with rich resources now have an object lesson in the heavy cost to be paid by one of their number which goes berserk with fanatical nationalism."[1] Spoken like a true slave-owner after the suppression of a revolt.

The language employed by the *New York Times* and other capitalist-owned media to demonize the democratically elected government of Dr. Mohammed Mossadegh in the early 1950s was nearly identical to the language used to portray the government of Saddam Hussein. This is not an accident, coincidence, or mistake. The U.S. ruling class cannot tell the truth about its motives and its interests in the Middle East because it will lose all public support.

The real issues in Iran in the 1950s were about the same as those driving the current U.S.-Iraq confrontation. The U.S. and Britain slapped an airtight economic embargo on Iran after the Mossadegh government nationalized the Anglo-Iranian Oil Co., known today as British Petroleum. Mossadegh wanted Iran's oil wealth to be used to develop the country and overcome its deep poverty.

The sanctions on Iran strangled the economy. Even the middle classes suffered greatly. They turned against the Mossadegh government. The CIA then took advantage of this social and political discontent and organized the bloody coup. Kermit Roosevelt, the grandson of Theodore Roosevelt, bragged openly in his book, *Countercoup: The Struggle for the Control of Iran*, about how he had led the CIA operation that overthrew Mossadegh. Having been returned to the Peacock Throne, the Shah promptly denationalized and privatized Iran's oil company, returning it to a consortium dominated by British and U.S. oil monopolies.

The U.S. and British aggression in Iran was not the result of a "mistaken" foreign policy or the actions of super-aggressive CIA operatives. It wasn't the result of a "bad" President. The destabilization of Iran started under the Democrat Harry S. Truman and reached its fruition under the Republican Dwight D. Eisenhower. This bipartisan strategy reflected the wishes of the billionaire class inside the United States to maintain its class dominance and super-profits by dominating the Middle East. The politicians then, like today, took their marching orders from Wall Street.

The Iran operation of 1951-1953 makes an almost casebook example of how the ruling class works. This intertangling of the White House, CIA, the oil monopolies, and the biggest U.S. banks is well described in William Blum's book, *Killing Hope*. Blum left his State Department position in 1967 because of his opposition to the U.S. war in Vietnam.

> One year after the coup, the Iranian government completed a contract with an international consortium of oil companies. Amongst Iran's new foreign partners, the British lost the exclusive rights they had enjoyed previously, being reduced now to 40 percent. Another 40 percent went to American firms, the remainder to other countries. The British, however, received an extremely generous compensation for their former property.
>
> In 1958, Kermit Roosevelt left the CIA and presently went to work for Gulf Oil Co., one of the American oil firms in the consortium. In 1960, Gulf appointed him vice president. ... Another American member of the new consortium was Standard Oil of New Jersey (now Exxon), a client of Sullivan and Cromwell, the New York law firm of which [Secretary of State] John Foster Dulles had long been a senior partner. Brother Allen [Dulles], Director of the CIA [at the time of the coup], had also been a member of the firm.
>
> Syndicated columnist Jack Anderson reported some years later that the Rockefeller family, who controlled Exxon [Standard Oil] and Chase Manhattan Bank, had "helped arrange the CIA coup that brought down Mossadegh." Anderson listed a number of ways in which the Shah demonstrated his gratitude to the Rockefellers, including heavy deposits of his personal fortune in Chase Manhattan, and housing developments in Iran built by a Rockefeller family company.[2]

This same U.S. capitalist class went wild twenty-one years later when the Iraqi government nationalized its oil. This is what led Richard Nixon, Henry Kissinger, the CIA, and the Shah of Iran to support the Kurdish insurrection inside the oil-rich northern part of Iraq in 1972.

Again, did the United States explain that its covert war against Iraq was retaliation for Iraq's recovering its own oil reserves from the imperialist oil monopolies? Of course not. It was explained that the United States was supporting Kurdish freedom. Suddenly, the rabidly racist Nixon administration was so concerned about the mistreatment of national minorities—in Iraq, not in the United States—that it had to spend billions to aid their cause.

This was not simply a case of hypocrisy. It is a reflection of a problem that the U.S. imperialist ruling class encounters as it repeatedly endeavors to carry out wars, plunder, and subversion to maintain its world domination. It can never tell the truth about its motives. It cannot tell its soldiers, "Be ready to kill and be killed to protect and extend our fortunes." So it relies on the demonization of its enemies by an all-powerful propaganda machine while declaring that its own aims are for "democracy" or "freedom" or "human rights" or "to protect small nations" or "to eliminate weapons of mass destruction."

To hide the imperialist character of U.S. capitalism and its government, this propaganda is designed to create a false consciousness. This false consciousness is important as a form of maintaining "public" support for government policies and actions.

When people come to understand the imperialist character of the government and the class it serves, this new and real consciousness can become an irresistible force. When large numbers of people reach their own conclusions about the way society operates and the nature of U.S. foreign policy, it becomes a dangerous and menacing problem for the rulers—who are, after all, a very small segment of the population. This is what happened during the Vietnam War, and it made the war unsustainable. The U.S. aggression in Vietnam, with all its attendant misery and suffering, led to a new consciousness. The anti-war movement went from being a few hundred in 1964-65 to a mass movement within a few years. By 1971, 25 percent of all U.S. soldiers worldwide had either deserted or gone AWOL.

All the Pentagon's firepower, its high-technology weapons of mass destruction, could not eliminate the Vietnamese people's conscious determination to be free, nor overcome the deepening polarization inside U.S. society that made the war effort so difficult to continue.

The specific tactic of economic sanctions against Iraq is at least partly fashioned with an eye toward preventing a powerful anti-war and anti-imperialist movement inside the United States. The U.S. ruling class wants to avoid a repeat of the Vietnam experience. The horrors of war and the seemingly endless casualties in a small, far-away third world country created a new consciousness. Tens of millions of people overcame the false consciousness spoon-fed them by the government. This led to the creation of a massive anti-war movement. *Time* magazine and the other media called this phenomenon the "Vietnam Syndrome."

This is a fundamental reason why the U.S. in 1991 wanted to end the Gulf War so quickly. After forty-two days of war, after wreaking such destruction on Iraq through air strikes, the Pentagon was afraid that actually occupying Baghdad to "take out Saddam," as they put it, would lead to a large number of U.S. casualties and the creation of a major polarization inside the United States.

One reason that the U.S. government relies on sanctions as a weapon of choice today is that it is a form of warfare—a form almost as deadly as open military hostilities—that is quieter, less dramatic, and less likely to arouse a storm of protest at home. All the dying, bleeding, and suffering is done by the "other side." Sanctions are a specific means by which to continue the 1991 war against Iraq without the threat of U.S. casualties and the backlash that would undoubtedly ensue. It is in reality a massacre of innocents, but in slow motion.

The Iraq Sanctions Challenge, which was actively supported by the donations and individual actions of tens of thousands of people in the United States, was an effort to deepen the anti-war and anti-imperialist movement that is finally taking shape around the country.

The sanctions have killed more than 1.5 million Iraqis. The casualty level is approaching that of the Vietnam War. But, for all the suffering they have caused, the sanctions have not accomplished their real political objective: the overthrow of the Iraqi government and its replacement by a Shah-like regime. Nor has the U.S. fomented a successful civil war or dismemberment of Iraq. Instead, the anti-colonial anger of the Iraqi people has only deepened against this U.S. and British aggression.

The people of the world, meaning all those outside of Iraq, are rapidly learning the true genocidal character of sanctions. It's been a longer process than with open military conflict, but the mood and consciousness are clearly changing.

The inability of the sanctions to impose imperialism's will on Iraq, coupled with the emergence of a new worldwide movement against sanctions, has laid the basis for a new crisis and a bigger struggle. The bold demonstration by the Iraq Sanctions Challenge at the U.S. Interests Section in downtown Baghdad may well be remembered as a harbinger of a new anti-imperialist consciousness.

---

[1] New York Times, 6 August 1954.

[2] William Blum, *Killing Hope* (Monroe, Me.: Common Courage Press, 1995).

REPORTS
ON
DAMAGE
TO THE
INFRASTRUCTURE

THE PROBLEM OF CHLORINE

DAVID SOLE

The images from the previous day were still in my mind. Hundreds of babies and children shrunken and dying at the Saddam Pediatric Hospital in Baghdad, most of them stricken with gastroenteritis and amebic dysentery, both water-borne diseases. Now we were walking through the April 7 Water Treatment Plant just north of the city. The plant was providing almost half the fresh water for a city of over five million people. Why were the hospitals so full? Perhaps the answer lay here.

Showing us around was Ferhan Mohson, the plant shift supervisor, and Dr. A. Al-Dabbagh, Assistant President of Baghdad University, an expert in water engineering. The facility was not that different from any fresh-water plant in Detroit, where I work for the Water and Sewerage Department. The huge pumps were roaring as they lifted water from the Tigris River. Settling tanks slowed the water and let solids sink to the bottom. Huge filtration tanks further reduced the contamination.

But unlike the procedures normally followed, this plant was not adding chlorine in the early stages of purification. "Importation of chlorine is restricted severely by the sanctions," explained our hosts. "As a poisonous gas, they say it can be used for military purposes." The chlorine now allowed into the country comes by way of UNICEF. But it is not enough.

The Tigris's water is very turbid, with minute solid particles suspended in it even after settling and filtration. Before the Gulf War the plant added alum, an aluminum salt, to the water to reduce these solids. Now alum is barred by U.S./UN sanctions and the plant adds an unprocessed ore that contains 50 percent impurities. Every day they have to use a mechanical shovel to clean out the tanks. Control of the turbidity is difficult.

As the water leaves the plant it gets what chlorine is available. Of the twelve chlorinators, six are working. Yet the chlorine is more than enough to purify the water. In fact, the chlorine residual (the amount of chlorine left in the water after the contaminants have been destroyed) is ten times that used for water leaving Detroit's Water Works Park. However, one official later told us that testing of tap water in homes around Baghdad showed that over 10 percent were receiving contaminated water. What's the problem?

The biggest problem comes from the massive bombing of Baghdad during the Gulf War. While the water-treatment plants in the city were not hit, the pumping stations were, and the entire network of underground water pipes was severely damaged. And, guess what? Pipes are considered potential military material and are restricted from import into the country by the sanctions. So many pipes are cracked and broken that 40 percent of all water leaving the water plants is lost to leakage, according to Dr. Adnan Jabrou, Deputy Mayor of Baghdad. This creates a low-pressure situation in the pipes. At many points, instead of water leaking out of the pipes into the ground, contaminated ground water is leaking back into the water delivery system's pipes.

That is why the water engineers are over-chlorinating the water as it leaves the plant. They are hoping to decontaminate the water as it runs through the broken pipes. But they do not have enough chlorine to completely purify the water. In fact, the Baghdad water engineers would like to double the amount of chlorine they use currently.

There is no rational reason to limit the chlorine coming into the country. UNSCOM inspectors visit the plant every two months to monitor the chlorine that is there. It is easy to keep track of the chlorine. It comes in huge one-ton containers that can have seals put on them. Pressure can be monitored daily if UNSCOM thinks it necessary.

Dr. Jabrou was proud of what Iraq had accomplished for the people before the Gulf War. "Before the aggression, when we tested the water at homes throughout the city, less than 1.8 percent failed the World Health Organization standards," he explained. "Our loss from leakage was only 15 percent, much better than many cities in the West or in Japan."

But now, because of the sanctions, diarrhea and dysentery are destroying an entire generation of children. These diseases are striking ten times as many people as before. Combined with malnutrition due to food shortages (again the sanctions) and the terrible shortage of medicine to treat these easily cured maladies, tens of thousands of children are condemned to death.

Waste water treatment in Baghdad is also minimal due to shortages of pumps, replacement parts, pipes, and chlorine. In fact, no chlorine is available for waste water treatment. An estimated 66 billion gallons of untreated sewage is being dumped into the Tigris annually without any treatment whatsoever. Industrial waste is also being dumped. And there are reports that hospitals, unable to sterilize the medical waste due to parts shortages for autoclaves and incinerators, are dumping their waste into the system, too. The long-term health and ecological problems this situation is creating are most alarming.

Everyone understands the need for clean drinking water. It is a cornerstone of modern life. To deny Iraq the necessary supplies to rebuild, maintain, and expand its water treatment facilities—especially chlorine—is a crime against humanity. There can be no legitimate objection raised to this on military or any other grounds. Only a desire to destroy an entire people can be motivating the U.S. policy makers. A worldwide outcry must be raised against this gross violation of human rights.

HOSPITALS PUSHED BACK IN TIME

SAPPHIRE MANN AHMED, M.D.

The Iraq health care system is largely a hospital-based curative structure. Except for a small, very affordable fee amounting to fifty cents, services are free in the public hospitals. In the capital there are twenty public hospitals. There are also private clinics that are expensive.

On 7 May we visited the Saddam Hussein Pediatric Hospital in Baghdad. It is the main teaching hospital and the best-equipped hospital in the nation. It has a four hundred inpatient bed capacity, but due to shortages of supplies, medications, and nursing, it is utilizing only about three hundred of these beds. There is a rapid turnover and a long waiting list, also due to limited resources and unpredictable supply deliveries experienced with the UN Oil for Food process and NGO medicine donations. The outpatient department sees an average of fifteen hundred to two thousand patients a day.

We toured the emergency room, isolation department, and cancer wards of the pediatric hospital. Most admissions nowadays are emergencies, chronic diseases, and malignancies—especially childhood leukemia cases, which have increased and for which there are limited oncology medications. In addition, there has been an increase in birth defects and congenital abnormalities, and a tenfold increase in kwashiorkor and marasmus since 1989.

Doctors feel that if they have nothing to offer the patients, there is no need to admit them simply to watch them suffer and/or die.

The general condition of the major hospital of Baghdad was equivalent to what one might have seen in a public hospital serving the poor and minorities in America in the 1950s. The hospital was fairly clean, but that was difficult to appreciate because the paint was very old, the lighting was limited, machinery was dusty, oxygen tanks were old and discolored, the bed sheets were off-white, and the patients' clothes were neither bright nor clean. It appeared that many of the patients were poor people. The scenario was what one would expect in a very poor African country, not in a developing oil-rich nation.

Al Qadissiya Hospital is a general hospital in a very poor area called Saddam City in Baghdad. The population in this area is about two million. Four hospitals serve this area. About twenty new patients are admitted a day and the outpatient department sees about one thousand a day. In addition to general medicine, there are gynecology; pediatrics; rehabilitation; ear, nose, and throat; dermatology, and general surgery departments. The doctors echoed the same story pertaining to shortages of medicines, medical supplies, and medical equipment as was reported by the doctors working at the Saddam Pediatric Hospital. However, all shortages were visibly more severe and the hospital and machinery more dilapidated.

In addition to the increase in medical problems mentioned above, the doctors reported an increase in crime-related injuries, social problems, homicides, and accidents. They also reported an increase in psychological, psychiatric, and social problems—including wife and child abuse and family fights, especially in the poverty-stricken areas. There is a large increase in malaria cases, but the supply of anti-malaria medications is limited. There is a shortage of all vaccines, especially DPT, and an irregular flow of all medications.

Doctors mentioned that the refrigeration system and electricity supply is poor and the generator is weak and breaks down often.

As for Iraq's food situation, we found that due to an increase in maternal depression, malnutrition, and other psychosocial effects of poverty, many mothers are not accepting medical advice to breast-feed their babies for longer periods. Consequently, the unreliable availability of four to six tins of artificial milk per child per month is not meeting the need; at least eight to ten tins of milk are needed per month.

General supplies we found lacking in the hospitals included bed coverings, air conditioners, ambulances, refrigerators, suture materials, sterilizing chemicals, pencils, pens, and writing pads.

As for the medical shortages, everything was lacking: intravenous fluids, all medicines including antibiotics, anti-tuberculosis medications to treat the increased incidence of extra-pulmonary TB, anti-convulsants, hypertension and anti-angina medications, to name a few. Many first-line cancer and leukemia drugs are not available.

Radiology, laboratory, and all specialty equipment and supplies are extremely limited or not available. For example, the defibrillation and ECG machines are limited, outdated, and broken. There is no functioning CAT scan or MRI.

Khaled Ahmad Al-Sudani, of the Islamic Relief Agency, and I had a very rushed meeting with Dr. Fakid Farhood at the World Health Organization in Baghdad. He and others thanked us for coming and said they welcomed our help. They repeatedly confirmed the pathetic medical situation of the Iraqi people. They believe that the Ministry of Health does a good job of distributing whatever supplies and services are available.

OBSERVATIONS OF A NURSE

SHARON EOLIS, R.N., M.S.

Imagine being a nurse in a hospital where there are no sheets, towels, gowns, diapers, or soap. The temperature is over 100 degrees and there is no air conditioning, not even a fan. Mothers are fanning their children to cool them and keep the flies away.

The hospital is a modern structure, with wall outlets for life-saving equipment. But nothing works. The emergency ward has seventy-five to one hundred children, two and three to a bed. A number have asthma, but only one nebulizer mask is shared by all of them. Each parent hopes her child will get treatment before the medicine runs out.

Imagine seeing one hundred to one hundred and fifty new admissions in a twenty-four hour period. They are referred from the outpatient department, which sees fifteen hundred to two thousand people daily. They send over only the sickest ones. Most of the children are there because of dehydration. Some get intravenous fluid infusing, but the amount available is not enough to properly hydrate them.

Imagine two isolation rooms, each of which would usually hold one patient. But one contains three children with whooping cough and the other has three children with measles. There is an epidemic of measles in adults and children. There are no vaccines to prevent communicable childhood diseases.

It's time to discharge one of the babies. The doctor has written a prescription but there is no medicine in the pharmacy to fill it. The child's family lives outside the city and the mother carries the family's drinking water from a contaminated river. Their stove is broken so she is unable to boil the water to mix the baby's formula. The baby was treated for amebic dysentery, contracted from the unsanitary water, but the treatment was only partial due to lack of medicines.

Now imagine a blockade on the American people that prevented us from having safe drinking water, food, milk for babies, antibiotics, and vaccines to fight infections and disease. These are the conditions the Iraqi people have been plagued with since the Gulf War in 1991.

When our delegation visited the Saddam Pediatric Hospital, we saw a modern hospital without adequate lighting, functioning elevators, x-ray film, anesthesia, or dialysis equipment. On the first ward, we saw infants and toddlers suffering from malnutrition, some with big bellies and listless eyes. In the second ward, we saw older children in acute renal failure with swollen faces, arms, and legs. Their mothers were sitting and watching, holding their children. Some were crying silently. Nearly all the children we saw in the hospital were suffering from malnutrition, dehydration, and renal failure, and many were close to dying.

According to one of the doctors with whom we spoke, amebic dysentery is the largest killer of these children, and 80 percent of the cases could be eradicated if they had clean water. Statistics compiled by the Iraqi Ministry of Health show that in 1989, there were 19,615 cases of dysentery; in 1997, there were 43,295 cases. In 1989, Iraq had no cases of cholera. Eight years later, there were 10,000 cases from contaminated water and food.

Dr. Samir Kalendar explained to our delegation, "Malnutrition is our number one problem. This problem is corroborated by the World Health Organization. All the children of Iraq are suffering from different degrees of malnutrition. This leaves them with a low immune system and vulnerable to diseases and infection." According to the Iraqi Ministry of Health, before the U.S./UN sanctions were imposed, there were 485 cases of kwashiorkor. By 1997 there were 28,475 cases per year. In 1991, there were 5,192 cases of marasmus; six years later, there were 139,346 cases. Kwashiorkor and marasmus are conditions caused by extreme malnutrition.

In Iraq, food is rationed and distributed through the Ministry of Trade. Families get six tins of powdered milk per month for babies up to one year of age. However, for infant growth and development, they need ten cans of milk per month. The mothers dilute the milk to stretch the supply for a month. Then the formula is so weak the babies cannot develop normally. The lack of sufficient food for pregnant and nursing mothers leads to low-birthweight infants and leaves some mothers unable to breastfeed their babies.

The infant mortality rate there is 92.7 per 1,000 live births. Maternal mortality is 117 deaths per 100,000 births. These abnormally high death rates are due to the draconian measures inflicted by the U.S./UN sanctions committee. Before the sanctions and the Gulf War, Iraq had a developed nationalized health system that provided free care to all the people. Its level of technological development in health care was on a par with industrialized Western nations. Iraqi doctors were doing open-heart surgery. Many Iraqi physicians learned the latest techniques by training in U.S. hospitals. In 1989, surgeons in Iraqi hospitals were performing 15,125 operations a month. But, by January 1998, the average was down to 3,795 procedures per month due to the lack of surgical supplies, anesthesia, heart valves, and antibiotics.

Before the war and sanctions, 50 percent of Iraq's nurses had come there from other countries. Most of them left after the sanctions were imposed. In Iraq, nursing is not viewed as a profession as we know it in the U.S. The prevailing religious and cultural traditions do not encourage the practice of nursing. It is customary for relatives to take care of sick family members in the hospital. Now doctors must carry out some of the tasks that usually fall to nursing.

In a brief conversation with a nurse at the Mansour Teaching Hospital for Children, I learned that there were similarities in our duties. The big difference is that in the U.S. we have up-to-date equipment to treat all life-threatening emergencies. In Baghdad hospitals, much of the equipment is broken or outdated.

The teaching hospital has a casualty ward for adults. We saw patients there with severe cardiac problems. Some needed surgery. Others needed pain medicine like nitroglycerin. Nitroglycerin is a major drug used to relieve chest pain. These tablets come in a dosage of grains 1/150. But nitroglycerin is considered a "dual-use substance" that can be used for explosives, so the UN sanctions committee refuses to approve it.

We delivered most of the medicines we had brought to the Ministry of Health. There, members of the delegation had an opportunity to meet with a ministry representative. He told us the UNSCOM sanctions committee had approved some medical aid to Iraq, but much of it had not arrived. In 1996 they received 70 percent of the aid promised; in 1997, 80 percent. In 1998 no aid had arrived as of May. The Ministry of Health had requested four hundred ambulances. Only two hundred were approved and none had been delivered. They are considered a "dual-use" item. Most of Iraq's ambulances are inoperable because they lack replacement parts after eight years of sanctions. We were told they need about two thousand ambulances to service 22.9 million people who live throughout the country.

In spite of the sanctions against Iraq, patients there are treated with dignity. The nurses and doctors do the best they can in the most desperate circumstances. They have the skills to cure, but not the means to do so. The only answer is to end the sanctions now.

VISIT TO A PSYCHIATRIC HOSPITAL

BERTA JOUBERT, M.D.

On our first full day in Baghdad—9 May 1998—I was able to visit, very briefly, the Ibn Rashid Psychiatric Hospital.

As a psychiatrist, I am very interested in knowing the status of psychiatry and its delivery in different parts of the world. In Iraq, where we went to see the effects of sanctions, I wanted to know their impact on the patients of this branch of medicine.

Since a visit to a psychiatric facility was not included in our incredibly tight schedule, I asked our hosts if one might be arranged anytime during our stay. Later on that first morning, during a press conference at the Ministry of Health, I was approached by one of our translators who said he could drive me to the Ibn Rashid Hospital. Without delay, I left behind my tape recorder to cover the press conference and set out to visit the hospital.

After a fairly short ride, we arrived at a white building surrounded by a white picket fence with a red crescent drawn on the front façade and the Ibn Rashid Psychiatric Hospital written in Arabic. I learned later that it is a teaching hospital serving 1,300 patients from the Baghdad area and providing both inpatient and outpatient services.

There I met with several psychiatrists: Dr. Natiq Kamal Khalil, the Directing Manager of the hospital who gave a brief overview, and Dr. R. H. Alkhaiat and Dr. N. J. Alhemyary. Also present were two other doctors and the head nurse, a very friendly young woman dressed in the classic white uniform and cap. When I arrived, they were conducting an interview with a patient and his relative and asked me to join them. Although the interview was in Arabic, it became clear that the patient was depressed. His wife was very attentive and obviously an integral part of the therapeutic process. They did not seem to be bothered by my presence.

This first contact with a patient underscored what the therapeutic team said afterwards. Because of the sanctions, there are hardly any psychiatric medications. They had always used family support as a key ingredient of therapy, but now because of the lack of drugs they sometimes have to rely exclusively on the patient's support system.

Psychotropics, commonly called psychiatric drugs, are a special class of medications that need to be administered very carefully under constant monitoring. Typically, they take two to four weeks to reach their full effect. In many cases the dose has to be constantly adjusted until the patient shows any significant improvement. Once the best dosage is found, the treatment has to last months and, in many cases, years. Many times they can cause unwanted and bothersome neurological reactions, in which case another drug (an anti-Parkinson) has to be added.

Because of the sanctions, even the most basic and widely used psychotropic medication, chlorpromazine, is not available in Iraq, at least not enough for a complete treatment. The medicines the hospitals receive each month are not necessarily the same ones they received the previous month, so there is no consistency in the treatment. There is no anti-Parkinson's medication to arrest the sometimes very painful neurological reactions that can happen even after the patient stops taking the psychotropic drug.

During the tour through the hospital, we visited the pharmacy. A pharmacist and her aide were working in a room with four or five cabinets. Some of them were completely empty. One had a pyramid of Mellaril tablet boxes on the upper shelf. These were all the medicines they had to treat the seventy-three patients, not counting the outpatients, admitted at that time. There must have been around fifty small boxes. Certainly not enough. Mellaril is an antipsychotic that tends to cause fewer secondary reactions, but it is very mild. For that reason it is generally given to elderly patients. There, it was the only drug available for every patient.

The other component of the treatment, family support, which is used to complement drugs and psychotherapy, now in most cases has to replace the medications. Unfortunately, this added pressure causes more destabilization in the family group, which is both unable to cope with the patient's more frequent and disruptive symptoms, and is suffering its own hardships due to sanctions—lack of food, electricity, general medicines, and so on. A vicious circle develops: patients have no medications, they get worse, the family support is missing, the patients deteriorate further.

In some cases, particularly when the patient is extremely depressed, agitated, or violent, the doctors resort to electroconvulsive therapy, which they have to administer in a very primitive way, without the drugs needed to counter the violent convulsions. Regardless of one's position on the use of ECT, the fact remains that it is still a form of therapy available in most countries. A general protocol exists to administer it in order to reap maximum benefits with the least amount of discomfort for the patient. The basis for its use is that it has produced significant improvement in patients with various severe mental symptoms—in particular, profound depression. Most often it is used when medications are not advisable. Part of the protocol is premedication first, with a short-acting anesthetic to sedate the patient, and then a muscle relaxant to prevent any violent convulsion and therefore a concomitant fracture. Oxygen is also administered, since the relaxant suppresses normal respiratory movement.

It is hard to fathom how ECT can be administered under the current situation in Iraq. The premedication or oxygen is often not available. Only an old-model ECT machine was available at the Ibn Rashid Hospital, and the physicians had to do their best. They have to weigh the psychological pain suffered by the patients against the consequences of the lack of premedications, which can be the pain of a fracture or the agonizing sensation that they cannot breathe.

One psychiatrist told me that sometimes, when the patient's relatives see their loved ones undergoing this treatment, they take them home. It is difficult to imagine the psychological pain these patients and their relatives go through. Patients with mental illnesses can be very vulnerable to other forces if they are not treated. Depending on the illness, they can become very careless and neglect their personal hygiene, health, and nutrition. Under the current conditions in Iraq, this neglect can be very dangerous for the overall health of the patient.

The physical condition of the hospital mirrored those of the other hospitals that we visited during our stay: bare rooms, lack of bed sheets and disinfectants, and so on.

Psychiatry, like any other science, is based on advances in other fields, including technology. Science is universal, and in the modern world, with the great leap in communication, discoveries in one part of the world are soon accessible in distant places. Iraq is completely isolated. Not only did mental health professionals ask us for medicines for their patients, but they requested literature in their field so they can keep up with the new treatments and advances. Many doctors were trained in England, France, the Soviet Union, Germany, and the U.S. Now, because of the sanctions, they train only in Iraq and cannot receive scientific journals because these are considered "dual-use."

It is particularly sad to see this development in a country with such a rich history. During the Assyrian-Babylonian era, the Iraqis together with the Egyptians were pioneers in recognizing certain depressive conditions. At the time they linked this to the idea of sin and therefore offered a treatment of confession. The history of medicine owes much to the Middle East, particularly to the autonomous schools of medical practice that existed during the Assyrian-Babylonian epoch.

THE IMPACT OF SANCTIONS: A MEDICAL EXAMINATION

ALLAN CONNOLLY, M.D.

As a Canadian physician and member of Physicians for Global Survival, the Canadian Affiliate to the International Physicians for Prevention of Nuclear War, I attended our congress in Stockholm in June of 1991. There I heard the medical and scientific report produced by the Harvard Study Team entitled, "Public Health in Iraq after the Gulf War." It was an appalling prediction of the death (murder) of 100,000 children per year in Iraq as a direct result of the UN sanctions. Unbelievable!

Time passed. As a physician, I followed the global issues related to peace and militarism, the latter, like an evil virus, destroying the people and resources of the world. In November 1997, I heard Kathy Kelly speak in Vancouver. I was appalled. It could not be. The number of dead over eight years due to the sanctions was higher than predicted. The UN, through various agencies, was reporting the results of its own sanctions. Experts and medical professionals had observed and confirmed the figures every two to three years. The most recent reports at the end of 1997 and early 1998 suggested that the number was increasing again, after a few years of improvement. Why?

The eight years of sanctions were finally overwhelming the host. Its immunological mechanisms were breaking down through a multifactor assault: foul, infected drinking water; bacteria and parasitic diseases running rampant; malnutrition; an embargo of medical supplies and food, and an embargo of medicine.

Clearly, unpredictable synergies were causing disease in the weakest—the young and the old. I was stunned by the details. I decided to join Voices in the Wilderness on one of their trips later in 1998. When the International Action Center extended an invitation early in April, I decided to make medical observations in Iraq. I left for Iraq on 5 May, taking one thousand pounds of medical supplies donated from local Vancouver hospitals and two thousand dollars worth of antibiotics paid for by collections taken up by several organizations.

Time was at a premium in Iraq, and I concentrated on making observations in the pediatric wards of four hospitals, two in Baghdad and two in Basra. I was the only physician in the group of fifteen who traveled south of Baghdad in an open bus for eight hours, following the heavily bombed route known as the Highway of Death. Remnants of that tragedy lined the highway.

In the last hospital in Baghdad, an erudite and kind Iraqi doctor said, "There is great sadness in my heart, but I cannot show it. I must be patient with my patients." She took me, as a doctor, into a side room where three children were in the terminal stages of marasmus. I took my last picture. It was too much. I couldn't look or listen to more. I distracted myself by reading the charts, literally scraps of used paper, with a few lab results and marginal progress notes. Each patient had a chart. Each chart had an initial medical history and examination record, printed in English.

"The children come to the hospital only to die—there is no medicine."

A Medical Examination of the People of Iraq

C.C. (Chief Complaint): A predicted slaughter of 1.3 million people by the embargo by the United Nations over the past eight years. Recent figures suggest the number of children dying is going up!

H.P.I. (History of Present Illness):
a) A sophisticated, socialized society isolated from the world community— August 1990.
b) Gulf War January 1991—Bombed for 47 days to intentionally destroy infrastructure; electrical power, water, and sewage distribution systems pulverized.
c) To break the will of the people and render them helpless to return to pre-morbid state ... cut off food supply and block medicine.
d) Reduce chlorine so they cannot sanitize their water ... hence infectious disease is killing a second generation ... a previous generation, one million young men, were killed in the Iran/Iraq war ... supported by weapons and logistics by the U.S.

O.E. (On Examination): Primarily at pediatric wards in hospitals ... two in Baghdad, two in Basra. Direct observation of sick children and of their mothers.

Other Sources:
a) Interviews: with doctors, patients, parents, government officials, and humanitarian workers.
b) UN Reports: WFP, FAO, and UNICEF.

UN Human Rights Commissioner Findings (General):
a) The young, the sick, the poor, and the elderly are bearing the brunt of the sanctions. Infant mortality rate has increased 6 times (16 times, in one report).
b) No medicine: limited medical supplies, e.g., no IV solutions.
c) No antibiotics.
d) No intravenous.
e) Lab inspections down 65%.
f) Surgical operations down 70%.
g) Medical response limited: no tools.

Head:
a) No educative supplies, doctor: "No journals since 1993."
b) Costs up.

Mouth:
a) Food distribution equitable, but limited to 1,000 K/day.
b) Vitamins and protein in short supply.
c) WFO has prevented nutritional crises in rural areas ... supplies spotty.
d) Water: infected and polluted.

Lungs:
a) Adult asthma and heart disease up. Air pollution>unusual skin conditions: i) oil fires>visual disturbances ii) microtoxins>congenital abnormalities. Possible chemicals released by UN Forces>rise in premature births. iii) DU dust>sheep: milk, wool, meat (300 tons) congenital defects up 10%.

Digestion:
a) Diarrhea>amebic and bacterial.
b) Increase in all water-borne diseases, in urban and rural areas.
c) Water distribution and sewage system useless.
d) Cities: leakage, pumps broken, low pressure, not enough chlorine, Al_3SO_4 contaminated.
e) Rural: 30% no sewage, raw into rivers and streams to drink.

Vascular:

a) Water is life blood, but is itself a source of disease.

Hematological:
a) Incidence of lymphoblastic leukemia increased 4 times.
b) Increased acute myelogenous leukemia.
c) Increased anemia; increased hemolytic uremic syndrome.

Cancer:
a) Males: Increased lung, bladder, bronchial, skin, and stomach.
b) Females: Increased breast, bladder, lymphoma.
c) Previously rare, now appearing: Sarcoma teratoma rabdomyosarcoma, nethroblastoma.

Diagnostic Impression:
a) An illegal genocide perpetuated by the world community on the people of Iraq (used by Saddam Hussein, their leader).
b) A medical emergency that demands the action of the global medical community!

Treatment Recommendations:
a) Lift embargo—the only solution.
b) Allow repair of water and sewage distribution system; restore medical system to full capacity.
c) Increase Oil for Food (SCR 986) to adequately allow for full function.
d) International medical response teams: training and research to ally with Iraqi doctors.
e) Diplomacy: UN Charter Article 50.
f) Public express concern to governments—write/phone/fax.

Prognosis:
a) Guarded. U.S. keeps changing the rules.
b) Media is silent?
c) People uninformed of preventable catastrophe and the Canadian government's active role in genocide.

Upon my return to Vancouver, I felt exhilarated and safe. Then I crashed, and experienced profound lassitude, giardiasis probably. I had taken a different route out of Amman, through Frankfort, to Canada. I was carrying fifty rolls of film and twenty-eight hours of videotape with me. This was to avoid their seizure when the IAC members returned to the United States.

Once I recovered, I went to work for three forgotten days, and reported my findings to the executive of End the Arms Race, my local medical group. I then went to Ottawa and reported my medical findings to the Board of Physicians for Global Survival at their annual general meeting, the first of many presentations.

In Ottawa I went to Foreign Affairs and met with officials at the Middle Eastern Desk. They told me, "There is no public concern about this issue in Canada, Dr. Connolly." I assured them I would raise public concern. I knew no sentient being would fail to be moved by the information and pictures of the children I had to share.

The public response has been overwhelming. People have a need to act and with the accurate information they will. I have received books, articles, and letters, new information that only makes the crime against humanity even more heinous, more duplicitous. All our governments are involved.

So far the medical response is deadening! The geopolitical evil dance may continue, but physicians of the world must rise up collectively, awakened to the slaughter of children which is Mengelean in its dimensions. Medical doctors predicted this. They have observed and confirmed it over time. This is no Spitzian experiment. Now they must act to end the sanctions. Only their end will allow Iraq to repair its infrastructure and save the next child from dying. To do less is to demean the profession of medicine!

SANCTIONS ON KNOWLEDGE

FATIMA ALI-KHAN

I wish lot of happines and long happy life and we are so grateful for your visit to our collage and I very sorry obout many speling mestakes.

Yaarob Falh Kalaf Saad Sabah
Iraqi university student, Baghdad

Education is an important form of investment for the future, providing people with a passport to greater economic security and enhanced life-chances. Schools are key agencies for the transmission of substantive knowledge and cultural values; further, they are generators of hope, windows to a different future, charged with a symbolic and emotional significance that journeys far beyond their job-creating potential.

For Iraqi society, education, which is the purveyor of progress and science, as well as the bookmark to the recovery of their suffering nation, has been criminally sanctioned. Alongside sanctioning food, water, medicine, and shelter—the very necessities of human survival—education has been denied to the people of Iraq because the United States government, under the auspices of the United Nations Security Council, does not consider the Iraqi people to be complete human beings.

I witnessed the breakdown of Iraq's education system when I visited the University of Baghdad, Iraq's oldest and largest university. Upon entering a biology class, the students' thirst for knowledge and energy illuminated the classroom. Despite the lack of microscopes, textbooks, laboratory equipment, and teaching materials, the class prevailed through the dynamism and creativity of the twenty-three-year-old biology professor. She brought new meaning to the fundamental philosophy of education by interacting with students and their families, initiating and instilling within each student solid values that blend with current realities, self-respect, and confidence.

Professors are struggling on monthly salaries equivalent to a meager three U.S. dollars, with outdated lesson plans and instructional materials. Yet they work persistently and creatively to keep students motivated and the learning process alive.

During the barbaric Gulf War and since the imposition of genocidal sanctions in 1991, Iraqi students have been robbed of an education, which is mandated by UNICEF as "the universally recognized, fundamental human right for all." The students I spoke with relayed heartfelt accounts of their dreams, career aspirations, daily lives, families, friends, love, and war. As a university student myself, I shared with them the common bonds of taking examinations, all-night study sessions, homework, social lives, stress, and achieving good grades to move ahead in life. Despite these globally recognized traits that accompany student life, there are unique differences between us that transcend such ordinary variations as language and clothing. Rather, they are tragic and cruelly manufactured differences.

Iraqi students have been isolated from the world for about eight years now, denied access to computers, books, journals, and other learning materials to further facilitate their knowledge. They're not able to participate in activities, symposiums, or study abroad. They're being robbed of knowledge simply because their passports are stamped with an Iraqi seal. These types of problems did not exist in Iraq before the implementation of the criminal sanctions.

In ancient times, Iraq was the center of learning. In modern times, too, education continues to be a top priority within Iraq's human resources development sector. As such, education in Iraq is compulsory and free, and the increase in investment for education was often three times that of the population growth. Undeniably, education has been sanctioned in order to cripple Iraq's ability to progress into the future. In the eyes of the West, a literate society armed with knowledge is the real "weapon of mass destruction." Furthermore, an educated Iraqi nation is in sync with the changing tides of technology, research, and development. If allowed to continue its development, it would not need a life-support system from outside—which the West can then heartlessly unplug when its brutal policies are not followed.

The professors, students, and administrative staff at the University of Baghdad reflect the epitome of heroism because, as everyday people, they are persevering against the evil forces of colonialism and immoral sanctions. As the president of the university relayed to us,

"There is an order to prevent any cooperation with us. When we contact other universities, they say we can't do anything with you or deal with you because you are Iraqi." He explained that "First, computers were eradicated. Therefore, we have learned to deal without computers. And since the December 1996 implementation of Resolution 986, Oil for Food, we haven't gotten anything [books, paper, pencils, etc.] as of yet. Resolution 986 is a very complicated resolution; the committee has to debate over every little item that we say we need. Even [drinking] glasses are sanctioned because they have decided that they are not needed for our university."

Those who make these decisions are the fat cats in Washington and New York. They would not survive one day, let alone almost eight years as the Iraqis have, without essential items. In every sense, "steadfastness" is a collective value embedded within the Iraqi culture, crystallizing an all-encompassing life of tenacious resistance to overcome oppression and preserve the Iraqi existence. I am angered that the world stands and watches while students' lives have been torn apart, education is left at a standstill, and racism and war prevail over peace and harmony.

Inshallah (God willing), the sanctions will be lifted soon. If that happens, the Iraqi people living in the paradoxical "cradle of civilization" will no longer be subjected to the barbarism of the West, which, in its crusade to become the king of the desert, is exterminating the Iraqi people, sending many to the "grave of civilization." Lastly, it would suffice to conclude with a *Hadith* (saying) from the Prophet Muhammad (Peace Be Upon Him): "For the acquisition of knowledge, if it requires, go so far, even to China." This explains Iraq's commitment to education in the past. For this to be part of Iraq's present and future commitment, it is up to us to work together in lifting the immoral and illegal sanctions.

WHAT TO TAKE TO IRAQ

BARBARA NIMRI AZIZ

It's hard to know, whenever I set out on a visit, what to take to Iraq. Whether old friends or new, they'll all help me, introduce me to others to interview, tell me the latest gossip about what their teenage son said to them one day when he felt so angry, or proud, or hopeless, discuss their rations, tell me what they saw in a hospital. They translate for me, comment on what they saw on TV, or mention a new book they heard about. They'll prepare a meal for a get-together in their garden. They'll help me understand what's happening in Iraq.

How can I thank them? What can I give in return?

What can I offer an Iraqi to give her or him hope? Of course I'll assure them that I'll press my government to lift the sanctions so Iraqis can be part of the world again, so they can all go to school again, so they can plan a career or a holiday in the scorching summer, or send their child to graduate school abroad, so they can receive visitors and show off their civilization, their beautiful rivers, and order a book from Beirut or London, and prepare a paper and fly to a conference to deliver it.

Fighting to lift the sanctions altogether is fine. But what about meanwhile? Something for the present. It must be something nourishing, something that can strengthen a woman and man because, I fear, they may still have a long road to walk. Besides, this gift has to weigh just a few kilograms—something concrete and compact that I can load on the plane with me, and transport in a car as I cross the desert from Jordan. We have no massive airlift underway there. There are none of the frantic collections Americans often launch in local schools, mosques, churches, or synagogues, or the YWCA, or Rotary Club.

After several years of visits and letters back and forth, and ten years of hearing Iraqis and interviewing them at their work, watching them, and then telling in newspaper articles and on the radio about what I saw and felt and learned in Iraq, I had a lot of experience. By this time, I could make a wise decision: a resolve to offer books.

For most people across the world, hope comes from a new baby. It comes from music, too—band music, gospel music, rhythmic recitation of the holy book, protest music, dance music. Besides this, for Iraqis especially, it's books. Books are a source of hope whether or not they are under embargo. Remember what books meant to the young James Baldwin? As a child, this man, who would become one of America's great writers, read every single book in his local Harlem library. He read them even though the books were not even about his own people or his culture.

In April of 1991, soon after the bombing ended, I reentered Iraq and found everyone still in a state of shock. Everyone I spoke with detailed their long nights, the waiting, then the familiar sounds of the bombers. They watched where the bombs unloaded, decided if and where they might go to escape. There was no water because pumping stations were bombed. There was no electricity because the bombs took out the entire electrical network of the country on the first night of the war. Families set up a place to cook in their hallways, away from any window. They brought their bedding there. They cooked in the dark halls and slept together with children and grandchildren. Farmers, artists, college students, diplomats, drivers, and teachers—everyone endured those deprivations.

So did Gaya. But Gaya drew my attention to a particular need. "I couldn't read," said Gaya, talking about the forty-two days of bombing. Gaya is an archeologist and she loves history, any history. She knows Iraqi history especially well. Nothing had unnerved this Iraqi more than being unable to read. She was the first who alerted me to that loss, and I have seen it grow more acute with time.

It has been eight years since Gaya's distressing remark. Today, conditions are better in some ways. Electricity is 75 percent restored in the cities so she and eighteen million others have light to read by—most of the time. Yet, more than ever, Iraqis cannot read.

Those who don't know Iraq will expect the fault lies within the country. We often hear how oppressive the government is, how little freedom exists, how severe the censorship is. Especially at a time when the leadership is under siege, we expect even more repression. The Baathists are surely to blame, we conclude. "Anyway, there's no food!" we argue. "Books should be a low priority at times like this. Forget about books."

But Washington's Iraq policy makers didn't forget about books. Neither did the U.S.'s staunch sanctions ally, Britain. The ban on books to Iraq lies squarely on the United States as chief architect of this embargo policy. Yes, Iraqis are bereft of books because of U.S. censorship! And it's worse than weeding out seditious reading material. It is a total ban.

When the embargo began, all deliveries of literature stopped. The U.S. and British governments decreed Iraq must have no books. Publishers and professional organizations were notified. Nothing over twelve ounces would be allowed through U.S. and British post offices. Above all, no professional journals.

The plan is likely devised on the basis of our government's intelligence about the importance Iraqis give to literature and knowledge. Everyone in the Middle East knows what voracious readers Iraqis are. The Arabs say, "Written in Cairo, printed in Beirut, read in Baghdad." Baghdad was neither a publishing center like Beirut nor a match for Cairo with its community of writers. But Iraqis admit they are fond of reading. They study foreign languages in order to read more, and they translate in order to know more, to keep abreast of current releases. They say this derives from their keenness, bordering on obsession, to know what is going on "outside."

Iraq is an almost landlocked nation, but it has many borders. It has been a crossroads for travelers from all directions. Iraqis took intense interest in whomever passed through. But their intellectual sensibility must be rooted in their ancient interaction with literature as well as their geography. Iraq's ancestors translated most of the Greek classics and scientific literature from Greek into Arabic. It was ancient Iraqis who introduced Hellenic and Byzantine thinking to the East, and then built on it. They criticized and synthesized those ideas and became great thinkers, inventors, and innovators.

Iraq's role in literature goes back even further—to the creation of humankind's first books, those inscribed clay tablets that have been preserved in the hundreds of thousands. The cuneiform script and the accumulation of recorded knowledge in those primordial books was a creation of Mesopotamia—their civilization. No Iraqi is unmindful of this.

They know that five-thousand-year-old dwellings, now buried deep beneath the sands, housed libraries with shelves and shelves of cuneiform-stamped tablets. As children, all Iraqis learn about their role in human history and they carry it with them—as Americans carry images of their war of independence, space explorations, and the voice of Dr. Martin Luther King Jr. This surely explains Iraqis' high standard of literacy in modern times and the priority they give education for boys and girls, from primary school through college.

My friend Dr. Walid el-Jadir, a professor of archeology at Baghdad University until his death after the war, excavated an ancient city called Sippar. Not only did Dr. Walid uncover a private library in one of the Sippar buildings, but in the corner of that room of tablets he found a set of cuneiform tablets that was the index to the library. So ancient Iraq had not only books but libraries, and the books in them were catalogued.

No Iraqis I have met are unaware of their ancestors' role in bringing literature to human civilization. At least before the embargo, most middle-class homes like Gaya's included a small library. It is part of a family's furnishings, their routine of life. Not only Arabic books, but volumes in English, German, and French are included. Iraqis collect books written about them by Europeans. They keep old gazetteers that list their city officials in the Ottoman times. They have art catalogues, music books, and cookbooks.

Who notices their absence? Iraqis felt it immediately. Their subscriptions from abroad stopped, their *Times Literary Journal* didn't arrive. There was no postal delivery at all for some months, so they thought maybe things were piling up at the border because Iraqi planes were banned from the skies. No one on that side was certain. Then shortages of other things became more pressing.

This loss began to show only slowly, two years after the war ended when the embargo really began to impoverish people. The intelligentsia was badly hit because most were government employees on fixed incomes who suddenly found they could not even buy food. A colleague told me his heartbreaking experience of helping a friend sell his *Encyclopedia Britannica*. "We sold it for only six hundred dollars," Sadoon said. "Can you imagine how hard it was for us to get this collection to Iraq in the first place? It took a lot of work, and it was costly." Few private libraries had such a set. "Now," he went on, "I had to help this same friend sell those books. He is heartbroken."

Have you ever heard of anyone selling their books to buy food? Few of us can imagine Iraqi homes having a library at all. Now think of all the universities in Iraq: eight medical colleges and twenty-two universities; the research centers, galleries, high schools—all of them government, and all furnished with up-to-date collections of books, magazines, and newspapers. And the museums and theaters.

Yes, there are many books in Iraq. Before, universities were amply supplied with all kinds of professional journals. Arabic books, especially literature, arrived from the Arab lands. College students had English-language textbooks—most of them from the U.S. Since medicine is taught in English, libraries of medical colleges were stocked mainly with English-language journals, all imported. Doctors and other specialists subscribed to whatever professional journals they needed.

Whatever books are available in Iraq now are recycled. Friends pass around a novel; schoolbooks, used by one year's students, are passed to the next and then the next. Professors need more than textbooks and so feel more bereft. One political scientist almost wept when he told me he hadn't read a single new book in his field in eight years. There have been no additions to the university libraries during this time, either. Magazines are rare. Families with private collections keep them as long as they can, then start selling their books, one by one.

It is ironic that pop culture is not as badly threatened. It's surviving the embargo through TV and videos, which are less expensive than books. Every house has a TV so Iraqis keep abreast of general world affairs. Movies are easily imported on videos and reproduced inside Iraq for distribution. Audio cassettes, too. So Iraqis are entertained by recent American movies and hit songs. No blockade there.

It's clear the embargo bullies do not care if Iraqis are exposed to influences from outside. This is a highly selective embargo, aimed at the nation's intellectual vigor, its professions, and its hope. Combine this ban with the ban on Iraqi participation in professional conferences. Combine the literature ban with the ban on Iraqi students studying any science in a foreign university. Combine this with the ban on Iraqi scientific articles being carried in international journals.

A recent meeting between members of the UN sanctions committee and several Iraqi deans, including one from a Baghdad medical college, pointed up the naked reality of the book ban. The meeting was to review their higher education budget, since Iraq must clear all its purchases with this sanctions committee. When it came to medical journals, the answer was a flat no. "No medical journals can be bought by Iraq for its colleges." The UN officer gave no explanation to the assembled deans. Just "no."

But Iraqis already know the purpose of these bans. It is to starve a nation's young minds. It is to drive out older, trained intellectuals and professionals. It is to reduce a civilization to a nation of farmers and clerks who simply work by rote, and consume.

It won't work, of course. Ancient civilizations like this have a residual store of knowledge that is hard for us from the young new world to understand. And people who know what they have achieved in the past will not lose the will to continue their tradition.

It's an acknowledgment of this capacity that motivates me to fill my baggage with books. A book is a way of acknowledging that Iraq belongs to the future, not only the past. It's a way of saying yes, Toni Morrison has done it again, or Michael Crichton's latest novel is not as daring as his earlier one, or this is a new theory about skin grafts. It's keeping a dialogue going. It's a way of looking to the future together.

Iraqi women and men want and need to be part of an international dialogue that should and can rise above these political ups and downs. Journalist Nirmeen al-Mufti told me, "We do not want your tears. We need you to acknowledge who we are."

A CASE OF ENFORCED POVERTY

MARIE BRAUN

When I retired from The Counseling Clinic in Brooklyn Center, Minnesota, in December 1997, I never dreamed that I would soon be carrying 140 pounds of medicine into Iraq in opposition to my own government's policy. However, when I learned that 4,500 children under the age of five were dying each month from hunger and disease, and that the eight-year-old United Nations economic sanctions against Iraq were threatening famine for four million people—one-fifth of the population—I was appalled and knew that I had to do something.

Following my decision to participate in the Iraq Sanctions Challenge, I wrote a letter to two hundred friends and persons in the peace and justice community asking for donations for medicine and medical supplies. The response was overwhelming: I received over $5,500 and an outpouring of moral support. The many supportive messages I received included the following:

"We all await your report on conditions in Iraq. You go with our blessing. P.S. A letter to President Clinton is in the mail."

"Thank you for your request. I've been looking for a way to help the children of Iraq. Seventy-five dollars of this check is from my third-graders, who raised it by recycling cans."

"Thanks for giving us the opportunity to participate in this wonderful effort to alleviate some of the suffering caused by the economic sanctions."

"Go with God. A blessed pilgrimage for you and friends."

"Enclosed is seventy dollars. Father Kroll talked about your trip at St. Otto's Care Center (Little Falls) in his sermon today. After Mass, many of the elderly gave money to buy medicine for the Iraqi children; others said they would contribute when they received their Social Security checks."

"Thank you for visiting our sisters and brothers in Iraq. May you and your group learn a lot and be filled with fire."

"Thank you for doing this in the name of many of us who abhor these sanctions."

"I appreciate what each and all of you have done in this endeavor to humanize the Iraqi situation for them and for the American people."

This outpouring of support convinced me that when the average Minnesotans learn the truth about what is happening in Iraq as a result of the sanctions, they will know that our government's insistence on maintaining these sanctions is wrong.

During my stay in Iraq, I visited several hospitals and schools and observed firsthand the devastating effects of the sanctions. The hospitals are wards of misery staffed by doctors with no medicine or medical supplies and few medical tools. Iraqi doctors, who are making heroic efforts to care for their patients, are forced daily to make decisions that no doctor should have to make. The director of Al Qadissiya Hospital in Saddam City told us that, while they know it is not good medical practice, they have decided they will divide the medicines they receive equally among the children. They have determined not to decide which child will live and which die.

In the hospitals, the children are two to a bed; their mothers sit on the beds ministering to them. Family members take care of the children and others who are hospitalized because they have no nurses. The suffering of the children and the grief on the faces of the mothers is heartbreaking. It was also heartbreaking to learn that most of the dying children I saw were dying because of preventable illnesses— from malnutrition, gastroenteritis, and vitamin deficiencies.

At Saddam Pediatric Hospital, a man with a small child in his arms held him out for us to see. The child cried continually in a very high-pitched voice. The doctor told us he was three years and three months old and had rickets. He could not walk because his bones were too soft. His neck could not support his head, which was too large for his shrunken body. He had no fat on his body. He had no muscle mass and was dehydrated. In all likelihood this child will die, another innocent victim of the sanctions.

Because of the sanctions, Iraq has not been able to import vaccines, so most of the children born after the Gulf War have not been vaccinated. Diseases such as measles, whooping cough, mumps, and chicken pox, which for the most part had been eradicated, are now being seen by doctors on a regular basis. One doctor told us a measles outbreak had occurred eight months earlier. In virtually every household, at least one member had contracted measles.

At the two elementary schools we visited, the teachers informed us that 50 percent of the children were malnourished. They had no school supplies—no paper, pencils, pens, or crayons, and few or no books.

The sanctions have affected every level of Iraqi society. Much of the country's infrastructure bombed in the war has not been rebuilt. In some areas, sewage runs in the streets and electricity, where available, is erratic. Inflation has reduced the salaries of even the middle class to almost nothing. The sanctions are inhibiting the importation of spare parts, chemicals, and the means of transportation required to provide water, sanitation services, and medical supplies—as well as chlorine to purify water and fertilizers and pesticides for crops. Polluted water has been the greatest cause of disease and death. A vibrant country on the edge of the first world in 1990, Iraq now compares in many ways to Somalia and other third-world countries.

I have become convinced that sanctions are deadlier than war. They must be recognized for what they are—a form of genocide, a weapon of mass destruction, and a crime against humanity. The most pervasive blockade of any country in modern history, the sanctions have been continued by the UN Security Council at the insistence of the U.S. and in the name of the American people. They have not hurt Saddam Hussein—instead they appear to be consolidating the people behind him. What the sanctions have done is hurt the Iraqi people—mostly children, the elderly, and the poor. People in the U.S. who are constantly bombarded with depressing facts about starving children around the world do not realize that this is a case of enforced poverty and starvation.

While frequently disappointed with the actions of my government, I continue to be hopeful and to work on a grassroots level because I still believe that the power is with the people, with us. We just need the courage and the wisdom to exercise it.

TWO YOUNG ENGINEERS

Jack Vahan Bournazian

In the hotel lobby a piano accompanies a violin. The song is the theme from *Titanic*. People mob the front desk asking for a room. The song finishes and no one claps. The musicians begin again.

Faris is Christian. Mohammed is Muslim. Faris is an Assyrian rediscovering his past. Mohammed is an Arab proud of his past. Faris lost his father in 1990 at age nineteen. Mohammed lost both of his parents at age six. Faris received his violin as a gift from his father at age six. Mohammed discovered a piano at the university and learned to play. Faris says, "When my father died I lost a friend that I can never replace." Mohammed says, "When I met Faris he was quiet, alone, and trusted no one." Faris says, "Mohammed restored my faith in people." They both say, "We are best of friends, we are brothers." They are both twenty-seven. They play music and people walk by.

Faris and Mohammed met at the University of Baghdad and both graduated as engineers. Neither works in his field. Faris has a small workshop in the city and repairs electric motors. Mohammed works at the hotel and plays piano in the lobby. He gets Faris extra work as a violinist from time to time. Faris owns a car his father gave him before the war and he gives Mohammed a ride home after work. Public transportation is difficult, but for one dollar an Iraqi can buy 150 liters of gasoline. They play music and wonder if anyone is listening.

Before the war Iraq provided free public education and university students received monetary stipends from the government. Now schools lack pens, paper, books, and pencils. Before the war Iraq provided quality medical care to the public free of charge. Now kidney patients go without dialysis, cancer patients go without morphine, and children die of dysentery. In Iraq people die in vain.

Mohammed practices piano two hours a day. Faris took violin lessons from the lead symphony violinist, an Armenian. Mohammed's family disapproves of his music, believes that it is frivolous, but accepts it for the time being as a means of income. The lead violinist told Faris that he had potential as a symphony musician. Mohammed has no piano at home and must go to the university when he wants to play. Faris has no money for music lessons and no time to practice; he is too busy trying to fix his car without spare parts, maintain his family's home without construction materials, and help support his family with his meager earnings. Both love to play classical music, but neither harbors any aspirations or illusions about composing their own music or playing for anyone other than hotel guests. People sit in the lobby—waiting, walking, talking. But are they listening?

"Are you married?" they ask. "Please excuse such a private question," they say. Both want to marry. Both are waiting to marry. Neither can afford to. Faris lives at home with his mother, his brother, and his sister-in-law. There is no place for a new wife and he cannot afford his own home. Mohammed lives with his ten siblings. Faris knows that he will marry a Christian. Mohammed, more of a romantic than he is willing to realize, is in love with a university student of an ancient Jewish sect. He captivated her with his music—he was practicing the theme from *Titanic*. Faris laments that this woman's family and Mohammed's family would never accept such a match. Both long for economic independence and for a chance to practice what they learned at the university.

The song is at rest. People wait in the hotel lobby. Mohammed and Faris are waiting, too. Everyone in Iraq is waiting. "Do you both know persons who have died because of the sanctions?" I ask. "Yes," is the answer, in a voice so strong and unequivocal that I do not ask more, out of courtesy for their pain. "My brother is a doctor. He says that at the hospital he does not practice medicine but rather show biz. Without medicine all he can do is try to convince people that he is helping them when he knows in truth that he is not." Silence is the only sound.

During the Mexican-American War, Henry David Thoreau refused to pay his taxes as a sign of protest. Ralph Waldo Emerson visited him in jail and reproachingly said, "What are you doing in there?" Thoreau replied, "What are you doing out there?"

DAMAGE TO THE INFRASTRUCTURE:
FOOD AND AGRICULTURE

HOW FOOD IS DISTRIBUTED

KEN FREELAND

Delegates of the Iraq Sanctions Challenge met with Dr. Moham-med Mahdi Saleh, Iraq's Minister of Trade, who turned out to be quite an engaging speaker. He spent a great deal of time with us and answered all the questions we put to him—despite the fact that we were late in arriving. According to Dr. Saleh, Iraq's annual imports prior to the Gulf War totaled $20 billion. At that time, Iraq depended on the operation of the free market, and on some price subsidies, to assure distribution of necessary items to the populace.

Since the imposition of the sanctions regime, Iraq has instituted a rationing system which the Food and Agriculture Organization of the United Nations has determined to be so fair and equitable that it has proposed to use it as a model for other countries where food short-ages necessitate a similar approach. The system is fully computer-ized, contains many checks and balances which protect against po-tential abuse, and emphasizes the principle of equality of quantity, quality, and price of all rationed items throughout the country.

The ration itself fluctuates from month to month, based on avail-ability of various items and price fluctuations. The monthly ration is announced publicly over radio stations at the start of each month. The per-person ration for the current month was set at 9 kilograms of wheat flour, 2.5 kilos of rice, 2 kilos of sugar, 1 kilo of cooking oil, 2.7 kilos of baby milk, 150 grams of tea, 250 grams of salt, and 350 grams of detergent. The cost of all this for a family of fifteen would be 1,500 dinars per month, or about one U.S. dollar. This comes to less than a dime (U.S.) per person.

In urban areas the retail centers that get government contracts to distribute rations to local residents are within easy walking distance. The retailers are kept honest by a system in which any complaint lodged by a consumer against a particular retailer leads to a plebiscite of local consumers. If 51 percent agree with the allegation, the retailer loses his franchise and is replaced.

During the Gulf War, agricultural centers in thirteen Iraqi provinces were targeted. In all, forty-eight flour mills were bombed, for a loss of productive capacity of 5,000 tons per day of flour, and 123,000 square meters of grain storage capacity. One way the Iraqis coped was by creating a kind of ersatz flour to replace the pure wheat flour they were accustomed to. They used a combination of wheat, barley, and corn flour, and the result was termed "sanction bread."

Iraqis have had to resort to smuggling to get food and medicine into their country. Dr. Mahdi Saleh related the story of a vessel with food bound for Iraq that was waiting to be unloaded in Jordan's port of Al Aqabah. Political pressure was put on the Jordanian government not to unload it. The cargo was eventually "donated" to a third country. Also interdicted were 2,000 pounds of powdered baby milk on order from the Nestle Company via Turkey.

Iraq's foreign assets, totaling some $4 billion, have been frozen since the original imposition of sanctions prior to the Gulf War. UN Resolution 778 prohibits any use of these assets, including for the provision of food or medicine. They can only be used (and are used) to pay the costs of UNSCOM.

Dr. Saleh was asked, "Why, if the rationing system is so equitable, are people so bad off nutritionally?" He noted the absence of animal or vegetable proteins in the ration basket. The ministry hoped to be able to include half a kilogram of cheese in the next month's ration basket, he said. However, this would be very costly—about $250 million for a six-month supply.

Prior to 1988, 25 percent of all U.S. rice exports were purchased by Iraq. Iraq is currently striving for agricultural self-sufficiency. There has been some progress towards this goal, with food production increasing in some sectors up to six-fold. However, this process is inhibited by four factors associated with the sanctions: 1) salinity of soil due to lack of irrigation (we witnessed this on the ride to Basra—you could actually see the salt on the soil surface in the salt-marsh); 2) not enough usable agricultural machinery because of a lack of spare parts; 3) a lack of pesticides, herbicides, and fertilizers; 4) a lack of irrigation due to reduced electricity—Iraq is currently operating at about one-third of its pre-war level of 11,000 megawatts.

DAMAGE TO THE INFRASTRUCTURE:
FOOD AND AGRICULTURE

THE SCREWWORM FLY

JENIFER DIXON AND GEORGE PUMPHREY

In the ancient story of Exodus, Joseph warns the Pharaoh that seven years of famine are to be followed by seven years of plenty, and that provision must be made. But in Iraq, after nearly eight years of U.S.-UN imposed sanctions, the famine that has already gripped the country is likely to be followed by plague. And unlike the Biblical tale, there is no provision left. And also unlike the Biblical tale, where bad years are followed by good, Iraq seems doomed to an indefinite siege of deprivation.

The condition of the country is far worse than the impression given by the mainstream media. The Oil for Food deal, recently doubled, still provides only $4 billion a year—out of which reparations must be paid and the UN operation financed—to import food and medicine into the country. But it would require at least $6.8 billion on an emergency basis to provide adequate food and medicine for the Iraqi people.[1] What this does not provide for is the rebuilding of the infrastructure largely destroyed in the Gulf War.

The countryside has become the very picture of post-Apocalyptic ruin. Following the war, U.S. and British planes sabotaged agricultural production by dropping dozens of incendiary bombs over wheat fields in Mosul.[2] In Sakhriya Al-Gharbiya, an agricultural area outside Baghdad, weeds grow taller than wheat and wilting cucumber plants are ringed by the telltale white trademark of salt, due to the high salinity of the soil. Irrigation systems have failed. A decrepit tractor and a water pump stand idle in the noonday sun. According to the UN's Food and Agriculture Organization (FAO), harvests of vegetables and cereals have shrunk by over one-third since 1990. Add that calamity to the fact that, before the war, Iraq imported two-thirds of its food, and you begin to see that the food situation is very grim.

The lack of oil revenue has made the country turn to local agriculture. But that, too, is a victim of the sanctions. Pesticides, fertilizers, and machinery that could conceivably have some military use have not been allowed into the country in the last seven years.[3]

Since all agriculture in the south and central parts of Iraq depends on irrigation, the restriction on imports has resulted in the abandonment of half the land in Sakhriya because of high salinity. FAO officials say it would take several years to rehabilitate the soil even if the sanctions were lifted tomorrow.[4] According to an article in the *Financial Times* of London, more than half the 8,000 chicken farms in Iraq have been running at 20 percent of their former capacity.[5] Production went from eighty-five eggs per person and fourteen kilograms of meat to ten eggs and one kilogram of meat.

With this situation in mind, the UN Security Council has allowed farming supplies to be imported under the Oil for Food deal. But with such a limited allowance, the Iraqi government has decided that farmers must come second to the immediate need for imported food, so only $94 million has been allocated for the agricultural sector, which the FAO considers "grossly inadequate."

Malnutrition in Iraq today, according to Denis Halliday, the chief humanitarian coordinator in Iraq, continues to be "acute" and "chronic." Fully 32 percent of the children under the age of five are chronically malnourished.[6]

According to an FAO report in December of 1995, a million people, six hundred thousand of them children, had already died due to the imposition of economic sanctions against the country. Take a poisoned water supply, an electrical grid operating at 40 percent capacity, hospitals without medicines or lights, an agricultural sector ground to a halt, then add a plague, and what do you get? Apocalypse. Or to put it more concretely, Iraq in 1998.

The world still awaits pictures of the thousands of Iraqi children with their swollen bellies, emaciated limbs, and tortured facial expressions—pictures that mysteriously never appear on American television sets. But even those pictures would be incomplete without the addition of flies circling the eyes. In this case it is the screwworm fly. An infestation of the screwworm has hit the country in the last two years and now affects an area of thirty thousand square kilometers.[7]

The plague targets the traditional animal farming that has survived the sanctions, unlike the modern animal husbandry which has been totally destroyed by the sanctions. According to the German paper *Sueddeutsche Zeitung*, commercial poultry production has dropped to 5 percent of the pre-war level and dairy to one-third of the pre-war level.[8] Those figures must be combined with the fact that before the war Iraq had to import two-thirds of its food. The result, according to the FAO, is that an Iraqi child gets 2.5 grams per day of animal protein in comparison to a German child, who gets 60 grams per day.

It is to this already desperate situation that the plague of screwworm has been added. The country does not have the pesticides or veterinary services necessary to combat this pestilence. Having been completely isolated from the world at large, Iraq has had few offers for help. The FAO itself has contributed $400,000 in emergency aid to Iraq and the Netherlands has given another $600,000, but this is a paltry amount in comparison to the $7.3 million the FAO estimates it would cost to effectively stop the spread of the parasite.[9]

The arrival of the screwworm (*Cochliomyia hominivorax*) in Iraq is not only tragic, it is peculiar. This parasite looks very much like a housefly but is twice the size and is greenish-blue with large reddish-orange eyes. Infestations can occur in any open wound, including cuts, castration wounds, navels of newborn animals, and tick bites. The wounds produce a dark, foul-smelling discharge. The screwworm feeds only on living flesh. The larvae can infest the wounds of any warm-blooded mammal, including human beings, and eventually kill their host by eating it alive. Multiple infestations can kill a grown steer in five to seven days.[10]

What is strange about its arrival in Iraq is that the screwworm is not native to that region of the world but is instead native to the tropical and subtropical regions of North, South, and Central America, and to Africa and southern and eastern Asia. Because of its devastation of the cattle industry in the United States over forty years ago, the Department of Agriculture initiated a program that was uniquely successful in fighting the pest. In the words of the Department of Agriculture on its Internet website:

> The United States-Mexico Joint Commission was formed in 1972 between Mexico and the United States with the goal of eliminating the pest from Mexico and pushing the barrier to the Isthmus of Tehuantepec, just north of Guatemala. A new sterile screwworm plant at Tuxtla Gutierrez, Chiapas, Mexico, was dedicated in 1976. With a production capacity of more than 500

million sterile flies per week, it replaced the former production plant in Mission, Texas, which was closed in January 1981. A barrier zone of sterile flies was set up along the 2,000-mile-long U.S.-Mexican border to prevent reinfestation from Mexico.[11]

By 1986 the U.S. Department of Agriculture had the bug under control.

The technique used to control the screwworm is simple but effective. The males of the species are radiated with gamma rays, rendering them sterile. They are then dispersed by aircraft over an area infected with screwworm. These male flies breed with the female flies on the ground, who then release unfertilized eggs.[12] Of course, in breeding the screwworm half of each generation, the female half, is not necessarily sterilized. In addition, some males must be preserved in their pristine state so as to be able to produce another generation. This produces both a possible danger, that of contamination, and a possible biological weapon. It is as easy to toss unsterilized flies of both sexes out of a plane as sterilized males. And it is the United States that pioneered this technique. Australia is the other country that also uses this technique. Australia has a plant in Malaysia where it raises sterilized "Old World screwworm" in contrast to the American plant, which deals with "New World screwworm."

It is not necessary to concoct a "conspiracy theory" that stretches the imagination when you look at the peculiar facts surrounding this infestation.

The first is that the screwworm is not native to the region. Both Brian Hursey, the FAO senior officer for vector-borne diseases, and Amir Khalil, FAO Representative in Baghdad, state the screwworm has no history in Iraq. They each say that they do not know how the screwworm arrived in the country, although the official supposition is that the warm weather coupled with the crippling of Iraq's agricultural sector are factors. Hursey mentions that the importation of ruminants into Saudi Arabia, especially during Ramadan, could account for the appearance of the pest. However, it would seem that the outbreak should then initially have begun in Saudi Arabia.[13,14]

Although the explanation seems somewhat insufficient, it becomes more so when other facts emerge. The first is the screwworm's predilection to target U.S. "enemies." In 1989 Libya suffered a screwworm infestation that killed twelve thousand head of cattle. This was the "New World screwworm" and not the "Old World screwworm," which would seem more likely as that is the breed native to Africa. The other countries that suffered particularly serious infestations in the early 1990s were other U.S. enemies—Nicaragua and El Salvador—where 138 (seventy of them children) and 500 cases, respectively, of screwworm in human beings were reported.[15]

The official explanation offered for the Libyan infestation was that it could have come from imported South American beef. But that would not explain the situation in Iraq, which does not import beef because of the sanctions. And although there is some movement of herds across borders, it does seem strange that the disease could have been imported from Africa or southeast Asia in this manner. Local herds are not likely to travel such a distance. In addition, the incubation period of the screwworm would seem to prohibit infected herds traveling such long distances. As has been noted earlier, the screwworm can kill a fully grown steer in five to seven days.

Another peculiarity of the screwworm is its tendency to move only within political borders. The bordering countries of Jordan, Saudi Arabia, Syria, and Turkey have reported no infestation during the time that Iraq has been hit, since 1995. The only other reported incidences in the region are in Iran, where four hundred cases were reported (in contrast to now over fifty thousand monthly in Iraq) in the region that borders Iraq, and in Kuwait, which reported a few incidents in November 1997.[16]

It is possible to conjecture that the same sterile border that the U.S. has created for itself along the Mexican border was created along the borders of Iraq, using the dispersal of sterilized flies to protect neighboring countries. The incidence of screwworm in Iran and Kuwait could be explained as two small breaches in the "firewall." It is possible that unsterilized flies could have been dispersed within the borders of Iraq itself. This would create a reverse of the situation along the U.S.-Mexican border. Here Iraq could have been bombarded with unsterilized flies that would cause an epidemic, while simultaneously the bordering regions could be protected using the same barrier zone that protects the U.S. itself from possible contamination from south of the border.

The infestation in Iraq is of the "Old World" variety, not native to the region but to Southeast Asia. Dr. Hursey feels it may have made the trek across the continent over a period of time, or be the product of global warming. However, it is interesting to note several things. The screwworm is being bred in Malaysia by the Australian government, presumably to protect its sheep industry. Another is the enthusiasm of the Australian government for the proposed bombing of Iraq this past February. And finally to be kept in mind is the aggressive role the chief weapons inspector for the UN, Richard Butler, who is Australian, has played with his continued call for maintaining the sanctions despite the latest round of inspections. In these inspections of the controversial palaces, no weapons of mass destruction were found. Despite this, Butler insisted that Iraq has not provided the full information needed to confirm Baghdad's claims that it no longer has chemical or biological weapons or long-range missiles. In that same interview Butler said that "It's against the rules for us to believe it just because you say it. You have to give us the material and verify it."[17]

By this statement, Butler shifts the burden of proof onto the defendant when it should be on the accuser. This puts the Iraqis in the position of having to prove a negative, which is logically impossible, but it does serve the purpose of extending the sanctions indefinitely—even though the official spin may say the opposite.

Another interesting coincidence in the saga of the screwworm concerns the use of airspace. Iraq has no control over its own airspace between Baghdad and the border of Kuwait. The U.S. does and has had since the Gulf War. The control over airspace in this region is so complete that the FAO flies the crop dusters, as Iraqis are not allowed to fly over this part of their own country at all.[18]

It was in 1992 that George Bush signed what CIA personnel term a "lethal finding." This directive gave the agency carte blanche to do whatever it took to remove Saddam Hussein from power, short of two actions—actual assassination or promising U.S. intervention to insurgents in case of an uprising.[19] The lethal finding certainly did not prohibit the use of lethal flies.

In the years following this order, the CIA did mount a series of campaigns to rid Iraq of Saddam Hussein. To date they have been unsuccessful. In 1995 CIA agent Marik Warren said they included flying over Baghdad and dropping leaflets ridiculing the leader of Iraq.

This brief summary of CIA activities in Iraq does indicate that the agency was trying a number of ways to depose Saddam Hussein. They certainly had the option to use aircraft to drop anything, including unsterilized flies, over the "no-fly zone" of Iraq without detection. (The "no-fly zone" refers to areas of the country where the U.S. and Britain—not the UN—ban Iraqi flights while reserving this right for themselves.) The first incidence of the screwworm was noted in the suburbs south of Baghdad, which is in the "no-fly zone" area.

A final interesting coincidence is that of the timing of the epidemic's "explosion." This occurred in December 1997, when the incidence of screwworm infestation nearly doubled in Iraq. It dovetails nicely with events of the month. The drums of war were again being beaten by the U.S. as it stepped up its campaign against Hussein. At that time Russia offered to take over the surveillance flights over Iraq to ease diplomatic tensions, but the U.S. rejected the proposal out of hand. Again it was the U.S. that had complete control over the skies of Iraq, as the number of incidences of screwworm nearly doubled. According to the FAO in Baghdad, the incidence of screwworm infestations in Iraq went from 31,703 in November 1997 to 56,121 in December, 57,166 in January 1998, 57,305 in February, and 57,857 in March.[20]

Two facts emerge from this data. One is that there was a significant jump in the number of cases reported in the month of December. And the second is that the incidence has leveled off but remains at the December level. The first is suspicious and the second is dangerous. According to FAO agronomist Henning Steinfeld, "This literally constitutes an explosion. By comparison, in the preceding fifteen months only thirty thousand cases were counted."[21]

In the final analysis one cannot be sure if the sudden, unannounced appearance of these pests is due to natural or deliberate causes. However the screwworm got into the country, getting rid of it under the sanctions will prove daunting if not impossible. "The apprehension of the agricultural experts in Rome is now that by the time the insecticides finally get into Iraq, it could be too late. We are racing against the clock," said Steinfeld.[22] He voiced that concern in December of last year. Already the country has had lengthy delays in the importation of anything mechanical. In talking about generator parts for a chicken farm, one FAO official said, "Things were sometimes held up for six to eight months when they weren't necessarily dual-purpose."[23]

Dr. Peter Pellett, Professor of Nutrition at the University of Massachusetts, Amherst, said in an interview with Jenifer Dixon on 20 May 1998, "As we traveled around the country, especially in the north, in our conversations I was assured of the seriousness of the [screwworm] situation."[24]

Hursey made the assertion in an interview in December of 1997 that although the official numbers stood at fifty thousand a month, the likely infestation rate was more along the lines of one hundred thousand animals a month. Heat and vegetation, both of which are in abundance in the affected region of Iraq, make it possible for the insect to thrive. He voiced concern that the next possible region to be contaminated might be the lowlands of the Arabian peninsula.[25]

As of a final "e-mail interview" on 8 June 1998, I was told by Amir Khalil of the FAO in Baghdad that the infestation has now spread to thirteen out of eighteen governorates in Iraq, and that Bahrain has now been infested. The human cases reported now stand at nineteen.

While writing this article, the authors engaged in an ongoing conversation as to how to present the story. We did not want to fall under the label of "paranoid conspiracy theory," and yet the coincidences described here are compelling. Even so, with limited resources, we cannot "prove" them.

In thinking about this, we began to wonder at our need to prove anything. There is now an infestation in Iraq that threatens to destroy what is left of the protein supply in the country. Whether that infestation is the product of malfeasance on the part of the U.S. government, or whether it is another development of environmental decay that is itself the result of war and sanctions, is almost not important. The continuing decay of Iraq is directly or indirectly the result of the sanctions, which have deprived the country of the means to cope.

The only real solution is to lift the sanctions immediately. If Iraq is to be given any chance to recover from the devastation of war and sanctions, it must do so before it is too late. Suffering from war, famine, and disease as it has, Iraq should not be subjected to a scourge of infectious parasites. The brutal isolation and punishment of the Iraqi people has gone on far too long. It seems to us that, in the attempt to play God, we as a nation have lost touch with our humanity.

---

[1] Roger Normand, "Sanctions against Iraq: New weapon of mass destruction," *Covert Action Quarterly*, Spring 1998.

[2] "Iraq's arable land hit by pests, says source," *The Baghdad Observer*, 30 October 1994.

[3] "Iraq: digging for defeat," *The Economist*, 2 May 1998, U.S. edition.

[4] Ibid.

[5] *Financial Times* of London, 6 March 1998.

[6] "Iraq industry: Fall in agricultural output exacerbates malnutrition," The Economist Intelligence Unit Ltd., 13 February 1998.

[7] Ibid.

[8] Ulrike Sauer, "Die Schraubenwurmfliege bedroht die irakische," *Sueddeutsche Zeitung*, 16 January 1998.

[9] "Screwworm epidemic threatens livestock in Iraq and neighboring countries, FAO warns," FAO Press Release (98/2), 15 January 1998.

[10] USDA Animal and Plant Health Inspection Service (APHIS): "Eradicating screwworms from North America" (http://www.aphis.usda.gov/oa/screwworm.html).

[11] Ibid.

[12] Ibid.

[13] From notes taken during a telephone conversation between George Pumphrey and Brian Hursey, 27 January 1998.

[14] From an e-mail interview between Jenifer Dixon and Amir Khalil, FAO official in Baghdad, 25 March 1998.

[15] U.S. Embassy, Costa Rica, "The Screwworm Eradication Program" (http://usembassy.or.cr/screwworm.html).

[16] A map showing the infested areas can be found at "Screwworm epidemic threatens livestock in Iraq and neighboring countries," News Highlights, Food and Agriculture Organization, 15 January 1998 (http://www.fao.org/news/1998/980102-e.htm).

[17] Craig Turner, "Iraq arms dispute still at slow boil," *Los Angeles Times*, 29 April 1998.

[18] See note 3, "Iraq: digging for defeat."

[19] Jim Hoagland, "How CIA's secret war on Saddam Hussein collapsed: A retired intelligence operative surfaces with details and critique of U.S. campaign," *Washington Post*, 16 June 1997.

[20] See note 15, e-mail interview between Jenifer Dixon and Amir Khalil.

[21] See note 8, *Sueddeutsche Zeitung*.

[22] Ibid.

[23] Raula Khalef, *Financial Times*, London Edition, International Section, 6 March 1998.

[24] From a telephone interview between Jenifer Dixon and Dr. Peter Pellett, Professor of Nutrition at the University of Massachusetts, Amherst, on 20 May 1998.

[25] See http://www.fao.org/news/1998/hursey-e.htm.

A WEAPON THAT KEEPS KILLING

HILLEL COHEN

When the bombs and shells blanketed Iraq during the U.S./UN war in 1991, tens of thousands were killed and injured. But the so-called "smart" bombs and high-tech shells had another remarkable feature: they could keep on killing long after being blown to bits. The dust that settled after the bombing and shelling was radioactive. And seven years later, people all over Iraq, especially infants and new-born children, are suffering from the effects.

As a representative of the 1199 health care workers' union in the Iraq Sanctions Challenge delegation, I was particularly interested in the health impact of the sanctions. For over twenty years, I have worked in epidemiological research. Before traveling to Iraq, I had read some material on depleted uranium.[1] I was looking forward to speaking to doctors in Iraq who were studying DU and its health effects.

There had been early indications that depleted uranium could become a major health problem. Although the Pentagon has been using the stuff for years to make bombs and shell casings, this was the first time that a huge amount had been used in actual combat. The Pentagon estimates almost a million shells with DU were used.

Even in 1991 there was speculation that the burned-out tanks and debris from the shells might be dangerous. But other, more immediate disasters demanded attention. For several years after the war, the Iraqis were still trying to recover from the enormous destruction of the bombings. Buildings had to be repaired or, if too damaged, torn down. Bridges had to be rebuilt and roads, water systems, and thousands of other necessities of everyday life attended to. Many things couldn't be repaired. The economic sanctions, back then and right through to today, have blocked Iraq from importing pipes, construction equipment, chlorine for water treatment, and medical supplies, as well as virtually all scientific instruments. The doctors, engineers, and health specialists had their hands full with daily emergencies.

As the years of sanctions dragged on, the doctors began to notice that they were treating unusually large numbers of cancers—such as infant leukemia—that had been relatively rare before the war. It was more obvious since there were little or no supplies of first-line medications for these cancers. With a huge increase in all sorts of simple illnesses, like childhood diarrhea, it took some time to see the big increase in cancer cases and deaths. Also, with the general breakdown of health services caused first by the bombings and then by the sanctions, many more people were getting sick than were coming to the hospitals. Parents were not always bringing their children to the hospitals because, with few supplies, not much could be done there. So it took a while for it to become clear that many were getting sick and dying from causes other than infection.

Depleted uranium is the remains of uranium ore after processing for the manufacture of nuclear bombs or fuel for nuclear reactors. Although most of the radioactive parts of the ore are removed, the tailings are still "hot"; that is, they still produce ionizing radiation, though at low levels. In addition to being radioactive, uranium is a heavy metal which is itself toxic to humans and other life if it contaminates food or water sources.

Getting rid of millions of tons of toxic, radioactive tailings was a huge problem for the Pentagon. So its scientists came up with the idea of "recycling" the toxic waste into weapons manufacture. In addition to being a heavy metal, DU is extremely hard. On impact it can penetrate steel. It can also prevent penetration from steel shells. The Pentagon used this property to harden its shells and bombs as well as to make armored vehicles more resistant to shells. The tailings were given to the weapons industry free to produce harder and more deadly weapons, while at the same time the Pentagon got rid of its waste. A "win-win" situation for Pentagon planners.

According to the U.S. military, the radioactivity in DU is very low and therefore harmless. (This claim sounds similar to what an earlier generation of military experts said about nuclear fallout from the Nevada tests. Now, some forty years later, they admit these tests led to large numbers of cancer deaths among GIs and civilians who worked near or down-wind from the test sites.) The claim that DU is innocuous is based on military tests of the substance in its ore or pressed metallic form. But something different happens in combat.

When a bomb explodes, the DU shell is pulverized into a fine dust that can be carried by the wind. Similarly, when an armor-piercing DU shell hits a tank, it actually burns its way through the metal. The DU is transformed into microscopic particles. The mildly radioactive dust can be breathed into the lungs or ingested with food and water, and then can accumulate in body tissue. Prolonged exposure even to low-level radioactivity can cause major medical problems, especially cancers and genetic birth defects. That's why Iraqi doctors suspected that DU might be a contributor to the big increase in cancers, spontaneous abortions, and birth defects they were noticing in the hospitals.

At a meeting at the College of Engineering of Baghdad University, Dr. Souad N. Al-Azzawi shared with us some data that she and her colleagues had collected. Starting in 1995, the scientists collected soil, water, and plant samples from areas in southern Iraq where DU weapons were used most widely. They reported finding excess concentrations of thorium-234 and radium-226, two radioactive byproducts from the decay of uranium-238. The concentrations ranged from seventy to five hundred times higher than what would be normally expected. There was a greater than ten-fold increase in radiation in areas near destroyed tanks, and a twenty-fold increase inside the wrecks.

Studies of fall-out from the atmospheric nuclear tests of the 1950s showed how radioactive byproducts, like the isotope strontium-90, could be absorbed by water, plants, and animals and increase in concentration up the food chain. Iraqi scientists reported a similar process taking place with the byproducts of DU. They estimate that over 200 million tons of soil and almost one million tons of edible wild plants have been polluted with these isotopes. As much as 31 percent of animal resources were exposed. While much of the wreckage was buried underground to prevent direct exposure to children playing in the hulks, it is unknown how much DU will still leach into the water, soil, and even the air.

Examining the same areas where the engineers did environmental testing, medical researchers have tried to measure excess cases and deaths from cancer that might be attributed to elevated exposure to radioactivity or to the heavy metal itself. The studies are still underway, hampered by a lack of resources and major population shifts which have taken place due to the hardships created by the economic sanctions.

However, preliminary statistics about cancers, spontaneous abortions, and congenital anomalies have been reported, with odds ratios of 4.6, 3.2, and 2.8, respectively. This means that, assuming all other things to be equal, the cases of cancer, spontaneous abortions, and congenital anomalies were that many times more likely to have occurred in the areas most exposed to DU.

These data were assembled from retrospective case-control studies, which are generally used as the quickest and least expensive method to estimate the risk of relatively rare illnesses, like cancer. More accurate studies require extensive observation of very large population groups over many years, since these illnesses often take a lot of time to show up and many other factors may be involved.

Pentagon scientists will say that such data can only suggest but not confirm a causal relationship—which is true. For the same reasons, however, tobacco company scientists can correctly claim there is only evidence but no "proof" that cigarette smoking causes lung cancer.

It is also impossible to tell if the higher numbers observed in these studies represent the crest of the damage done, or merely the first signs of an even greater problem as the slow accumulation of radioactive particles in human tissue begins to show effects.

The clinical doctors we met at the hospitals have made their own observations. The wards are full of children with childhood leukemia, which before 1991 was extremely rare. Without access to medications that can help treat this deadly disease, the doctors try to make the children, and the mothers who attend to them in the wards, as comfortable as possible. The increase in deaths from these cases is not as dramatic as the huge numbers of children who have been dying from the infections and weakened resistance brought about by the economic sanctions. Nonetheless, the knowledge that the left-over DU might poison the environment for decades or even centuries is frightening.

In some ways, the DU story is not unlike that of land mines, which have recently become a focus of international attention. Land mines left over from a war can keep killing years after the fighting stops. The U.S. government, which is the biggest producer and user of land mines, has been reluctant to sign the international treaty that would ban them. But the State Department and the Pentagon are even more reluctant to ban DU or even acknowledge its dangers. U.S. weapons stashed all over the world use it. The Pentagon has sold DU weapons to at least 15 countries. DU has been found in towns in Bosnia where fighting has occurred. So there has been a big effort by the Pentagon's public relations department to quash the story about DU.

This is of particular concern for U.S. veterans of the Gulf War. It is possible that Gulf War Syndrome may be due in part to the effects of DU exposure. Similarities of birth defects in Iraqi children and in children of "Desert Storm" veterans are striking. Some of the symptoms reported by veterans—including fatigue, rashes, lowered resistance, and incontinence—are similar to those of low-level radiation poisoning. After denying for years that Gulf War Syndrome even existed, the Pentagon is now trying to avoid even looking at DU as part of the answer.

U.S. and UN arms inspectors have been scouring Iraq for traces of "weapons of mass destruction" and have used the inspections as an excuse to keep up the sanctions. But the weapons that have done the most damage, and that keep on killing, were the ones used by the U.S. military. And these same DU weapons are in depots all over the world while Pentagon generals decide where to use them next. The evidence so far from Iraq shows that no matter which corporations profit from the next war, there will be big losers among the civilian population at the receiving end and even among the GIs conscripted to do the shooting.

---

[1] See *Metal of Dishonor—Depleted Uranium* (New York: International Action Center, 1997).

FROM AGENT ORANGE TO DU

FREDY CHAMPAGNE

As a veteran of the Vietnam War, I have to say the trip to Iraq with the Iraq Sanctions Challenge was not pleasant, not fun, and not an adventure. The trip for me personally was horror, destruction, devastation, helplessness, depression, embarrassment, pain, and suffering. I cannot atone for the sins of my government, but that did not stop me from feeling the bitterness and overwhelming anger towards our elected leaders and their genocidal policy of exterminating third world peoples of color. I am ashamed of my government.

One of my purposes on this trip was to gather more information on the effects of the first use of depleted uranium weapons against the Iraqi people—soldiers and civilians. I am appalled at the data we are receiving.

There is a parallel to the use of Agent Orange in Vietnam. For years after the war, the Vietnam veteran was told there was no connection between exposure to Agent Orange and the health problems our veterans were experiencing. Our Vietnam vets used Agent Orange with little training and no protective gear. We were exposed and sacrificed. Those exposed were "friendly fire" casualties.

Now we find the same thing happening with depleted uranium poisoning. Our Gulf War vets were not warned or protected. In fact, those who sent them into battle knew they would be contaminated, knew that a great percentage would be permanently damaged and disabled. They were contaminated with atomic poisoning just like the atomic veterans of World War II and its aftermath.

We, the veteran community, call on our brothers and sisters to join with us in the campaign to ban the manufacture, sale, deployment, and use of all types of depleted uranium ammunitions, armor, and landmines.

We have been invited to return to Iraq in December 1998. We are inviting veterans of the Gulf War, and veterans of other wars, from any countries, to join with us in the largest delegation of veterans to visit Iraq since the Gulf War. Our purpose is to set up ongoing communications, study, and cooperation on the issues of depleted uranium, the health effects on veterans, and problems related to their exposure. As many of the Iraqi veterans were more severely wounded, and therefore have correspondingly greater health problems, we wish to learn as much as possible in Iraq.

We will also work on issues such as a post-traumatic stress disorder study of the Gulf Vets returning to the war zone and meeting with Iraqi veterans, and the consequent healing process. And we as veterans will seek ways to work together to end the sanctions in place against Iraq.

THE AMARIYAH BOMB SHELTER

SAM MARCY

According to the claims of the allied imperialists, almost all of Iraq's significant military installations, so-called biological and chemical weapons centers, and supposed nuclear capabilities were either effectively crippled or demolished in the first month of the Gulf War. Yet there was no capitulation by the Iraqi government, nor any significant signs of a break in the morale of the embattled Iraqi people. So another phase of the imperialist assault upon the Iraqi people was begun.

Up until 13 February 1991, the unprecedented massive air assaults on Iraq seemed to be directed against military targets. There was, of course, what the imperialist military refers to as "collateral damage," meaning civilian casualties. But the civilian casualties, even according to the Iraqi government, were not so massive as to convey the impression that the U.S. was specifically aiming at civilian targets.

The air assault of 13 February changed everything. It did not of course change the war's class character as a war of the leading monopoly capitalist imperialist countries against an oppressed people. But it did change the character of the war's conduct from a military standpoint. For on 13 February the U.S. unleashed an unprecedented massive assault, a pinpoint attack by two missiles launched from a stealth bomber against not a military target, but a civilian establishment—an air raid shelter, no less. The U.S. claim that the shelter was a cover for a military outpost was ridiculous on its face.

It would have been entirely in order, even customary, for the U.S. Air Force to give a warning of even a few minutes if not some hours before attacking the facility so its inhabitants could vacate the premises. This they failed to do.

They also failed to answer a reporter's key question at a military briefing: Why didn't they show the video that supposedly showed military personnel going in and out of the bomb shelter? The U.S. military refused to produce the pictures or allow an independent investigation of the incident. Within the space of twenty-four hours the Pentagon announced that its own internal investigation, conducted in secret, of course, was over and the case closed.

Thus, the character of the war had changed from attacking military targets to the fascist-like mass destruction of the civilian population. Soon the British joined in, killing 130 civilians in a market while attacking a bridge supposedly used for military purposes. The mass destruction of the civilian population has gone on steadily in the week since.[1]

What is the significance of the swift change from attacking military targets to wholesale attacks on the civilian population? It foreshadowed the beginning of a genuine genocidal war against Iraq. This was a turning point in the war. It elicited an announcement and an offer from the Iraqi government, which for the first time stated it would withdraw from Kuwait and offered to begin discussions toward that end. The 13 February attack was a deliberate, premeditated move that couldn't be explained away. So within the space of a few days, this mass murder carried out by the U.S. military against a civilian population all but disappeared from the capitalist media here.

Here it is necessary to recall another military "incident" that will shed considerable light on the meaning of the bloody 13 February attack. It took place toward the close of the Iran-Iraq war when both the belligerents were nearing exhaustion.

The U.S. had for a considerable period secretly supported the Iraqi side of the war. The U.S. aim during the early period of the Iran-Iraq war was to allow both belligerents to exhaust themselves in a conflict that could only benefit the imperialist ruling classes in the end. But by the summer of 1988, the U.S. had decided that its secret support of the Iraqi regime was inadequate for its sordid purposes. And it had to send an unmistakable message to Iran that the U.S. had shifted its support to Iraq, in order to curb and possibly destroy Iran's economic and political influence in the Gulf.

On 3 July 1988 the USS Vincennes launched a surface-to-air missile at an Iranian civilian airliner. It was on a scheduled commercial flight from Bandar-Abbas to Dubai. The attack resulted in the deaths of 290 passengers and crew members. The U.S. proclaimed the whole thing was an "error" by the crew of the Vincennes. Further investigation found no fault and resulted in no punishment. The incident was dismissed and forgotten. However, it was precisely this act of mass murder of civilians that compelled the belligerents in the Iran-Iraq war to call a halt to military hostilities. It effectively ended the war.

The 3 July 1988 mass murder was an attempt by the U.S. to demonstrate that it would go to any lengths to achieve its predatory imperialist objectives. It is a precise parallel to the 13 February 1991 mass murder of civilians in Iraq under a similarly veiled cover of a supposed attack on a military target, which showed that the Pentagon and White House were at one in the goal of subjugating the Iraqi people to U.S. imperialism.

Up until 13 February, the U.S. was unable to subjugate or vanquish the small country of Iraq, even though the war conducted by the imperialists was of a collective, coordinated character, concentrated on one small country fighting alone.

---

[1] This chapter is an edited version of an article that originally appeared in *Workers World* newspaper, 28 February 1991.

THERE WAS NO MILITARY FACILITY

SONYA OSTROM

I have been in the pediatric wards of Kings County Hospital in Brooklyn a number of times, but nothing could ever have prepared me for what I saw in Baghdad. It wasn't just the number of children at the hospital, but what they looked like. We were told they were dying from diseases we no longer suffer from, like whooping cough and measles, and amebic dysentery because of the lack of clean water. I am not a doctor and could not tell if these diagnoses were correct, but almost every child I saw lay there listless and emaciated.

Child after child I saw was skin and bones, and lay there staring up—the saddest I have ever seen. Clearly, they were not properly medicated and were severely undernourished.

I am also not an engineer, so I cannot totally assess the damages to the infrastructure caused by the lack of material, but as we traveled through the city and the environs (I went to Babylon), I did see building after building that seemed to have been started but not completed. There was no equipment to indicate they were being worked on. There were no work crews, yet the city seemed to be full of men without jobs.

Cars and trucks generally exhibited the lack of parts and paint that the sanctions have imposed. Unlike buses in Jordan, our buses in Iraq were not air conditioned. The taxis we saw and rode in were rusty. We often saw cars and trucks on the side of the road with people trying to get them working. Our own truck, full of medicine, broke down on the way to Baghdad. The whole city had a grim appearance, with rusty, dented, dilapidated cars and trucks everywhere. I have been told this was once a beautiful city, the gem of the Middle East.

I was taken to the Amariyah bomb shelter, now a memorial. During the Gulf War it was bombed, not once but twice, and almost everyone inside was killed. Americans were horrified by this, but our government claimed there was a military facility underneath it. The pictures of the women and children killed were truly sad, as was the story told by our guide, who lost nine children in the raid. One thing was certain, there could not have been a military facility there. The hole in the floor made by the missile and the debris around it would have revealed a basement if there had been one.

People everywhere were warm and friendly, especially when they learned we were from America. When they heard of our mission, they thanked us profusely. This was true at the University of Baghdad, where we paid an almost unexpected visit. Not much time to fake things, if that was their desire. The biology lab was woefully deficient—in need of basic equipment and with a nonworking air conditioner. I was even more impressed by student complaints about the lack of paper and books and how they must do all their work on paper because they have no lab equipment.

I asked the president of the school about computers, and he said they could not teach even a basic freshman computer course because UNSCOM had canceled their orders for PCs.

IMPRESSIONS OF IRAQ UNDER SANCTIONS

Children at one of Iraq's historic ruins. "The Iraqi civilization goes back thousands of years. Our mission to Iraq was not of mercy or sympathy. It was a message of gratitude to those great people for their contribution to human heritage, a message of support and solidarity, and a strong commitment to break the walls of their prison."
—Nabil Migalli

Street scene in Basra. "I remember it as a beautiful city of one million people. But by May 10, 1998, it was a completely different scene. The city's infrastructure was in shambles." —Kadouri Al-Kaysi

Water-treatment plant in Baghdad. "Clean drinking water is a cornerstone of modern life. To deny Iraq the necessary supplies to rebuild, maintain, and expand its water treatment facilities, especially chlorine, is a crime against humanity." —David Sole

Photo by Sharon Ayling

Guide at Amariyah bomb shelter points to bomb hole. "Our guide, Umm Reyda, lost nine family members when two smart bombs blasted the Amariyah bomb shelter. Exits were sealed when the bombs exploded and the temperature rose to 500 degrees centigrade. Overhead pipes burst, sending water cascading down on innocents who slept. My stomach turned as she pointed out skin and hair fragments remaining on the walls as well as the burn imprints of children's bodies." —Kathy Kelly

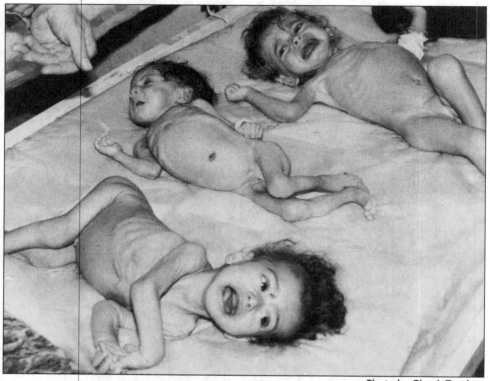

Mashgal Anur, Adraa Hussein, and Misal at Basra Pediatric Hospital. They all suffer from the malnutrition disease marasmus. "Dr. Feras Abdul Abbas told us, 'If you stay here for two days you will go to your country with a broken heart.' Many illnesses are caused by extreme malnutrition and a contaminated water supply. One mother, with tears in her eyes, showed me that her little daughter was suffering from bloody diarrhea, a treatable disease, and other complications. But due to lack of medicines this child, along with the other children in the hospital, would likely die." —Michelle Kimball

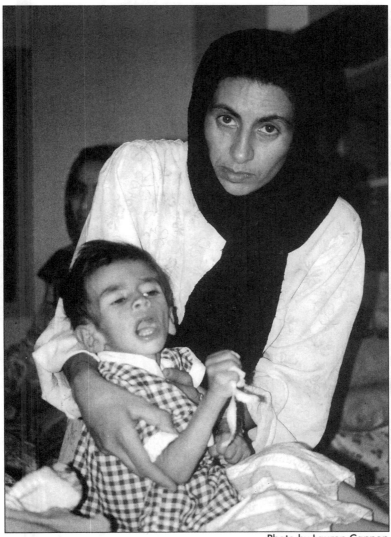

Photo by Lauren Cannon

Mustafa Hussein, two, at Al-Mansour Teaching Hospital in Baghdad. Diarrhea led to kidney failure, which brought on seizures, crippling this child for life. "Should I describe these ghosts that float through the hallways? In Al-Mansour Hospital I passed three rooms full of children under ten waiting to die." —Melysha Sargis

The emergency room at Saddam Pediatric Hospital, Baghdad. "We saw a modern hospital without adequate lighting, functioning elevators, x-ray film, anesthesia, or dialysis equipment. Nearly all the children were suffering from malnutrition, dehydration, and renal failure, and many were close to dying. According to one of the doctors, amebic dysentery is the largest killer of these children, and 80 percent of the cases could be eradicated if they had clean water." —Sharon Eolis, R.N.

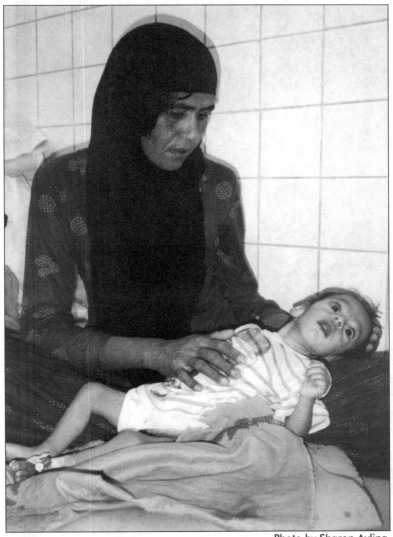

Mother with child, Saddam Pediatric Hospital. "Each parent hopes her child will get treatment before the medicine runs out." —Sharon Eolis, R.N.

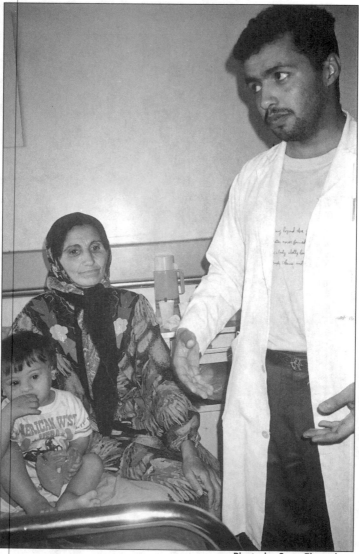

Photo by Sara Flounders

"The hospitals are wards of misery staffed by doctors with no medicine or medical supplies and few medical tools. Iraqi doctors, who are making heroic efforts to care for their patients, are forced daily to make decisions that no doctor should have to make." —Marie Braun

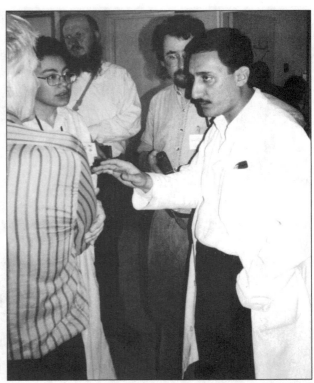

Delegates with Iraqi doctor.

The pharmacy in a Basra hospital. "I filmed the contents of the hospital's pharmacy. Most shelves were bare, except for a few containers of intravenous fluid, tubing, and some bottles of ampicillin. Before the 1991 bombing and imposition of sanctions, this prosperous country enjoyed high-quality health care with well-equipped hospitals."
—Michelle Kimball

"Iraq had one of the best educational systems in the world. Today, like the medical services, it has been nearly destroyed. We visited schools that previously had thirty students per classroom; now there are sixty students to a classroom, and school is in session for only three hours a day. The embargo includes such innocuous and basic items as pens, pencils, paper, books, and even toys. There can be no doubt that the intent of this embargo is to destroy not only the health but the minds of future generations." —Manzoor Ghori

Graduates at Baghdad University. "The professors, students, and administrative staff reflect the epitome of heroism because, as everyday people, they are persevering against the evil forces of colonialism and immoral sanctions." —Fatima Ali-Khan

Iraq Sanctions Challenge delegates at JFK airport, May 6, 1998, with four tons of medicine.

Bishop Thomas Gumbleton with boxes of medicine in transit through Amman, Jordan.

Delegates transport medicine. (Bottom) Rev. Lucius Walker, Bishop Thomas Gumbleton, Dr. Sapphire Ahmed and Manzoor Ghori at the Ministry of Health.

Photo by Lilia Velasquez

Photo by Sara Flounders

Photo by Monica Moorehead

(Right) Ramsey Clark, Bishop Thomas Gumbleton, Rev. Lucius Walker and Sara Flounders lead protest at U.S. Interests Section in Baghdad. (Below) Delegation members in front of U.S. Interests Section.

Photo by Sharon Ceci

Photo by Sara Flounders

Delegation members give press conference in Baghdad. "The delegation symbolized a wide spectrum of grassroots America. I saw Americans of all ages, ranging from seventeen into the eighties. They were a group of labor leaders, professionals, students, homemakers, senior citizens—who differed in many aspects, even in their political views. From all walks of life, they had nevertheless gathered on a common ground."
—Nabil Migalli

Iraq sanctions delegation headed back home.

To Whom It May Concern:

Despite my almost empty stomach, despite my half-dressed body, I still have the will and strength to hold the pen and write down these few words that uncover the ideal motto the (UN) raises. We say that "Petrol" is not that "worthy" to be compared and measured to my life and other children's. I should have the "milk" needed and food as well, but since the embargo is still imposed, there won't be a chance to have a life as the American child has and the British child, because I am an Iraqi child.

Taif Mahdi
First Class

LETTERS AND DRAWINGS FROM IRAQI CHILDREN

Calling from the children of Iraq to the Children of the World. We ask you to raise your voice to those who killed our childhood and prevent milk and medicine from us. We ask you again to call the United Nations to lift the siege from our country Iraq.

Taif Naji

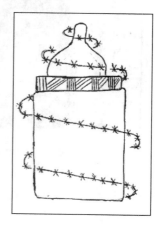

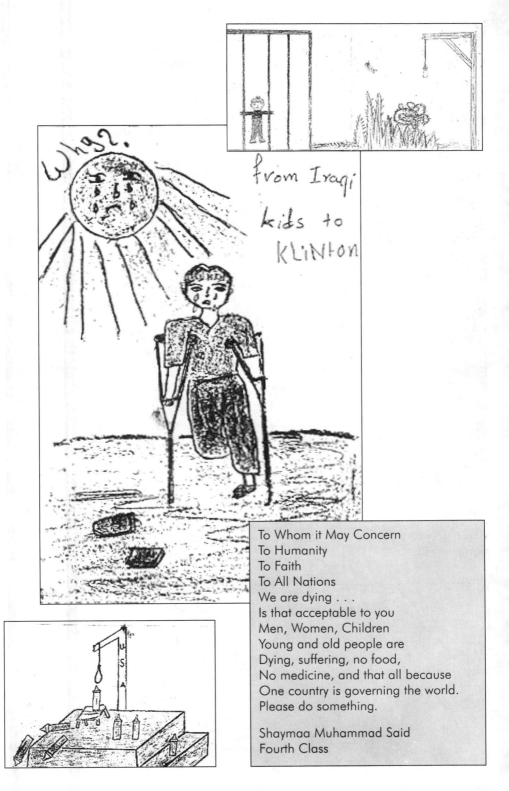

Kouthar Al-Rawi, 10, and Marwa Al-Rawi, 9, are sisters who have initiated a campaign called "Remember the Iraqi Children." Their goal is to send one million postcards to President Clinton calling for an end to the sanctions. The sisters visited Iraq and collected drawings by Iraqi children to send to Clinton. They are also collecting postcards from people in other countries.

You can send postcards to:
Kouthar and Marwa Al-Rawi
One Million Postcards to
President Clinton Campaign
P.O. Box 1141
San Pedro, CA 90733, USA

http://members.aol.com/hamzaha/
iraqichildren

MEMOIRS
OF
CHALLENGE
DELEGATES

THE ADVANCE TEAM

PRESTON WOOD

I was happy to be asked to leave for the Middle East in advance of the main Iraq Sanctions Challenge delegation, along with Kadouri Al-Kaysi from the International Action Center in New York, Kathy Kelly from Voices in the Wilderness, and David Sole, a water-treatment specialist and president of a UAW local in Detroit. The four of us flew to Amman, Jordan, on the night of 3 May 1998.

Our assignment was to arrange transportation for the overland journey from Amman to Baghdad, acquire the needed water and food for the trip, organize a press conference for the main delegation when it arrived a few days later, and arrange for the delivery and transport to Iraq of medicines purchased in the Middle East and Europe.

When we got to Jordan, a whole group of new friends worked with us over the next few days helping us get ready for the arrival of the delegates. These included many activists, journalists, and professionals from the Association of Professional Unions in Amman. For the next four days, we worked together at their offices.

Wherever we went in Jordan, we were greeted with great warmth and hospitality. The news media there and throughout the Middle East carried front-page stories about the upcoming challenge to the U.S. sanctions. People all over Amman seemed excited and anxious to help us. In restaurants, stores, everywhere we went, people waved in solidarity with our mission. Kathy, who had come through Amman before on many trips to Iraq, led us to the tiny and wonderful Al-Monzer hotel, where our hosts did everything in their power to help us.

In addition to Ahmed Shruf, Emad Maali, and many others, Khaled Ahmad Al-Sudani from the Islamic Relief Agency made sure that all the arrangements for transportation and medicine were carried out. On one beautiful day, he took us to visit the magnificent Roman ruins at Jarash, just outside Amman.

The next day, while Kadouri, Kathy, and Dave worked on arrangements in Amman, Al-Sudani took me with him to check on some water conservation projects his agency is developing north of Amman.

Here we visted several Palestinian refugee camps in the Irbid area, including the camps of Irbid, Husn, Jerash, and Souf. These camps house more than 60,000 of the over 3.2 million Palestinian refugees living in Jordan, Syria, Lebanon, the West Bank, and Gaza. Fifty years after the dispossession of the Palestinian people, they are still struggling for a free and independent Palestinian state.

Seeing these camps, where generations of Palestinians have been forced to live since being uprooted from their lands, it was clear to us that the struggle against the Iraq sanctions is not separate from the Palestinian struggle for full self-determination. The U.S. government is maintaining sanctions against the people of Iraq to force its will on the Iraqi people. At stake is control of the vast oil reserves in Iraq and elsewhere in the Middle East. The promotion of the Zionist state of Israel has been central to U.S. and European policy. The lands of the Palestinians were stolen in order to control the vast resources of the Middle East by securing a military base of operations against the popular nationalist regimes in the region.

In the camps and throughout Jordan, Palestinians told us about how their families were uprooted by the Israelis fifty years ago. It was easy to see why they have great sympathy for the people of Iraq.

We also drove to the Syrian border, where we could see the Israeli-occupied Syrian territory of the Golan Heights in the distance.

As we drove back to Amman, Al-Sudani talked about many of the projects he is involved in to help the Palestinians and others in the region who struggle to live day by day without adequate food or water. It became clear that our struggle against the sanctions was an important part of all this.

Within a few days, our entire delegation left for Iraq, armed with $4 million in medicines and, more importantly, armed with the truth. We were committed to carry out the Iraq Sanctions Challenge and defy the U.S. rulers who have caused so much suffering in Iraq and throughout the Middle East.

SEEING IS BELIEVING

Manzoor Ghori

Before my trip to Iraq, I had heard a lot about the embargo and its effect on the Iraqi people. I felt it was my duty to join this courageous effort to challenge the sanctions.

These sanctions are not only immoral, but illegal. The Geneva Convention, of which the United States is a signer, specifically prohibits both an embargo of the general population and genocide against a people, even in a state of war. Sanctions on Iraq are clearly both.

The second purpose of this delegation was to convey the message to Iraqi people that the American public does not support these inhumane sanctions. In a recent survey, over 60 percent of the Americans surveyed opposed a new bombing. Third was the goal to urge Iraq's neighbors not to honor the immoral sanctions. To that end, members of the delegation entered Iraq through Jordan, Syria, and Lebanon. There, the delegation was widely covered by the media.

Although I had read extensively about the sanctions and their devastating toll, nothing prepared me for what I witnessed during my short stay in Iraq. My first visit to a children's hospital in Baghdad— with 340 beds for over 1,200 children—left me drained and speechless with sorrow at the condition of the innocent children, who were being punished merely for being citizens of Iraq. There, in 100-degree heat, without air conditioning, lie hundreds of children surrounded by flies and their anxious parents. I witnessed sights I could have imagined only in my worst nightmares.

I met fourteen-month-old Noha Jawad, who is dying of meningitis due to the lack of medicine. She shares a room with nine-month-old Ahmed, whose tiny body is wracked with whooping cough. I saw Asim, a two-year-old child weighing what an eight-month-old baby usually does. His helpless mother waits for him to die. I shook the hand of another two-year-old, Ali Mahmoud, and kissed the sweaty foreheads of two wasted babies, Shaima and Abbas. I could only meet a few of the hundreds of malnourished children who filled this and other hospitals throughout Iraq. Their emaciated frames and bloated bellies are evidence of the rampant increase in diseases of malnutrition—kwashiorkor and marasmus—diseases unheard of prior to the embargo.

While malnutrition is one major cause of death among children, with over 4,500 under the age of five dying every month, infectious disease is a second. There are rampant epidemics of childhood diseases like whooping cough and measles. These diseases could be prevented with vaccines, which have only recently become plentiful after a period of interrupted availability. My group, Global Peace, was able to obtain $1 million worth of diarrhea medicine for only a fraction of its cost. We distributed the medicine to every hospital we visited, and gave the remainder to the Ministry of Health. There was enough of the drug, *Al-hamdu lillah*, to treat 200,000 children, but 500,000 more are in need of it.

One memory will be permanently seared into my heart and mind: a visit to the Amariyah bomb shelter in Baghdad. A place of refuge for women, elderly, and children, it was bombed during the Gulf War. Twelve hundred people perished in a horrendous and barbaric attack. The building has been made into a memorial. The first floor still boasts the gaping hole where a missile penetrated. On the cement wall, the impression of a mother nursing her baby still stands, permanently engraved into the wall when she was incinerated by the extreme temperature when the bomb hit. Images of the unfortunate refugees who had sought shelter there on that tragic day cover the cement walls. In the basement, where hundreds of others had taken refuge, water in the pipes boiled, burst out of exploding pipes, and drowned them in the boiling fluid. Their scalded skin and eyeballs are still affixed to the surrounding walls, a testament to a crime that boggles the mind. It took me hours to get myself together again after being guided through that building by one of the thirteen survivors. It was a sight from which I will never totally recover.

One of the major causes of such diseases as diarrhea, worms, and dysentery is the water. Four of the five chlorine plants were bombed during the war and the UN has not allowed them to be repaired. Because there are insufficient amounts of chlorine, combined with the fact that pumping stations, water pipes, and sewage facilities were also destroyed during the war, raw sewage now flows into the Euphrates, making for a mixture that is lethal. Without the medicines necessary to treat the diseases produced by this contaminated water, the rise in disease and mortality has been astonishing but not surprising.

One of the most heart-wrenching sights I saw in the hospital was a long line of desperate mothers standing at the pharmacy window begging for medicine that nobody in Iraq possesses. Prior to the embargo, Iraq imported $20 billion worth of food and medicine a year. In recent years, because of the sanctions and the consequent degradation of the oil industry, Iraq has only been able to spend about $2 billion a year, of which only a small percentage reaches the average Iraqi citizen. The price of a chicken is now equal to a whole month's salary. People survive on government rations—rice and what is called flour, but which is really a mixture of flour, corn, and barley.

There is a tragic rise in childhood leukemia and other diseases believed to be caused by the use of depleted uranium shells during the war. According to the U.S. Army's own statements, about fourteen thousand high-caliber shells alone were fired during the Gulf War. The British Atomic Energy Authority reports that about forty tons of this type of ammunition are scattered on the border between Iraq and Kuwait. When rain falls on these toxic remains, the DU seeps into the ground and contaminates the ground water, thus entering the food chain. DU contamination may be behind the alarming rise in congenital deformities, immune-deficiency diseases, and leukemia.

Prior to the Gulf War, Iraq had one of the best educational systems in the world. Today, like the medical services, it has been nearly destroyed. During the Gulf War and its aftermath, 40 percent of Iraq's educational institutions were badly damaged. The materials needed to repair them are unavailable due to the embargo. More than 50 percent of the schools in rural areas have been closed due to lack of teachers. We visited schools that previously had thirty students per classroom; now there are sixty students to a classroom, and school is in session for only three hours a day. The embargo includes such innocuous and basic items as pens, pencils, paper, books, and even toys. There can be no doubt that the intent of this embargo is to destroy not only the health but the minds of future generations.

Iraq, the cradle of civilization from time immemorial, has suffered a travesty of the most terrible proportions. To bomb a country to the ground—including hospitals, schools, milk factories, electrical plants, bridges, and water pumping stations—and then to place an embargo on the entire people struggling to recover from this devastating attack, is nothing less than genocide. All people of morality and conscience must join together to speak out against this terrible injustice that continues to kill, maim, and destroy an entire generation. As it says in the Holy Qur'an, "Whoever saves one life, it is as if he has saved the whole of humanity."

EAST MEETS WEST

NABIL MIGALLI

During our mission to Iraq, a reporter from a French radio station asked me whether there were Republicans among the delegates. "Possibly," I answered, "but I do not know." The question made me turn around and look at the faces of the delegates.

I saw Americans of all ages, ranging from seventeen to eighty-five. Some seemed to be physically fit and healthy, while others had obvious limitations. They were a group of labor leaders, professionals, students, homemakers, senior citizens—who differed in many aspects, even in their political views. From all walks of life, they had nevertheless gathered on a common ground. Muslims, Christians, Jews, and others carried out their commitment to respect the value of every human life. You saw a Catholic bishop next to a Bahai, a Baptist minister next to a Muslim leader, a blonde woman in an Indian sari and an African-American doctor in traditional Islamic dress. Catholic Workers displayed a banner of St. Francis saying, "Always have mercy." Others carried signs in Arabic and English condemning the sanctions. And at a distance, in a quiet corner, a delegate was practicing yoga.

Their individual differences ranged from personal beliefs to the ways they were dressed. Some were in traditional costumes, others in suits and ties, simple two-piece outfits, tee-shirts, and jeans. This diversity created a colorful and beautiful harmony. For a moment, you might think it was Central Park or Main Street in any American town or village, not the lawn of a Baghdad hotel. The delegation symbolized a wide spectrum of grassroots America.

Not enough attention has been given to the thousands of people who donated money for the medicine. School children spent weeks collecting empty soda cans for recycling to support the children of Iraq. Senior citizens, residents of nursing homes, gave portions of their badly needed Social Security checks. Not to mention sizable donations from some organizations, and Jim who drove a truck loaded with medical supplies from Georgia to New York. A grandmother in the heartland of America bought dozens of teddy bears for the deprived children of Iraq, and Nancy designed and produced hundreds of beautiful greeting cards for people to sign and send to these children.

The mission represented the commitment and hard work of thousands of unknown soldiers, and served as a vehicle of love, support, and solidarity with the people of Iraq, the victims of America's silent war.

Most of the delegates took a commercial flight from JFK airport to Amman, Jordan. Some told their fellow passengers about the mission. As a result, some $300 was raised on the plane from sympathetic passengers, mostly Jordanians. I was part of the "Syrian group," so called because we entered Iraq by way of Syria. We flew to Beirut, then took a bus to Baghdad. The trip from New York to the Iraqi capital took forty-four hours. On the way back, we returned via Jordan. In Beirut, Damascus, Amman, and every other part of Arab soil, we felt the solidarity with the people of Iraq.

In Amman airport the delegation was greeted by hundreds of members of the Association of Professional Unions. A press conference turned into a massive rally of support. On the Lebanese and Syrian borders, security officials were moved by our mission. As we were leaving, they shook hands with us warmly. A Syrian captain in his military uniform hugged me tightly with tears in his eyes.

Prior to our mission, delegates from Egypt, Jordan, Morocco, and other Arab countries had delivered medicine and medical supplies. At the Central Pediatric Hospital in Baghdad, I noticed that Egyptian medicine was used. Doctors mentioned the Egyptian team led by film director Youssef Shaheen and told me that the movie star Raghda has been a frequent visitor to the hospital and is well known by many families.

Solidarity with the Iraqi people was not limited to the Arab countries. In Baghdad we met with visiting French and Belgian delegations, and a joint statement was issued calling for the end of sanctions. A Russian medical team also arrived in Baghdad with medical supplies. At the time of our visit to Iraq, an international conference was held in Oxford, England, to discuss the devastating results of the sanctions on the Iraqi people. News was released in England at that time about the use of depleted uranium by the allies during the Gulf War. Obviously we were not alone!

More and more the world is realizing the impact of the sanctions on Iraqi children and other civilians. Visits and humanitarian missions may reduce the suffering or save lives for some time, but the devastation of Iraq is beyond comprehension and there is no solution but to end the sanctions.

We visited hospitals, water-treatment plants, food distribution centers, elementary schools, and colleges, and saw first-hand the devastating results of the sanctions. We met, touched, and spoke with Iraqis, and developed a human attachment to them. Some of these people will die if the sanctions continue. In our hearts and minds the victims are not just numbers anymore.

The bus trip from Baghdad to Amman took sixteen hours. After a week in Iraq, everyone was physically tired and emotionally drained, but with a strong feeling of a mission accomplished. It is oversimplifying to describe it as a humanitarian mission, because the most important part is the political message. The sanctions could be challenged. We broke the silence and the voice in the wilderness was heard. It was the voice of people from all corners of the world. We returned with more determination to end the sanctions.

During the trip I looked at the land, the trees, and the buildings and felt as if the twenty-three million Iraqis were captives in a huge concentration camp. They are physically isolated from the world because of the ban on travel and flying. They are victims of a war of starvation, without adequate medical treatment or even clean drinking water. In Islam, as in other cultures, water is a symbol of life. Medical professionals told us that 80 percent of the ailments now rampant in Iraq could have been prevented by proper treatment of the water.

The Iraqi civilization goes back thousands of years. Our mission to Iraq was not of mercy or sympathy. It was a message of gratitude to those great people for their contribution to human heritage, a message of support and solidarity, and a strong commitment to break the walls of their prison. At the Jordanian border, we stopped at a modest cafeteria. I had a little chat with Khaled, the manager. When he learned that we had returned from Iraq, Khaled refused to charge me or others for tea and sandwiches. It was not just traditional Arab hospitality but another sign of support for what we had done.

A BLIND PERSON GOES TO IRAQ

EDWIN R. LEWINSON

I have long felt that one of the most important accomplishments of the United Nations and its specialized agencies has been consciousness raising on a wide variety of issues. The 1996 report of the World Health Organization on the devastating effects of UN sanctions on Iraq caused me to become aware of the need for their repeal as well as the evil consequences of sanctions generally. When the opportunity to join the Iraq Sanctions Challenge arose in the spring of 1998, I felt that learning about conditions firsthand would enable me to bear witness more effectively.

I have been totally blind all my life. As I filled out the application for the Iraq Sanctions Challenge, a small twinge of fear lurked in the back of my mind. Not fear of going to Iraq, as I had made a number of overseas trips, usually alone. I had participated in a Pastors for Peace Caravan to Cuba, and, as a volunteer at the International Action Center, I personally knew the people who would pass on my application. The twinge of fear was that before I could go to Iraq, I might have to enlighten the organizers on the provisions of the Americans with Disabilities Act and on the competence of blind people.

My fears were groundless. On previous trips I had sometimes traveled with my guide dog and sometimes with my white cane. I determined, and the people from the International Action Center agreed, that this should be a cane trip. The heat of the desert would not complement my dog's long hair, and the uncertain state of the water might play havoc with his digestive system. I found friends who were willing to keep the dog, and my white cane accompanied me to Iraq. Because of the nature of the trip, I did not have to use my cane. In Iraq as well as going back and forth, delegates traveled in groups.

Sighted delegates gave me vivid descriptions of conditions. They told me of the death throes of children in hospitals, of crumbling buildings, and of vehicles rusting for lack of spare parts. Some conditions did not need to be described. I traveled with a group to Basra, and Archbishop Gabriel Kassab told of the 87 percent unemployment rate. When I first found out that we were staying in an expensive international hotel in Baghdad, I ascribed it to Iraqi attempts to curry favor. But I soon learned that staying in a first-class hotel taught as much about the effects of sanctions as other experiences. The hotel suffered from having very little business. The TV was old and barely worked. We had to ask for toilet paper. The food was well cooked, but very limited in variety. We were told that despite being in a Muslim country, the hotel used to have a bar, but had one no longer.

As I looked back on the trip, my blindness caused no special problems of which I was aware. For me as the others, the plane and bus trips were long and tiring. I was one of the delegates who experienced diarrhea.

I had hoped to meet with Iraqi blind people and learn about conditions for them. We did not stay long enough for this or for other individual desires of delegates. I hope that I will meet Iraqi blind people on my next trip, because I do plan to go on the next delegation and to keep going until the sanctions are repealed.

Sanctions will only be repealed by a groundswell of public opinion in the U.S. and in other countries. Saddam Hussein has been demonized, but his role is really irrelevant to the need for the repeal of sanctions. Sometimes news stories give the impression that Saddam Hussein is the only person living in Iraq. It is a nation of twenty-three million people, a million and a half of whom have died since the end of the Gulf War. Germany and Japan were devastated as a result of World War II, but eight years after the war ended, they were well on their way to recovery. Although the sanctions have been imposed by the UN, they almost certainly would be repealed if the government of the U.S. did not pressure other countries to keep them. As Americans, we must not blind ourselves to the effects of wrong-headed and destructive policies of our government, and we must use our power as citizens and as voters to change these policies.

HOW WAS YOUR TRIP TO IRAQ?

Lee and Phil Booth

People ask the strangest questions. They ask if we had a good trip. Or how we liked Iraq. Sometimes they're really asking if the trip was a success, but we're glad for every question since it opens the way to talk about genocide.

We tell them how sadly hurting that country is. The hospitals are full of the sick and dying, and have little or no medicine. Phil tells them about the protein deficiency diseases, the malnutrition, and all the other horrors in the hospital. He describes the crowding, the dis-abled ventilation system, and the bare pharmacy shelves. All are a result of the sanctions.

I tell them about the valiant teachers. Valiant because they are teaching pupils without pencils or paper—poor boys and girls with not enough to eat, judging from their thin bodies, wearing shabby clothes, in a pathetically bare and crowded classroom with Disney cartoon characters painted on the wall.

Like the people of every country, Iraqis want to be friends, but the U.S. government wants them for slaves. We tell people about the food rations the Iraqi government gives every Iraqi family at almost no cost. It's not enough. The poor children aren't getting enough to grow on. The result is malnutrition, stunting, and diseases never be-fore seen in that rich country. The poor are getting poorer, and the government, too.

The government now has to charge tuition for the previously free colleges and universities. Our Iraqi bus driver told us he'd been studying French when the government began charging tuition and he had to drop out. How badly he had wanted to be a French teacher. "I have to drive bus. Spring, summer, fall, winter," he said. "Over and over." His anger was in his face and in his voice, breaking when he talked about his three children. Their cheeks are thin, not round like children's should be, he said, drawing his own cheeks down with his hands. Then, hunching his shoulders, he turned away.

We've heard Arab Americans discussing the U.S. purpose there. Many of them say the U.S. government doesn't really want to kill Saddam Hussein—it wants to destroy Iraq's progress. I see they're right. The U.S. government has sentenced a whole generation of innocent children to grow up inadequately educated, without pencils and paper—much less the computers and technology of this decade.

The Iraqis know who is causing their pain. They know our risk and our stand against the sanctions. At the art academy I received an outpouring of their love. Not close enough to the mural to hear the speech well, I walked across the court to listen to the students' music. It was a combination of rock and Arab sounds. Some of the students began pointing at me, and one asked with signs if I liked their music. I signed back that I did. Later a young woman stopped in front of me and, pointing to my sanctions buttons, said, "I like you." When we were heading back to the bus, the students who had pointed surrounded me. One looked up at the roof and spoke in Arabic, and I was doused with water. Someone near me said in English that pouring water on you is an act of love. The water is brought from Babylon and considered special.

We can't get over the horrible memory of the Amariyah bomb shelter. The imprint of the hands and hair washed against the walls by the boiling water haunts us. We remember the anger we felt when we saw pictures of the burnt bodies alongside photos taken when they were still healthy, happy children. We saw the anger in the face of our guide, and didn't wonder. She had lost family there. We went away with heavy hearts.

I happened to ride down on the elevator at the al-Rashid hotel with two UN inspectors. I could see they weren't Iraqi, and when they said they were from Sweden and Denmark, I was thrilled. My grandfather immigrated from Bornholm, Denmark. Then remembering I hadn't told them my purpose in Iraq, I touched my pins and said I was a member of the American delegation that brought $4 million worth of medications. I told them we had broken the sanctions and were working to get them lifted.

One lifted his hand in a weak gesture and said their job is with the sanctions. He said they inspect what comes into Iraq. I was shocked and upset and said, "Shame on you. Why don't you get a job that helps people? You're hurting people."

They looked down at the floor and didn't respond at all, but I got the impression they felt that way, too. Now, I tell everyone if you're going to a foreign country or know someone who is, tell the people in that country to bring home their UN workers from Iraq. They're hurting the Iraqi people terribly. They should quit in protest, and help force the lifting of the sanctions.

When we applied to go on the Sanctions Challenge, we wondered whether we shouldn't instead contribute all the money to the International Action Center for medicine. But, as in the case of Cuba, gifts of medicines or food can go on for decades. It can never be enough. These countries don't deserve to have to live on charity. They must have the rights of every other country to trade. Iraq must have the right to sell its rich oil, and buy what it needs and wants. We concluded the money would be better spent taking us to Iraq to witness and challenge the genocide.

Knowing brings responsibility. We must do all we can to lift the sanctions.

VENICE OF THE EAST

KADOURI AL-KAYSI

Basra, the largest city in the south of Iraq, is situated along the west bank of the Shatt-al-Arab River fifty-five kilometers from the Persian Gulf and about 552 kilometers from Baghdad. It is bordered on one side by the desert, so you may hear the jingling of camel bells mingled with the horns of ships passing nearby. This is al-Qurna where the Tigris joins the Euphrates. It is the legendary spot of the Garden of Eden.

Basra had a prominent place in the history of Iraq and Islam. It was built by the Arabs in 636 A.D. on a site a few miles from the present city. It soon became an important commercial town as well as a great center of Islamic and Arabic culture.

Basra is sometimes called the Venice of the East because it is laced with canals. Sinbad, the sailor of *Arabian Nights* fame, is associated with Basra, whence he started each of his fabulous seven journeys.

On 10 May 1998 a group of American citizens, including Bishop Thomas Gumbleton of Detroit, Kathy Kelly, Walter Black, and I, visited hospitals in Basra, including the Basra City Center Hospital. We toured two hospitals and found no medicines in the emergency rooms. It is like this every day. The emergency room is full of children but the hospital beds are empty. The reason is that the mothers realize the doctors have nothing with which to help their children, so the children are taken home to die.

So many pieces of equipment in the hospitals are broken. They need spare parts but the U.S. and UN refuse to allow Iraq to import them. Dr. Abdel-Amir Al-Thamiri thanked us for the medicines we gave to the Basra City Center Hospital. However, he told us that this ton of medical supplies would be used up within twenty-four hours. He needs a steady supply of medicine, but most of all he needs medical textbooks and current medical journals. However, he said, all their problems would be solved if the embargo were lifted.

I am an Iraqi-American who left Basra in 1960. I remember it as a beautiful city of one million people. It was very well maintained with greenery everywhere. The people were happy. Even during the eight years of war with Iran, the city did not lose its beauty. But by 10 May 1998 it was a completely different scene. The city's infrastructure was in shambles. Roads, bridges, buildings (including hospitals and schools), and electricity and water services were destroyed.

For the first time in Basra's long history, there are homeless people. Even fully employed people struggle for their daily existence. A couple, both employed as teachers, receive a wage equal to three dollars per month each. Even with additional government food rations, there is nothing left after the first half of the month. They subsist on tea and bread for two weeks.

Whenever I speak to my friends or relatives, they always ask me when the sanctions will be lifted. I always answer them: "I hope soon." Most of them say they have nothing against the American people, but they are against the U.S. policy towards Iraq. They know that their children are dying and that all the people of Iraq are suffering because of the U.S. insistence on keeping the sanctions in place.

LET THE CHILDREN LIVE

MICHELLE KIMBALL

On 10 May 1998 a small group of U.S. delegates headed to Basra, located in the south of Iraq near the border of Iran and Kuwait, and the site of heavy bombing in 1991. I met and talked with more mothers and their children that day than on any other day during our trip. Our encounters were filled with a great outpouring of love, but also with deep grief. It was Mother's Day. We arrived in Basra in the early afternoon after passing through the biblical sites of Ur, where Abraham is said to have been born, and the shrine of Ezra near the town of Amara. Our group of fifteen agreed to forego lunch and eat only crackers to have time to visit the pediatric hospitals.

One kind doctor, Feras Abdul Abbas of the Basra Pediatric Hospital, was beaming when he greeted us. "I thank you for your visit. I am very happy. I smile from my heart and feel the world is with me. I am happy to see you. You make me strong." And he added, "If you stay here for two days you will go to your country with a broken heart." We told him that we already had broken hearts.

I sat with adoring and sometimes numbed mothers holding beautiful babies who were doomed to die for no reason of their own making. Many illnesses are caused by extreme malnutrition and a contaminated water supply. One mother, with tears in her eyes, showed me that her little daughter was suffering from bloody diarrhea, a treatable disease, and other complications. But due to lack of medicines this child, along with the other children in the hospital, would likely die. Two of her other children had already recently died, and this was her only daughter. She pleaded with us to please save this precious child.

I filmed the contents of the hospital's pharmacy. Most shelves were bare, except for a few containers of intravenous fluid, tubing, and some bottles of ampicillin. Before the 1991 bombing and imposition of sanctions, this prosperous country enjoyed high-quality health care with well-equipped hospitals. It had a low infant mortality rate.

Dr. Abbas told us of a recent case in which a woman had experienced infertility for ten years, and then was blessed with a baby. But her baby died for lack of something as basic and inexpensive as IV fluid. The miserable conditions the doctor and patients must endure make these doctors heroes in the eyes of many. Dr. Abbas remarked about the patients: "They look to our eyes for hope. But we have no hope." Five thousand children die a month.

The lack of coverage in the United States of this humanitarian crisis, coupled with widespread misinformation, has effectively reduced the credibility of those opposing these sanctions. In the meantime thousands of loving people die. Many efforts by the international community, including those of three Security Council members—France, the Russian Federation, and China—have promoted the lifting of these sanctions.

When I asked Gabriel Kassab, the Archbishop of Basra, if he had a message for the American people, he referred to an earlier message he had sent to the Catholic bishops and cardinals in the U.S. (many of whom have since voiced their opposition to President Clinton).

During Christmas 1997 he wrote, "We appeal to people of conscience to work to end the blockade of Iraq. Let it be known that Resolution 986 (Oil for Food) has served to divert world attention from the tragedy while aggravating it. We appeal to all Catholics and to all Christians [and people of conscience] in America and the world. The sanctions are killing our people, our children, the ones [God] has given us to protect. They are killing our beloved Muslim brothers and sisters. They strike at our poor and our sick most of all. In the name of God's people, we ask you: Tell your government to end the sanctions against the Iraqi people. End the seven years of war against Iraq."

He then said to me, "You, you go and say what you have seen here. You have seen the suffering caused by the sanctions, the effects of no food, no medicine, no water, no electricity. Sometimes they don't believe us. They think we are speaking this way because it is our country, but we are speaking in the name of all humanity. "

Vatican envoy Cardinal Roger Etchegaray has asked for "an end to the sanctions which contradict God's laws calling for clemency, pardon and respect for humanity." He is working on arranging a visit by the Pope to Iraq in the hopes of drawing international attention to the plight of Iraqis.

Voices in the United States can be raised in unison with the voices of millions in the international community who call for an end to the genocidal sanctions. For the love of all humanity we, too, can walk in the spirit of Gandhi's message: "All of us are one. When we inflict suffering on others, we are bringing suffering on ourselves. When we weaken others, we are weakening ourselves, and weakening the whole [of life]."

HOW DO YOU DESTROY A PEOPLE?

MELYSHA SARGIS

If you were to destroy an entire people, where would you begin? A friend reminded me of this question posed to us several years ago in the film *The Land and a People*, analyzing the destruction of Palestine. If we are to grasp the enormity of the travesty in Iraq, it is mandatory to ask this. So where would *you* begin to destroy a people?

Would you begin with the economy? Perhaps you would discover a method of mass destruction that could stun the economy so brutally that paralysis would remain for years. Let's suppose we implement this for several years, maybe seven or eight. And we place limitations on basic necessities such as antibiotics, penicillin, light bulbs, pencils and pens, and books. This creates havoc in the primary social institutions of a civilization.

Historically, one of the first methods of colonial attack is within the educational systems and higher learning. Whether we live in South Africa or Chicago, illiterate children and adults can be manipulated and controlled. Education, formal or informal, results in knowledge that can challenge and overcome oppression.

Hospitals are the vitality of our existence. Technology within these institutions determines the average life span of a people. If these resources and information are attacked, we can easily revert to a much lower life expectancy. Without medicines such as antibiotics, ammonium nitrate, and fluid nutrients, diseases such as typhoid and yellow fever would reemerge, along with many women dying in childbirth.

If we were to destroy a people, should we begin with women, who are blessed with the ability to reproduce humanity? Or our elders, who contain histories of a past and stories of our futures? Or our children, who are the future and offer hope and insight even in the midst of despair? We need not reflect any further than the Vietnam War on these forms of devastation. There are countless tales of women being raped to death and children tortured to death by soldiers. But technology does not simply influence our health, it also enhances our military abilities.

Shall I assist you by offering methods? We could first create mass starvation throughout a region. Women are affected, so that at feeding time their breasts are empty and lifeless. The country lacks resources for baby formula and bottles; therefore, we witness their infants' deaths.

Shall I inform you of three-year-old Amira in Saddam Children's Hospital? She was regurgitating blood due to an infection created by polluted water systems. Twenty minutes later, I held her sobbing mother as the child died before my eyes. I could state the case of thirteen-year-old Mohammed, who had a waist of forty-five inches during Ramadan in January. Now it was down to twelve inches. The doctor matter-of-factly stated he would be dead in a matter of weeks.

Should I describe these ghosts that float through the hallways? In Al-Mansour Hospital I passed three rooms full of children under ten waiting to die. Six children with infectious diseases, who in the U.S. would be placed in isolation, were together in one room. The doctor remarked that all would be dead over the next few months due to cross-infections.

Can you listen to the rates of leukemia? In the U.S. we boast a 95-percent cure rate. Iraq once had a 76-percent chance of survival; now Iraqi doctors estimate 25 percent will live. Can you envision three to five babies daily being removed in body bags from one hospital alone? Can you gaze at the ghosts in the hospital and truly comprehend the reality that over three-quarters of them will be dead upon your return in the fall?

This might be the method. We can combine it with other approaches that assault immediately.

I know of a shelter built with steel so thick it was thought impossible to rupture. Doors that weigh forty tons. A protective system devised for women and children during times of war. Could we ensure its destruction by dropping two pinpoint bombs? First, we must delineate an effective goal. We acquire the blueprints of the structure from the Finnish manufacturing company. Locate the air ducts and the water tanks. Our boys are extremely talented and could certainly position a bomb to destroy both features. This takes care of three surefire methods of extinction: the impact of the bomb, suffocation due to air loss, and the liquefying of the human beings from water temperatures exceeding 2000 degrees Fahrenheit.

Shall we discuss the shadows of these ghosts permanently engraved on the walls? Women holding children, children embracing one another, children standing alone. Only thirteen survived.

Do we destroy the people or do we destroy their minds? Is it worse to die or to survive? How many of your own children can you witness dying before it becomes overwhelming? How many nights can you endure hunger without your mind collapsing? How long can you drink polluted water and eat infected food? Could you tolerate the humiliation of being an educated person who is compensated less than three dollars a month to sustain an entire family? What would your response be to your children when they weep from starvation?

Bismillah Ir-Rahman, Ir-Rahmin: "We are born from one soul into male and female and into various nations and tribes so that we may come to know one another and not destroy each other. Verily, the most honored in the face of Allah is the one most righteous among you." "Allah created us from the same red clay earth but into various nations and tribes."

Why is this repeated constantly throughout the Qur'an? Everything is intentional. And just as we are mandated to understand *salaat,* we are expected to grasp that we were created as one but separated differently.

Why? Why weren't we all created Muslim to perform the righteousness of our Creator? Why did Allah give us free will? Why does Allah permit so much evil and destruction?

These are the questions secularists constantly bombard me with as the foundation of their rejection of *iman* or faith. These are the same questions practicing Muslims also endure. But the answers to these questions are entirely different. I offer the world of Iraq, where we witness Islam as the sustaining force of the community. It provides hope of rescue, it is an integral part of society, and offers love and compassion in the midst of annihilation. It is the neighbor I spoke to who passes up bread to offer it to the children next door. It is the family I saw seeking food who share it with many others rather than saving it for themselves. It is the mothers who witnessed my sobbing as I stared at their children in hospital beds, who rubbed my back and held me as I wept, telling me, "May Allah bless you."

Our Creator has posed us the challenge of a lifetime. In Iraq are the cries of Palestine, Algeria, Mexico, Vietnam, Cuba, Guatemala, China, Japan, India, Pakistan, Afghanistan, El Salvador, Nicaragua, Haiti, Ireland, Somalia, Ethiopia, South Africa, and America. These tests are everywhere. Do we create a continuum of pain and struggle? Do we determine which is worse: Africans forced as slaves to America, stripped of their religion, dignity, hope, and lives—or the countless Africans killed, isolated, and tortured in the apartheid-ridden South Africa?

Allah did not create evil, we did. We constructed the bomb, nuclear weapons, sanctions, occupations, land mines, and we are destroying the rain forest. The suffering inflicted on us is not God on human but human on human. This is the purpose of free will. Evil is permitted to flourish, as is good. We were blessed with intellect, emotions, hearts, spirits, sense, and a conscience. We make our own choices. But as Muslims, deciphering right from wrong is insufficient. We most respond actively and aggressively to injustice to assure the equality of all people.

A doctor in Iraq stated, "Our children are entitled to laugh and play, eat and sleep, read and learn, be safe and kept, just like American children." Yet the children of Iraq lead a strikingly different life. Will we permit this? Or will humanity overcome and rise above it all? We must prove to our Creator, to ourselves, and to each and every human being in Iraq that we are prepared to conquer this bitter situation. We are willing to listen and learn and offer everything within our power to eliminate the sanctions in Iraq and permit the children of Iraq the right to life.

The only question that remains is: Are we ready for the challenge?

FOR THESE THINGS I WEEP

CHRISTOPHER ALLEN-DOUÇOT

In May I joined fifteen other Catholic Workers, Bishop Thomas Gumbleton of Detroit, former U.S. Attorney General Ramsey Clark, and many others on a trip to Iraq. Dubbed the Iraq Sanctions Challenge, eighty-four of us traveled to deliver $4 million worth of medicine to various hospitals to alleviate suffering and to challenge the legality and morality of the embargo.

Our action was a direct violation of U.S. law; however, it was in direct obedience to God's law requiring us to "feed the hungry and comfort the ill." From a legal perspective, the sanctions violate the Nuremberg Principles, the First Protocol Additional to the Geneva Convention (1977), the International Conference on Nutrition—World Declaration on Nutrition of the UN FAO/WHO (1992), UN Resolution 44/215 (1989), the Constitution of the World Health Organization (1946), the Universal Declaration of Human Rights (1948), the Charter of Economic Rights and Duties of States adopted by the UN in 1974, and Title 18-2331 of the U.S. legal code regarding International Terrorism.

These laws and treaties prohibit the targeting of civilians and/or the use of starvation as a method of political coercion. The sanctions are directly responsible for nine thousand civilian deaths every month. Half of the victims are under five years old.

Before the Gulf War the health and welfare of most Iraqis was secure. Nearly the entire population had access to clean water, sewage was treated, and electricity was available to everyone. According to UNICEF, before the war malnutrition was statistically nonexistent in Iraq.

The situation in Iraq today is a nightmare. During the Gulf War we dropped 88,500 tons of unguided bombs on Iraq. We hit 688 schools, ninety-five hospitals or clinics and seven of eight hydroelectric dams. Our bombs destroyed 80 percent of Iraq's farm production. All eleven major electrical stations and 119 substations were bombed, cutting off electricity in every city and village in Iraq. Incubators went cold, food and medicine spoiled.

Before the embargo, on average, 600 children under five died each month due to respiratory infections, diarrhea, gastroenteritis, and/or malnutrition. In March of 1998, 4,947 died from these causes. In 1990 there were 102,487 cases of malnutrition (kwashiorkor, marasmus, and other caloric and/or vitamin deficiencies). In 1997 there were 2,132,729 cases.

The current ration received by Iraqis is grossly inadequate.[1] Vitamins A and C are barely present, and people are receiving less than 40 percent of the Recommended Daily Allowance of calcium, zinc, riboflavin, and vitamin B6. Prior to the war Iraq imported two-thirds of its food annually at a cost of about $2 billion. Because of the sanctions all of Iraq's assets in foreign accounts are frozen, so Iraq is unable to use those funds to purchase food and medicine. *"All her people groan as they search for bread." (Lam. 1:11)*

Through the Oil for Food (Resolution 986) deal, Iraq is allowed to sell $2 billion of oil every six months. About half of the money in the deal goes to the UN and Kuwait. The remaining money is spent on food, medicine, spare parts for water works and sewage plants, and medical equipment. However, some of the items that Iraq tries to purchase are vetoed by the U.S.

For example, the U.S. has prevented shipment of powdered milk. Moreover, the FAO reports that Iraq needs at least $2.7 billion just to import sufficient food. Denis Halliday, UN humanitarian coordinator for Iraq, stated on 12 January 1998 that Iraq needs $30 billion a year to meet its current requirements for food, medicine, and infrastructure.

Meanwhile, Dr. Habib Rejeb, WHO head in Iraq, stated on 18 May 1998 that medicines bought through Resolution 986 are received "one hundred percent of the time, yes, definitely," by hospitals and clinics, not the "black market." Because of the devastated infrastructure, particularly regarding water, the people are starving to death and dying from preventable disease.

The acreage of available farmland is rapidly decreasing because of increased salinity in the soil due to a lack of water for irrigation. During our bus trip from Baghdad to Basra, we all saw the white salt that covered the land. Crop yields are also decreasing because of a lack of fertilizers, pesticides, herbicides, and spare parts needed to repair farm machinery. We saw hundreds of vehicles stripped bare for their parts.

Before the war and sanctions, Iraq produced and imported an annual average of 5,626,000 tons of grains. In 1997/98 they had 5,356,000 tons (43,000 pledged, not yet received). Red meat supplies have decreased from 245,000 tons to 45,000 tons; poultry 245,000 tons to 33,000 tons; fish 67,000 tons to 5,000 tons; eggs 1,228 million to 150 million; milk 401,000 tons to nearly nothing.

Criminally compounding the severe and chronic (eight years and counting) shortage of food and nutrients is the increased incidence of water-borne diseases. An FAO report in October 1997 explained:

> Water availability in its widest sense involving drinking water, irrigation, salinity, and sewage disposal is absolutely fundamental to the future of agricultural productivity and health of the population. A recent UNICEF survey on the availability of water and sewage systems reported that more than half of the rural population did not have adequate access to potable water, while for sewage disposal some 30 percent of the total population were without adequate services with much of the waste being discharged directly into rivers and streams. In addition, much of the supplied water was contaminated or below acceptable standards. Such lack of water and sanitation has a direct link with the prevalence of infantile malnutrition.[2]

Because of the sanctions, Iraq is unable to purchase enough chlorine to adequately treat drinking water and sewage, or the parts necessary to repair the pumps at water and sewage-treatment plants. With insufficient pressure the sewage often backs up onto city streets, into homes, and into water lines, which also are insufficiently pressurized. The convergence of malnutrition and disease has led to the current annihilation of the people, especially the children, of Iraq.

Walking the wards of several hospitals in Baghdad and Basra, I was among hundreds of children lying in pain and waiting to die. Their mothers, usually in tears, sat on their bedsides shooing the flies out of the mouths, eyes, and noses of their emaciated babes.

I met Hasan, a six-year-old girl who weighed only thirty-seven pounds and suffered from dysentery because of the dirty water. In Basra I met Jafra. Her mother had her in a cute pink dress. Jafra was five months old and dehydrated due to chronic vomiting. She weighed 6.6 pounds. I met Hasa, a fourteen-month-old who suffered from dysentery and weighed a mere twelve pounds. I met Hawraat, who had entered the hospital a week before with a fever, rash, and bloody diarrhea. At admission he weighed twenty-six pounds; when I saw him he weighed 17.6 pounds.

Most of the children with dysentery end up with bloody diarrhea, which leads to anemia and then renal failure; without treatment, this leads to death. The children need dialysis, but the machines are broken and no spare parts are forthcoming. The children need blood and platelet transfusions, but often the hospital lacks the simple collection bags or the appropriate needles to draw blood.

We met many children with leukemia. The incidence of leukemia has quadrupled since the end of the war. Many suspect this increase is related to the widespread use of depleted uranium weapons by the U.S. during the Gulf War—350 tons of depleted uranium were left behind. We met an eight-year-old with acute lymphoblastic leukemia. The child's eyes and joints were swollen from bleeding; he was sobbing in pain. The doctor told us he had no medicine to treat the disease or alleviate his pain and that the child would die in a few days.

I met Husan, an 11-year-old boy with leukemia. Because of his low white-blood-cell count he is susceptible to infection. Because of the sanctions the hospital lacks proper needles and antiseptic swabs. Husan had a raw, open wound on the back of his hand from an infection he got from an intravenous treatment. The infection was eating away at his hand and the hospital did not have antibiotics to treat it.

I met a seven-year-old girl with leukemia who weighed twenty-four pounds. I met premature babies born with leukemia. The preemie unit had two attendants for thirty babies; the standard is a one-to-one ratio.

In Basra we met Feras Abdul Abbas, M.D. The mounting pile of lifeless little bodies has visibly distressed Dr. Abdul Abbas. The hospital he works in was dimly lit. The fans and air conditioners did not work. Electricity frequently goes out. Wiring is exposed and paint is flaking. The air is heavy with the emanations and discordant timbres of the dying. The pharmacies and medical libraries are mostly barren and void of the latest drugs and literature. Much of the machinery is broken and most of the beds lack sheets.

Often unable to treat the diseases, the doctors are further frustrated by a lack of pain medicines. Their weekly pay wouldn't buy them a Coke at the hotel where we stayed. Dr. Abdul Abbas greeted us: "I smile from my heart when I see you. You make me strong.

You will be sad when you leave here. If you were to stay here for two days it would break your heart." We kept asking the doctor about the prognosis for each child we met. After continually repeating the refrain, "He will die soon," the doctor blurted out: "They are all going to die." Asked what he tells the mothers, he said, "I can't tell the mother, 'Your baby will die,' I can't tell them there is no hope. They look for hope in our eyes but we have no hope." Later he said he thought the "U.S. government wants the next generation of Iraqi children to be weak and retarded." *"My eyes are spent weeping; my soul is in tumult; my heart is poured out in grief because of the destruction of the daughter of my people, because infants and babes faint in the streets of the city." (Lam. 2:11)*

Leaving one hospital, we walked past a woman wrapped in black from head to toe. She knelt on the street corner in front of the hospital, rocking back and forth as her tortured wail rose above the din of the city and pierced my heart. After we boarded our bus, she approached the side, opened her garments and revealed to us the fount of her anguish: nestled against her breast was the withered body of her child, who had just died. *"They cry to their mothers, 'Where is bread ...' as their life is poured out on their mothers' bosom." (Lam. 2:12) "For these things I weep; my eyes flow with tears; for a comforter is far from me ... my children are desolate for the enemy has prevailed." (Lam. 1:16)*

I had to stop going into the crowded patient rooms because I couldn't gain my composure. I went to be alone, thought of my children, and wept for their brothers and sisters. I cannot tolerate the image of Micah and Ammon writhing in pain, their ribs exposed, hair thin, bones brittle, and flies crawling up their noses when our government builds nuclear weapons and sends troops into other countries—the very justifications they gave for the bombing and embargo against the people of Iraq.

The ghastly images I experienced have seared themselves into my consciousness. I have had several nightmares involving the children I met and my own children suffering with them. Like never before I feel an almost unbearable burden of responsibility to stop this crime.

If a madman were to enter a nursery school in my home town and open fire on the children, we would all be shocked and outraged by the massacre of innocents. My friends, we have massacred nearly one million Iraqi children. How dare we consider ourselves Christians or people of good will if we remain silent?

For heaven's sake, the specter of death is frantically taking our children; many of us are inexcusably oblivious, others are sadistically supportive. Have we become a nation of cold-hearted sociopaths unmoved by the image of hundreds of thousands of children imploding from starvation and crumbling from diarrhea? *"Happier were the victims of the sword than the victims of hunger, who pined away, stricken by want of the fruits of the field." (Lam. 4:9)*

I have to believe there is no widespread dissent regarding the sanctions because most Americans are not aware of what is happening. The mainstream media have largely neglected their duty to report the truth. Much of what I have written here cannot be found in the *New York Times* or the *Boston Globe*. The *Hartford Courant* did not cover the Iraq Sanctions Challenge even though four Connecticut residents were participants. It won't even print my letters to the editor. *"Those who dwelt of old in your holy land you do hate for their detestable practices ... their merciless slaughter of children, ... these parents who murder helpless lives ... but even these you did spare, since they were but human ... by judging them little by little you gave them a chance to repent." (Wisdom of Solomon 12:3-10, apocrypha)*

If we are sane, caring people of good will we must repent and take definitive action to protect the children. I beg your assistance in exposing this genocide.[3] Please arrange for me to make my slide presentation to any group that will listen. Write to me for a picture of one of the children I met; hang it on your refrigerator as a reminder to pray and act. Please contact your elected officials and tell them to lift the sanctions. Write letters to the editor. Join us in our weekly vigil at the Hartford Federal Building. Hang a sign on your house and hold a sign in your town. Fast and pray. Talk to your friends. Send medicine to Iraq.

In May I returned from a holocaust. The children I met have surely since perished.

---

[1] Special Report of the UN Food and Agriculture Organization, 3 October 1997.

[2] Ibid.

[3] To communicate with any of the Iraq Sanctions Challenge delegates, contact the International Action Center in New York; see Appendix 1.

IRAQ PAST, PRESENT, FUTURE

SAAD KHADIM

My trip to Iraq wasn't exactly a vacation. I have a great deal of feelings for the seriousness of the tragedy the Iraqi people are suffering because of the most immoral collective punishment: sanctions.

I come from Iraq. Before the sanctions it was an oasis with a booming economy, rich culture, and great diversity. Baghdad on its own harbored more than three million workers—Arabs and other ethnic and racial groups. Growing up in Iraq was a wonderful time; education to the highest level and health care were available and free for everybody. Housing was affordable, living conditions were comfortable, and society was crime-free.

Being in Iraq in 1998 was a depressing experience. In the first five minutes I was confronted with five children no older than six years, one carrying a one-year-old infant who hardly breathed. They begged me and kissed my hand to give them anything to buy milk for the baby because he was dying and their mother was home sick.

Driving through Baghdad's streets, you can definitely see the effects of the sanctions on the daily life of the Iraqi people: the poverty and homelessness is very noticeable, begging and selling of furniture takes place all over, the schools are over-crowded and school buildings are deteriorating, three or four children share one school desk, three babies with three kinds of infections share the same hospital bed.

This is not the prosperous Iraq where I grew up. Iraqis are a very proud people. With the little they have they are trying to rebuild after the devastating damage caused by U.S. "smart" bombs and missiles. They have been under siege since 1990. The most notable change is the devastation to the social structure and the breakdown of the ethical and moral values for which the Iraqis were well-known.

This most uncivilized, silent war should be stopped immediately to give the Iraqi people the chance to rebuild their country, reestablish their position in the Middle East and be able to trade freely with the rest of the world. Once the sanctions are lifted, in a matter of months the Iraqi people, as productive and hard-working as they are, will begin to rebuild their future so that it will be as great as their past, if not better. Iraq by no means was or will be dependent on foreign aid. The country has all kinds of resources and good will to flourish.

GO, YOU WILL SEE THE TRUTH

JOHANNA BERRIGAN

The "Ramah" spoken of by the prophet Jeremiah can easily be replaced with "Iraq" in this era of continued UN/U.S.-enforced sanctions. As part of the Iraq Sanctions Challenge of 6-13 May, I was one of the delegates who chose to deliberately break the sanctions and deliver medicine and medical supplies to this devastated country.

"Go to the hospitals, you will see the truth," admonished the gift shop attendant at the al-Rashid Hotel in Baghdad. I not only saw but heard the truth—the cries and moans of pain were the background noise to every conversation and lingered on my tape recorder as I later transcribed the words of medical personnel.

At Saddam Pediatric Hospital, a bustling establishment akin to the busiest U.S. city hospitals, Dr. Ghian Al-Habehni, the director, explained that, of the nearly one thousand patients seen daily, "every other patient is a malnourished child." The staff has experienced a "tenfold increase in nutritional problems," he explained, since sanctions were imposed in August of 1990. Typhoid, cholera, and spontaneous abortions are on the rise. Children die of measles and diarrhea. To visit any ward is to meet death—in the faces of the children, who often lie two or three to a bed, and in the faces of parents, especially the mothers who sit on the beds, hour after hour, day after day, shooing flies away from their dying children.

This was a formerly high-tech hospital. Today, surgery, if performed at all, is frequently done without anesthetic. Medical journals have been denied by the sanctions, as have parts to repair machines. There is one working MRI machine in a country about the size of California. Air-conditioning is nonexistent.

One of the attending Iraqi doctors just laughed at questions from a physician on our delegation about the availability of multivitamins for children and whether leukemia patients could get bone-marrow transplants. The problems are much more elementary, he explained.

The water is so polluted he cannot be assured of not carrying bacteria after washing his hands, and could be spreading germs just by touching the children. The cost of canned milk is so expensive that mothers too ill to nurse attempt to "stretch" it by adding water, which can be full of bacteria.

I had seen the pictures of emaciated children taken by others on visits before me, but still I was not prepared for the first little girl we encountered. She looked as no human should ever have to look. I made eye contact with her mother, requesting to take a photo, but still I felt like an intruder.

Those in the delegation who had visited Iraq before noted an anger in the doctors not previously encountered. Due to the shortage of intravenous solutions, doctors perform a triage process in deciding which patients can receive what is available. In addition to shortages of ampicillin, penicillin, and such basics as aspirin, there is a shortage of medical personnel. Any non-Iraqi nurses and physicians employed before the sanctions have left the country. Delegates who visited Basra reported that hospitals there lacked even sheets.

Our delegation brought nearly four tons of medicine and supplies worth $4 million in wholesale value, yet we knew even this was a mere drop in the bucket compared to the endless needs. When the International Action Center approached U.S. pharmaceutical companies for donations, only one responded positively, then reneged on a promised shipment after being informed by the U.S. Treasury Department that it would be fined $175,000 per medication donated to Iraq.

While the children at Al-Monsour School appeared healthier than those in the hospitals, I was aware that toys, pencils, and books are banned by the sanctions. Disinfectant is also banned, explained the principal, apologizing for the condition of the school.

While some evidence of Gulf War bombing remains in Baghdad, there are newly constructed bridges and roads. Yet the Iraqi dinar, the currency, which bought three U.S. dollars before the war, is currently worth $.00058 or less. One needs a plastic bag to hold the 1,170 dinars now purchased with one U.S. dollar. Rusted cars abound. Of those that run, all had windows rolled down in the 105-plus-degrees desert heat. I saw people in parks and on street corners attempting to sell household belongings. I did not see buyers. Street corners were also staffed by children selling cigarettes and soft drinks.

Dr. Barbara Aziz, an anthropologist and member of the delegation who has traveled back and forth to Iraq for ten years, told me that the middle class has all but disappeared. She explained that there is an emerging "nouveau riche," comprised of those who have made money on the illegal market and of rich farmers who manage to maintain machinery through "black market" connections.

I was part of a group that met with Dr. Souad Al-Azzawi, an environmental engineer at Baghdad University. She presented us with an abstract of a newly completed study on "Environmental Damages Resulting from the Usage of Depleted Uranium Bullets Against Iraq." During the Gulf War U.S. troops and allies used a new generation of radioactive weapons for the first time. Their use was especially concentrated in areas in southern Iraq. According to the U.S. Army Environmental Policy Institute, over 940,000 30-millimeter uranium-tipped bullets and more than 14,000 high-caliber DU rounds were consumed during Operation Desert Storm/Desert Shield.

Dr. Azzawi's voice changed dramatically when she stopped reading the abstract and referred to the "Highway of Death" in southern Iraq. For miles there are burned skeletons of twisted metal—all that remains of vehicles, including cars and trucks full of refugees, that were hit by DU shells. A large number of leukemia cases has developed in the area. Depleted uranium burns into a fine ash that can be mixed with soil, water, and plant life or be airborne and taken into the lungs. She referred to the process as "killing people quietly" and suggested that some people might find the lingering radioactive death sentence "acceptable," because there was no spontaneous damage as with a nuclear bomb. Depleted uranium is roughly 60 percent as radioactive as naturally occurring uranium and has a half-life of 4.5 billion years. As an alternative to being stored in low-level waste repositories, it is given *free of charge* to arms manufacturers.

We met with Umm Reyda, a woman who lost nine family members when two smart bombs blasted the Amariyah bomb shelter. Exits were sealed when the bomb exploded and the temperature rose to 500 degrees centigrade. Overhead pipes burst, sending water cascading down on innocents who slept. My stomach turned as she pointed out skin and hair fragments remaining on the walls as well as the burn imprints of children's bodies.

Why did I travel halfway around the world to immerse myself in holocaust conditions? Why subject myself to a possible twelve years in prison, a $1 million fine, and a $250,000 administrative fine that could be imposed without a trial proceeding? Why spend thirteen hours on a plane followed by nineteen hours on a bus just to get to Baghdad? Why bother?

The command of the Gospel is quite clear to me. I am required "to love my neighbor as myself." I love by feeding the hungry, comforting the ill, and giving drink to the thirsty. The sanctions are not an expression of neighborly love. Indeed, they are an act of war imposed against a civilian population. I have never experienced such shame as being an American in Iraq. If we are to love God, then we must love all of God's created people, including those our government has declared "enemy." If I remain silent, accept the genocide, I will be judged by God.

On the application for the delegation, I wrote, "I am motivated by a spirituality of nonviolence, one that abhors the violence of war and suffering. I believe that faith requires action in addition to prayer. ... The only way to deal with encountering pervasive feelings of hopelessness is to suffer with, to enter into the suffering of the Iraqi people and feel their agony and not to pretend that I am somehow other or better because I enjoy a great deal of economic security as a white woman religious who lives in the United States. The invitation to agony is never easy, yet I have found that it leads me to necessary conversion step by step."

On 12 May, the morning I left Baghdad, the Gospel reading was from John 14:27-31. In it, Jesus says, "Peace I leave with you; my peace I give to you. I do not give to you as the world gives." I reflected that I was leaving peace with the brothers and sisters I had met in Iraq, also knowing that God's intended peace for them was frequently not the same as the world's notion of peace. I have been called to follow the nonviolent example of Jesus and compelled to place my faith not in gods of metal, but in the God of mercy, justice, and peace.

BANNING CHILD SACRIFICE: A DIFFICULT CHOICE?

KATHY KELLY

From several trips I have made to Iraq, it is obvious where one should go to find overwhelming evidence of a weapon of mass destruction. Inspectors have only to enter the wards of any hospital to see that the sanctions themselves are a lethal weapon, destroying the lives of Iraq's most vulnerable people. In children's wards, tiny victims writhe in pain on blood-stained mats, bereft of anesthetics and antibiotics. Thousands of children, poisoned by contaminated water, die from dysentery, cholera, and diarrhea. Others succumb to respiratory infections that become fatal full-body infections. Five thousand children under age five perish each month. Almost a million children who are severely malnourished will bear lifelong consequences of stunted growth, brain deficiencies, disabilities. At the hands of UN/U.S. policy makers, childhood in Iraq has, for thousands, become a living hell.

Repeatedly, the U.S. media describe Iraq's plight as "hardship." Video footage and still photographs show professors selling their valuable books. Teenage students hawking jewelry in the market are interviewed about why they aren't in school. These are sad stories, but they distract us from the major crisis in Iraq today, the story still shrouded in secrecy. This is the story of extreme cruelty, a story of medicines being withheld from dying children. It is a story of child abuse, of child sacrifice, and it merits daily coverage.

When I traveled to Iraq in February 1998, a Reuters TV crew accompanied our delegation to Al-Mansour children's hospital. On the general ward the day before, I had met a mother crouching over an infant named Zayna. The child was so emaciated by nutritional marasmus that, at seven months of age, her frail body seemed comparable to that of a seven-month premature fetus. We felt awkward about returning with a TV crew, but the camera person, a kindly man, was clearly moved by all that he'd seen in the previous wards. He made eye contact with the mother. No words were spoken, yet she gestured me to sit on a chair next to the bed, then wrapped Zayna in a worn, damp, and stained covering. Gently, she raised the dying child and put her in my arms. Was the mother trying to say, as she nodded to me, that if the world could witness what had been done to tiny Zayna, she might not die in vain? Inwardly crumpling, I turned to the camera, stammering, "This child, denied food and denied medicine, is the embargo's victim."

I felt ashamed of my own health and well-being, ashamed to be so comfortably adjusted to the privileged life of a culture that, however unwittingly, practices child sacrifice. Many of us westerners can live well, continue "having it all," if we agree to avert our gaze, to look the other way, to politely not notice that in order to maintain our over-consumptive lifestyle, our political leaders tolerate child sacrifice.

"It's a difficult choice to make," said Madeleine Albright when asked about the fact that more children had died in Iraq than in Hiroshima and Nagasaki combined, "but," she continued, "we think the price is worth it." Iraqi oil must be kept off the markets, at all costs, even if sanctions cost the lives of hundreds of thousands of children.

Camera crews accompanied us to hospitals in Baghdad, Basra, and Fallujah. They filmed the horrid conditions inside grim wards. They filmed a cardiac surgeon near tears telling how it feels to decide which of three patients will get the one available ampule of heart medicine. "Yesterday," said Dr. Faisal, a cardiac surgeon at the Fallujah General Hospital, "I shouted at my nurse. I said, 'I told you to give that ampule to this patient. The other two will have to die.' " A camera crew followed us into the general ward of a children's hospital when a mother began to sob convulsively because her baby had just suffered a cardiac arrest. Dr. Qusay, the chief of staff, rushed to resuscitate the child, then whispered to the mother that they had no oxygen, that the baby was gasping her dying breaths. All the mothers, cradling their desperately ill infants, began to weep. The ward was a death row for infants.

Associated Press, Reuters and other news companies' footage from hospital visits was broadcast in the Netherlands, in Britain, in Spain, and in France. But people in the U.S. never glimpsed those hospital wards.

I asked a cameraman from a major U.S. news network why he came to the entrance of a hospital to film us, but opted not to enter the hospital. "Please," I begged, "we didn't ask you to film us as talking heads. The story is inside the hospital." He shrugged. "Both sides use the children suffering," he explained, "and we've already done hospitals." I might have added that they'd already "done" F-16s lifting off runways, they'd "done" white UN vehicles driving off to inspect possible weapon sites, they'd "done" innumerable commercials for U.S. weapon displays.

While political games are played, the children are dying and we have seen them die. If people across the U.S. could see what we've seen, if they witnessed, daily, the crisis of child sacrifice and child slaughter, we believe hearts would be touched. Sanctions would not withstand the light of day.

Upon return to the U.S., customs agents turned my passport over to the State Department, perhaps as evidence that according to U.S. law I've committed a criminal act by traveling to Iraq. I know that our efforts to be voices in the wilderness aren't criminal. We're governed by compassion, not by laws that pitilessly murder innocent children. What's more, Iraqi children might benefit if we could bring their story into a courtroom, before a jury of our peers.

We may be tempted to feel pessimistic, but Iraq's children can ill afford our despair. During the Gulf War, I wasn't in the U.S. I was with the Gulf Peace Team, camped on the border between Saudi Arabia and Iraq and later evacuated to Baghdad. I didn't witness firsthand the war fever and war hysteria. But people told me, when I returned to the U.S., that the war had often seemed like a sporting event. Some people went to bars, raised mugs of beer and cheered when "smart bombs" exploded on their targets. "Rock Iraq! Slam Saddam! Say hello to Allah!" they shouted.

When I hear those accounts I think of Umm Reyda, a mother who lost nine of her family members when, on 13 February 1991, two astonishingly smart bombs blasted the Amariyah community center. Families in the Amariyah neighborhood had gathered to commemorate the end of Ramadan. They had invited many refugees to join them and had made extra room in the overnight basement shelter so that all could huddle together for a relatively safe night's sleep.

The smart bombs penetrated the "Achilles heel" of the building, the spot where ventilation shafts had been installed. The first bomb exploded and forced seventeen bodies out of the building. The second bomb followed immediately after the first, and when it exploded the exits were sealed off. The temperature inside rose to 500 degrees centigrade and the pipes overhead burst with boiling water, which cascaded down on the innocents who slept. Hundreds of people were melted. Umm Reyda greets each of our delegations, just as she greeted me when I first met her in March 1991. "We know that you are not your government," she says, "and that your people would never choose to do this to us." I've always felt relief that she never saw television coverage of U.S. people in bars, cheering her children's death.

On 18 February 1998, a vastly different cry was shouted by college students in Columbus, Ohio. They didn't cheer the bombers, and they may well have prevented their deadly missions. "One, two, three, four, we don't want your racist war," the chant that confronted Madeleine Albright, crackled across Baghdad. People on the streets smiled at me, an obvious Westerner, and counted, "One, two, three, four ..."

A week later, UN Secretary-General Kofi Annan, at the conclusion of his remarks introducing a peaceful resolution to the weapon inspection crisis, urged young people around the world to recognize that we are all part of one another, to see the world not from the narrow perspective of their own locale but rather from a clear awareness of our fundamental interdependence. What a contrast between his vision of a new generation that wants to share this planet's resources and serve one another's best interests, globally, and the vision that Secretary of State Albright offers: "If we have to use force, it is because we are America. We are the indispensable nation. We stand tall. We see further into the future." Ms. Albright's reference to "use of force" is the stuff of nightmares, given the ominous comments some U.S. military officials have made about preparedness to use even nuclear force.

I doubt that other nations will accept that the U.S. "stands tall." It's more likely that international consensus will conclude that the U.S. lacks the moral standing to be prosecutor, judge, and jury in the dispute over Iraq's policies. Most people in the Arab world believe that the U.S. favors Israel and is unwilling to criticize its actions, even when it violates international agreements or United Nations resolutions. People throughout the world point to the hypocrisy of the government of the U.S. in other aspects of international relations. The U.S. is over $1 billion in arrears in payments to the United Nations; it has ignored judgments by the World Court and overwhelming votes in the UN General Assembly whenever they conflict with its desires; and despite its rhetoric about human rights, the U.S. record of support for ruthless regimes is shameful.

Is it outlandish to think that courage, wisdom, and love could inform the way in which we arrive at foreign and domestic policies? Is it overly optimistic to think that we could choose to ban the production and sale of weapons of mass destruction? Is it too much to ask that economic sanctions against Iraq be lifted and never again used as a form of child sacrifice?

INDELIBLE IMAGES OF IRAQ

DENNIS APEL

Incidents which remain embedded in my memory and heart include a woman sitting in an overcrowded emergency room with her dying infant child, tears streaming down her face as she looked up and said, "You come here and take pictures and go back home, but nothing changes." I felt helpless. On the bus leaving Saddam Pediatric Teaching Hospital, by the wall of the exit gate, two women sat on the asphalt crying. One woman stood up, approached our bus, and unfolded her black garment to reveal an infant in her arms. Her child was dead.

In the hospital in Mosul I stood next to the bed of a seventeen-year-old student with aplastic anemia and no treatment available. The doctors had told him they would try to keep him as comfortable as possible until he died. I took his hand in mine as tears came to my eyes. He looked at me peacefully, no tears. I feel responsible to do what I can to end the sanctions and these people's sufferings.

JOHANN CHRISTOPH ARNOLD

Brothers and sisters, I have traveled to many countries but nothing prepared me for the poverty of Iraq. There everyone, everywhere, let us know they were hungry. Even the liveried workers for Baghdad's leading hotel asked us for food, and turned down a tip in U.S. money. It was useless to them. They signaled us by pushing away our hand and pointing to their mouth and stomach.

We visited a soup kitchen in Iraq. As the kitchen closed down for the day, we joined the exiting crowd. Around the corner we came upon what looked like a street riot. Looking closer, we saw the riot's strange focus: one spot in the gutter. An old lady had been carrying her precious bowl of rice home from the soup kitchen, had stumbled and dropped the bowl. As the jostling people thinned out, we could see the last few grains of rice being picked out of the filthy water and slime in the gutter. The people ate the grains immediately. The point is that the people have nothing, absolutely nothing. But, brothers and sisters, they have one thing and that should not be taken from them, not by us, not by anyone: they have their patriotism. Respect this patriotism. Allow them their patriotism. It is all they have. I thank God that I had the chance to go to Iraq. I am ready to go anytime again.

WALTER BLACK

The significance of this trip for me was being able to personally deliver much-needed medical supplies and gifts to some of the suffering people of this planet who need it the most. Seeing the genuine joy on the faces of the people was my most important experience and I truly hope we can do it again.

To see hope come alive on the faces of people who are victims of sinful, wicked life-destroying sanctions—I would not trade that for anything on earth. We must do all we can to offset this dastardly war being waged against the poor people on this planet. The insane and life-destroying drive to rake in larger and larger margins of profit and wealth is making life on this planet virtually unbearable for those of us who desire only to live plain and simple lives.

When I was in Iraq I entertained very vivid ideas of somehow finding a way to return to the United States with every citizen of Iraq who is ill or suffering as a result of sanctions and place them in U.S. hospitals to be properly treated for the rest of their lives at the expense of the U.S. government.

PATRICK CARKIN

Two children, a boy and a girl, sat in the hotel lobby with their father, who wanted us to take them back to the U.S. for treatment. Both kids had double sickle-cell anemia. The girl wore what appeared to be her finest dress. I gave them both a box of crayons. The girl could only shrug. She was hot to the touch, too thin, and obviously very sick. She is just one of the thousands of children who are being harmed by the sanctions. I will always remember her father's desperation, how sick that little girl was, and knowing that it was preventable. The U.S. is killing those kids and we have to stop it.

EDITH ECKART

In the crowded wards we visited, babies on beds without sheets, their mothers fanning the flies off their faces, were dying of dysentery, pneumonia, renal failure, leukemia. A doctor from our delegation, conversing with an Iraqi doctor, learned that potable water, antibiotics, immunizations, sterile syringes, and IVs were unavailable. Our doctor asked, "How many of these babies will die?" The Iraqi doctor threw up his hands and answered, "All of them."

MARY ELLEN McDONAGH, BVM

I was particularly struck by the women of Iraq. One woman I met at Saddam Pediatric Hospital wore a beautiful beaded dress and smiled as she fanned her dying child. She was the only one who smiled. Most gave off an aura of strength through sad faces. I was appalled to hear Dr. Souad Al-Azzawi speak of the long-term effects of depleted uranium bullets.

MARIA MOHAMMED

It was my first trip to Iraq. I was impressed by the beauty and hospitality of people. In the stores that were in the hotel, they would offer me tea. But sanctions made me remember Poland under German occupation: hospitals without medicine, children without milk, schools without paper and pencils. It was very hard to see the Amariyah bomb shelter, where so many children lost their lives. It felt as if the whole country had been placed in a concentration camp.

P. J. PARK

At the Saddam Pediatric Hospital, the number one hospital for children in the country, I asked one beautiful mother, Sajeedal Ahmal, how the sanctions have affected her. She was in the casualty ward holding her three-year-old son Adi, who had measles. "We are dying out. Everything is very, very hard to get. Without Tylenol, we cannot bring Adi's fever down." To the American people, she said, "Enough is enough. Get your government out of this place."

REV. LUCIUS WALKER

It was truly empowering to challenge the most senseless and monstrously evil U.S. policy toward Iraq. I saw genocide in the mutilated bodies and anguished faces of Iraqi babies who were at the threshold of death because of U.S. sanctions.

APPENDIX 1: ORGANIZATIONS OPPOSING SANCTIONS

International Action Center

The Iraq Sanctions Challenge was initiated by the International Action Center, founded in 1992 by former U.S. Attorney General Ramsey Clark. He and other anti-war leaders and organizers had rallied hundreds of thousands in street protests before and during the U.S. war against Iraq.

Although it is best known as an anti-war, anti-imperialist activist organization inside the U.S., the IAC is motivated by a broad vision of radical social change as an alternative to the current society's class domination by the military-industrial complex. With U.S.-based transnational banks and Big Oil at its core, the U.S. ruling establishment has proven itself to be endemically warlike abroad and racist and anti-worker at home.

Unwilling to accept the current status quo, the IAC believes that power can really belong to the people, but only by challenging the political supremacy currently exercised over society by a small elite representing the richest sectors in Corporate America.

The rest of the world is currently suffering from U.S. domination. Military invasions and endless threats of military action, economic sanctions and blockades, and IMF-imposed economic austerity programs are just some of the methods used by the U.S. to maintain this modern world empire. History has shown that all those who seek empire, and use the bloodiest methods to maintain it, are eventually consigned to defeat and ruin. Human society has evolved and developed on the scrap heaps of defeated empires that had grown rich off slavery and other forms of bondage.

The IAC's view is permeated with optimism because it believes that the "power of the people" can eventually overcome injustice and the war-drive that flows from the current economic and social system. But the people must become politically conscious, mobilized, and militant to see the fruits of this now latent power.

Advancing political consciousness requires telling the truth to overcome the propaganda of the U.S. "war" establishment. This is a great deal of the work of the IAC, especially with regard to Iraq, which has been so effectively "demonized" by the propaganda machine.

The IAC was the first U.S. organization to expose the U.S. bombing of innocent Iraqi civilians and the massive destruction of the Iraqi infrastructure. This evidence was compiled and published in the book *War Crimes*.

The IAC coordinated an International War Crimes Tribunal that held hearings in twenty countries and thirty U.S. cities probing the Pentagon's systematic destruction of Iraq. Evidence presented at this War Crimes Tribunal, which implicated the United States in gross violations of international law, was published in Ramsey Clark's ground-breaking book *The Fire This Time*.

For the last eight years the IAC has been a leader of the movement to unconditionally end U.S./UN sanctions against Iraq. It has coordinated international meetings and teach-ins, held demonstrations, published news releases and fact sheets, and, in collaboration with the Peoples Video Network, produced several educational video documentaries on sanctions.

In addition to *The Children are Dying*, first printed in 1996 and now in a second edition, the IAC also published the groundbreaking book on depleted uranium use in Iraq, *Metal of Dishonor: Depleted Uranium—How the Pentagon Radiates Soldiers and Civilians with DU Weapons*. Each of these books has come out of cooperative research, networking, and educational work in the activist tradition of the IAC.

In early 1998, the IAC launched Medicine for Iraq, a campaign to set up a pipeline for medical supplies and medicines to offset in a small way the desperate conditions created by the sanctions on the beleaguered Iraqi people, especially the children unfortunate enough to be born at this time in Iraq's history. The tragedy of these small lives, the innocents, the future of a people, is the direct result of that cruelest of weapons—economic sanctions. The Medicine for Iraq campaign has as its second purpose educating the people in the U.S. on this point.

The IAC has also mobilized opposition to the thirty-seven-year U.S. blockade of Cuba, and organized shipments of medical aid to the socialist island, including $2 million worth of vitally needed insulin in 1994.

The IAC continues to actively oppose U.S. military involvement throughout the globe. In 1998, the IAC published an important contribution to the discussion of the changing role of NATO in Europe, *NATO in the Balkans*.

One of the main purposes of the IAC is to expose the intricate web of lies the Pentagon weaves before, during, and after each military intervention. The IAC shows that U.S. intervention is dictated by big business's drive for profits, and that even as military funding continues to grow, schools, hospitals, and social programs are slashed in the U.S.

The IAC is a volunteer activist organization. In its campaigns opposing U.S. intervention, it relies totally on the donations and assistance of supporters around the country. To be part of a growing network, or to make a donation, request a speaker, or volunteer your support, contact the IAC.

National Office: 39 West 14 St., Suite 206, New York, NY 10011; phone: (212) 633-6646; fax: (212) 633-2889; ; website: www.iacenter.org; e-mail: iacenter@iacenter.org.

West Coast: 2489 Mission St., Room 28, San Francisco, CA 94110, phone: (415) 821-6545; fax: (415) 821-5782 e-mail: afreeman@igc.apc.org

Organizations opposed to sanctions

The following list covers a number of groups that have organized some form of opposition to sanctions against Iraq, especially those based in countries that were part of the alliance that waged war on Iraq in early 1991. The list is by no means complete, but consists of those groups that have been in direct contact with the International Action Center. The activities carried out by the organizations described here cover a wide variety of approaches to opposing sanctions: providing humanitarian assistance, organizing political opposition, publishing books and other educational material, and taking direct action. They illustrate both the growing opposition to sanctions and the variety of tactics to fight them.

Al-Bushra (Arab American Roman
  Catholic Community)
website: www.al-bushra.org

American Arab Anti-Discrimination
  Committee, Task Force for Iraq
4201 Conn. Ave. NW, #300
Washington, DC 20008
phone: 202 244 2990
fax: 202 244 3196
e-mail: adc@adc.org

American Friends Service
  Committee, Mideast Committee
1501 Cherry St.
Philadelphia, PA 19102
phone: 215 241 7000
fax: 215 241 7275
e-mail: afscinfo@afsc.org
website: www.afsc.org

American Muslim Council Midwest,
  Shifa International
Ahmed El-Sherif
P.O. Box 6092
Leawood, Kansas 66206
phone: 913 541 0404
fax: 913 541 8808
e-mail: shifa@juno.com

American Muslims for Global Peace
  and Justice
800 San Antonio Road
Palo Alto, CA 94303

phone: (650) 856 2912
fax: 650 856 0444
e-mail: global-peace@global-
  peace.org
website: www.global-peace.org

Arab Lawyers Network
Sabah Al Mukhtar, LL.B.
phone: 011 44 181 670 3698
fax: 011 44 181 670 7337
e-mail: sabah@arablaw.demon.co.uk

Arab Women's Solidarity Assn.
Nawal el-Saadawi, Director
19 Maahad Nasser St., Bldg. 61
El Sahel, Cairo, Egypt
Fax: 202 203 5001

Association EquiLibre
23, Allée du Mens
BP 1613-69606 Villeurbanne Cedex
Lyon, France
phone: 33 33 79 78 4 (33)
fax: 02 50 79 78 4 (33)
e-mail: embargo@equilibre.org
website: www.equilibre.org/
  embargo

Bridge to Baghdad/un ponte per ...
Campaign of Solidarity with the
  Civilian Victims of the Gulf War
via della Guglia 69/A-00196
Rome, Italy
phone: 06 678 0808

fax: 06 679 3968
e-mail: abridge@mbox.vol.it

Bruderhof, Spring Valley
P.O. Box 260, Route 381 N
Farmington, PA 15437
phone: 412 329 1100
website: www.bruderhof.org

Campaign Against Sanctions on Iraq
Sebastian Wills, Clare College
Cambridge CB2 1TL, Britain
e-mail: saw27@cam.ac.uk

Campaign Against Sanctions and
    War on Iraq
Hugh Stephens, coordinator
BM 2966, London WCIN 3XX,
    Britain
phone: 011 44 171 436 4636
fax: 011 44 171 436 4638
e-mail: justice@easynet.co.uk
(continuing the work of the International
Commission of Inquiry on Economic
Sanctions)

Campaign to End Sanctions Against
    the People of Iraq
c/o End the Arms Race
825 Granville St., #405
Vancouver, B.C. V6Z-1K9 Canada
phone: 604 687 3223
fax: 604 687 3277
e-mail: info@peacewire.org
website: www.peacewire.org

Campaign for the Iraqi People, Bos-
    ton
Wells Wilkenson, Mobilization for
    Survival
11 Church St.
Cambridge, MA 02138
phone: 617 354 0008
e-mail: salaamg@aol.com

Catholic Worker New York
Jane Sammon
55 E. 3rd St.
New York, NY 10003
phone: 212 777 9617

Coalition for Social Justice
c/o Sadu Nanjundiah
Central Connecticut State University
Physics Department
New Britain, CT 06050
phone: 860 832 2942
fax: 860 832 2946
e-mail: sadanand@ccsu.edu

Conscience International, Inc.
Dr. Jim Jennings, President
4685 Chamblee-Dunwoody Rd, A-7
Atlanta, GA 30338
phone: 770 454 9109
fax: 770 936 0996
(health care professionals and medical
doctors opposing continuation of sanctions against Iraqi people)

Desert Storm Think Tank
Patricia Axelrod
2601 N Street #3
Sacramento, CA 95816
phone: 916 441 4397
(ad hoc committee of soldiers and scientists analyzing impact of Gulf War)

The Edge Gallery, Hugh Livingstone
2 The Circle, Queen Elizabeth St.
London, SE1 2LP, UK
phone/fax: (+44) 171 403 4198
e-mail: edge@easynet.co.uk
(a working documentary project about
depleted uranium)

Felicity Arbuthnot
23 Nisbet House
Homerton High Street
London, England E9 6AJ
phone/fax: (+44) 0181 985 0058

Fellowship of Reconciliation
P.O. Box 271
Nyack, NY 10960
phone: 914 358 4601
fax: 914 358 4924
e-mail: Doug Hostetter or Clayton
    Ramey dhostetter@igc.org
website: www.nonviolence.org/for

German Anti-Imperialist Forum
An Der Nesselburg 91
53179 Bonn, Germany

Gesellschaft Kultur des Friedens
Am Lustnauer Tor 4, 72074 Tuebin-
gen, Germany
phone: 07071 52200
fax: 07071 24905
e-mail: culture_ofpeace@GAIA.de

Houston Coalition to End the War
Against Iraq
c/o Lee Loe, chair of Fellowship of
Reconciliation
1844 Kipling
Houston, TX 77098
phone: 713 524 2682
(publish the newspaper *Iraqi Notebook*)

India Anti-Imperialist Forum
77/2/1 Lenin Sarani
Calcutta 700013, India

International Action Center
39 West 14th St., #206
New York, NY 10011
phone: 212 633 6646
fax: 212 633 2889
e-mail: iacenter@iacenter.org
website: www.iacenter.org
and
2489 Mission St., #28
San Francisco, CA 94110
phone: 415 821 6545
fax: 415 821 5782
e-mail: afreeman@igc.apc.org
and
5920 Second Ave.
Detroit, MI 48202
phone: 313 831 0750
(there are IAC offices in many cities; call
NY or SF for the one nearest you)

International Movement for a Just
World
P.O. Box 288, Jalan Sultan
46730 Petaling Jaya
Selangor Darul Ehsan, Malaysia

phone: 603 7583614
fax: 603 7583735
e-mail: muza@po.jaring.my
website: www.jaring.my/just/

International Nino Pasti Foundation
C.P. 7218 Roha-Nomentano
00100 Rome, Italy
phone: 39 6 817 3247
fax: 39 6 817 4010
e-mail: s.lacommare@agora.stm.it

International Relief Association
24522 Harper Ave.
St. Clair Shores, MI 48080
phone: 810 772 2357
fax: 810 772 3159
1-800-82-RELIEF
e-mail: ira97@mainnet.com
website: www.ira-usa.org

Iraq Action Coalition
7309 Haymarket Lane
Raleigh, NC 27615
phone: 919 848 4738
fax: 919 846 7422
e-mail: IAC@leb.net
(can automatically subscribe to list by
sending e-mail to "majordomo @ leb.
net" with the command "subscribe iac-
list")
website: www.leb.net/IAC/

Iraq Action Network—Canada
P.O. Box 40052
75 King St. S.
Waterloo, ON N2J 4V1
phone: 519 746 5851
fax: 519 746 4096
e-mail: gccwat@web.apc.org
website: www.web.net/~gccwat/iraq

Iraq Crisis Anti-War Homepage
website: www.nonviolence.org

Iraq Help
e-mail: Nawaralsaadi@yahoo.com
website: husky1.stmarys.ca/
   ~n_alsaad/iraq.html
("a personal effort by an Iraqi citizen to
give help and support to his country at
this dark moment in history")

Iraqi Canadian Friendship Assn.
455 Wilbrod St.
Ottawa, Canada K1N-6M7
phone: 613 241 5389
fax: 613 241 2415

Islamic Center of Long Island
website: members.aol.com/
   icli/iraq/index.html

Karbala Hospital Fund
c/o Dr. Barbara N. Aziz
160 Sixth Ave.
New York, NY 10013

Labor Art and Mural Project
Mike Alewitz
c/o Rutgers Labor Education Center
Ryders Lane and Clifton Ave.
New Brunswick, NJ 08903
phone: 732 220 1472
fax: 732 296 1325
e-mail: lamp@igc.apc.org
website: www.igc.apc.org/laborart

Mennonite Central Committee—
   Assistance to Iraq
website: www.mennonitecc.ca/
   mcc/index.html

Minnesota Alliance for Iraqi
   Children
Pres. Abdulwahab M. Asamarai
351 Purce St. NE
Minneapolis, MN 55413
phone: 612 331 5276
e-mail: samarrai51@hotmail.com

Muslim Peace Fellowship
P.O. Box 271
Nyack, NY 10960
phone: 914 358 4601

fax: 914 358 4924
e-mail: mpf@igc.apc.org
website: www.nonviolence.org

National Council of Churches
website: www.ncccusa.org

Organization in Solidarity with the
   People of Africa, Asia, and Latin
   America (OSPAAAL)
Valverde, 28-28004
Madrid, Spain
phone/fax: 01 523 18 29

Pastors for Peace/Interreligious
   Foundation for Community
   Organization (IFCO)
402 W. 145th St.
New York, NY 10031
phone: 212 926 5757 (New York
   City); 773 271 4817 (Chicago)
fax: 212 926 5842
e-mail: ifco@igc.apc.org
website: www.ifconews.org

Pax Christi USA—National Catholic
   Peace Movement
532 West 8th Street
Erie, PA 16502-1343
phone: 814 453 4955
fax: 814 452 4784
e-mail: info@paxchristiusa.org
website: www.nonviolence.org/
   pcusa/

Peace Action, Metro New York
Sonya Ostrom, President
475 Riverside Dr., #242
New York, NY 10115
phone: 212 870 2304
fax: 212 870 2243
e-mail: metropeace@aol.com

Peace and Justice Works
P.O. Box 42456
Portland, OR 97242
phone: 503 236 3065
website: www.teleport.com/
   ~copwatch/Iraq.html

Peace Suitors at Tokyo
c/o Bongadou, Kudan-kita 1-10-2-
  402
Chiyoda-ku, Tokyo, 102, Japan
phone: 81 3 3234 2127
fax: 81 3 3234 2166
e-mail: peace-st@jca.ax.apc.org
website: www.jca.ax.apc.org/
  peace-st/

People's Fight Back Center
3030 Euclid Ave., #LL1
Cleveland, OH 44115
phone/fax: 216 426 0851
e-mail: pfcenter@aol.com

Persian Gulf Peace Network
  / AFSC-KC
Ira Harritt
4405 Gillham Road
Kansas City, Missouri 64110
phone: 816 931 5256
fax: 816 561 5033
e-mail: afsckc@oz.sunflower.org

Physicians for Social Responsibility
  / Washington
Gerri Haynes
4554 12th Ave. NE
Seattle, Washington 98105
phone: 206 547 2630
fax: 206 547 2631
e-mail: psrwase@igc.apc.org

ProActivist.com
website: www.proactivist.com
(photographic essay by Iraq Sanctions
Challenge delegate Patrick Carkin)

Remember the Iraqi Children
Kouthar and Marwa Al-Rawi
P.O. Box 1141
San Pedro, CA 90733
e-mail: Iraqikids@aol.com
website: members.aol.com/
  hamzaha/iraqichildren/
(children's campaign to send 1 million
postcards to President Clinton)

Santa Barbara Peace Coalition
c/o Michelle Kimball
900 Mission Canyon Rd.
Santa Barbara, CA 93105
phone: 805 569 3738
fax: 805 569 2391
e-mail: mfkimball@aol.com

Save the Children of Iraq
Fisal Hammouda, Chicago
phone: 630 240 3655

Save the Iraqi Children
422 Southwestern Ave., #202
Los Angeles, CA 90020
phone: 213 487 2368
e-mail: npcla@earthlink.net
and
Orange County Office
P.O. Box 1056
Stanton, CA 90680
phone: 714 626 1323

Social Action Network
P.O. Box 4480
Chica, CA 95927
phone: 530 343 2570
e-mail: joel@c-zone.net

Society for International
  Communication
Gesellschaft fuer Internationale Ver-
  staendigung (GIV)
c/o Gerhard Lange, Im Hassel 38
37077 Goettingen, Germany
phone/fax: 0551 37 20 48
e-mail: G.Lange@LINK-GOE.de
website: www.germany.net/
  teilnehmer/101.88843/index.htm
  (click on British flag for English)

South Movement
e-mail: davemull@alphalink.com.au
website: southmovement.
  alphalink.com.au/

Spanish Campaign for Lifting the
    Sanctions on Iraq
Apart. de Correos 14.180, 28080
Madrid, Spain
fax: 1 531 75 99

Student Coalition for Peace with the
    Iraqi People
1164 Templeton Place
St. Louis, MO 63017
phone: 314 434 3473
fax: 314 434 6146
e-mail: peaceiraq@aol.com
website: www.artsci.wustl.edu/
    ~urahmad/index.html

Um So'Mundo—Apelo a Favor do
    Iraque
website: www.aliasoft.com/iraque

United Campaign in Solidarity with
    the People of Iran
P.O. Box 7519, FDR Station
New York, NY 10150
phone: 212 620 4283
email: ucspi@igc.apc.org

Veterans for Peace
5011 "K" St. NW, #525
Washington, D.C. 20005
phone: 202 347 6780
fax: 202 347 6781
e-mail: vfp@igc.org
website: www.nonviolence.org/vfp

Vietnam Veterans Restoration Proj-
    ect
Fredy Champagne
P.O. Box 69
Garberville, CA 95542
phone/fax: 707 943 1874
e-mail: fchampagne@humboldt.net
(organizing Gulf War veterans' trip to
Iraq)

Voices in the Wilderness
1460 West Carmen Ave.
Chicago, IL 60640
phone: 773 784 8065
fax: 773 784 8837
e-mail: kkelly@icg.apc.org
website: www.nonviolence.org/vitw/
(sends delegations to Iraq)

West Harlem Coalition
P.O. Box 660
Manhattanville Sta.
New York, NY 10027
phone: 212 666 6426
fax: 212 280 7832

Women for Mutual Security
Coordinator, Margarita Papandreou
1, Romilias Str.
GR. 14671 Kastri, Greece
phone: 01 88 43 202
fax: 01 80 12 850
North American Coordinator:
    Lenore Foerstel
510 West Pennfield Road
Columbia, MD 21045
fax: 410 964 9248

Women's International League for
    Peace and Freedom (WILPF)
1213 Race Street
Philadelphia, PA 19107
phone: 215 563 7110
fax: 215 563 5527
e-mail: wilpf@wilpf.org
website: www.wilpf.org

Women's Strike for Peace
110 Maryland Ave. NE, #102
Washington, DC 20002
phone: 202 543 2660
fax: 202 544 9613

Where to Send Your Protests

Permanent UN Security Council members:

H.E. Ambassador Qin Huasun
Permanent Mission of China to
 the UN
155 W. 66th St.
New York, NY 10023
phone: 212 870 0313
fax: 212 870 0333

H.E. Mr. Alain Dejammet
Permanent Mission of France to
 the UN
245 E. 47th St., 44th Fl.
New York, NY 10017
phone: 212 308 5700
fax: 212 421 6889

Mr. Sergey Z. Lavrov
Permanent Mission of the Russian Federation to the UN
136 E. 67th St.
New York, NY 10021
phone: 212 861 4900
fax: 212 628 0252

H.E. Sir John Weston
Permanent Mission of the UK to
 the UN
885 2nd Ave.
New York, NY 10017
phone: 212 745 9334
fax: 212 745 9316

H.E. Richard Holbrooke
Permanent Mission of the U.S. to
 the UN
799 UN Plaza
New York, NY 10017
phone: 212 415 4404
fax: 212 415 4443

Others:

H.E. Kofi Annan
Secretary-General of the UN
United Nations Headquarters,
 Room S-3800
New York, NY 10017

H.E. Richard Butler, Chairman
UN Special Commission on Iraq
United Nations Plaza
New York, NY 10017

H.E. Mr. Nizar Hamdoon
Permanent Mission of Iraq to the
 UN
14 East 79th Street
New York, NY 10021

President Bill Clinton
The White House
1600 Pennsylvania Ave. NW
Washington, DC 20500
phone: 202 456 1414
fax: 202 456 2461
White House Comment Line: 202
 456 1111 (1-1-0)
e-mail: president@
 whitehouse.gov

U.S. Department of State
Secretary of State Madeleine
 Korbel Albright
2201 "C" St. NW
Washington, DC 20520
phone: 202 647 9640
Iraqi Desk
NEA/NGA Rm. 4515
Washington, DC 20520
phone: 202 647 5692

Capitol switchboard
202 224 3121

U.S. Senate Committee on For-
    eign Relations
Washington, DC 20510
R-phone: 202 224 4651
fax: 202 224 0836
D-phone: 202 224 3953
fax: 202 224 5011

U.S. House of Representatives
    Committee on International
    Relations
Washington, DC 20515
R-phone: 202 225 5021
fax: 202 225 2035
D-phone: 202 225 6735
fax: 202 226 3581

APPENDIX 2: APPEALS AND RESOLUTIONS

An International Appeal to the United States Government and the Security Council of the United Nations

Economic sanctions and blockades, as now applied as the weapon of choice by the United States and by the Security Council of the United Nations at the urging of the U.S. and its allies, are weapons of mass destruction directed at a whole people.

These blockades have been used only against poor countries, and while the entire people is punished by their economic impact, the greatest harm is overwhelmingly on the poorest and weakest, infants, children, the chronically ill, and the elderly.

There is no crueler violation of fundamental human rights than this sanctions policy. The case of Iraq has demonstrated that the U.S. and its allies do not stop short of the deliberate creation of a new zone of death and destitution, with thousands of deaths monthly, dehydration, organ failure, and pain without relief, permanent physical or mental disability, and generalized shortening of life.

All humanitarian law from its inception has endeavored to limit violence to combatants, to prevent use of cruel and unfocused weapons, to protect civilians from the scourge of war, and to outlaw the principle of collective punishment. The sanctions policy is clearly a "Crime Against Humanity" as defined under the terms of the Nuremberg Principles. It also clearly violates the Charter of the United Nations, the Geneva Convention, and other fundamental documents of contemporary international law.

Ahmed Ben Bella, first President of Algeria • Daniel Ortega, former President of Nicaragua • Clodomiro Almeyda, former Deputy President of Chile • Karmenu Mifsud Bonnici, former Prime Minister of Malta • Romesh Chandra, President, World Peace Council • Roosevelt Douglas, Member of Parliament, Dominica • Ben Dupuy, former Ambassador at Large, Haiti • Sir Gaetan Duval, former Deputy Head of Government of Mauritius • Sheikh Mohammed Rashid, former Deputy Head of Government of Pakistan • Morad Ghaleb, former Foreign Minister of Egypt • Fr. Miguel D'Escoto, former Foreign Minister of Nicaragua • Tony Benn, Member of Parliament, Britain • Ramsey Clark, former Attorney General of the United States • Margarita Papandreou, former First Lady of Greece

The above Appeal was drafted by Ramsey Clark and introduced by the International Commission of Inquiry on Economic Sanctions.

Detroit City Council—Testimonial Resolution

The following Testimonial Resolution to Ramsey Clark was passed by the Detroit City Council on April 14, 1998.

WHEREAS Ramsey Clark, former United States Attorney General, attorney, author and distinguished humanitarian, has embarked on an effort to deliver medical supplies to the people of Iraq, and

WHEREAS Hospitals in Iraq are currently unable to provide antibiotics, anesthetics, dialysis or even aspirin to millions of people who are in desperate need of these basics, and

WHEREAS The policy of sanctions against Iraq by the United States government and the United Nations has resulted in the deaths of one and one-half million Iraqi civilians, mainly children, due to lack of food and medicine over the past seven years, and

WHEREAS The policy of sanctions unjustly victimizes the population of an entire country, especially children and the elderly.

NOW, THEREFORE BE IT RESOLVED That the Detroit City Council salutes the humanitarian efforts of Ramsey Clark and welcomes him to Detroit on April 14, 1998. We commend his challenge to the genocidal policy of sanctions and join him in urging the immediate end to this policy.

Berkeley City Council—Resolution of Support

Resolution No. 59,227-N.S.

Supporting actions to provide humanitarian relief to civilians in Iraq, particularly to Iraqi children.

WHEREAS, in 1990, the United Nations Security Council at the behest of the United States imposed severe sanctions on Iraq after its hostilities with Kuwait; and

WHEREAS, after seven years there is now occurring in Iraq according to United Nations Agency sources, including UNICEF, WHO, FAO, WFP and others, such severe civil dislocation that one-fourth of the children under the age of five suffer from extreme chronic malnutrition (UNICEF 1997 Report), 4,500 children under five die every month due to malnutrition and a total of one million Iraqis—600,000 of which are children—have died as a direct result of the sanctions (FAO December 1997); and

WHEREAS, Protocol 1 additional to the Geneva Convention of 1997 states that starvation of civilians as a method of warfare is prohibited, as is the destruction of a nation's ability to produce food for itself; and

WHEREAS, Iraq was a secular nation with a modern infrastructure that employed not only a large working population, but also provided employment to three million guest workers from third world countries; but after seven years of economic sanctions, Iraq has no functional agriculture, medical, communications, water, sewer or energy infrastructure causing diseases, starvation and social disorder;

NOW THEREFORE, BE IT RESOLVED by the Council of the City of Berkeley that in order to safeguard the human rights of the Iraqi people, and the civilian populations of all countries targeted by sanctions, the Berkeley City Council calls on the United States President, United Nations Secretary General Kofi Annan, and President and Members of the Security Council, to:

1. Modify the oil-for-food deal to remove the limit on oil revenues for humanitarian needs. Since the United Nations controls the bank account and will monitor distribution of humanitarian supplies, Iraq should be allowed to sell enough oil to meet all civilian needs. It does not make legal or ethical sense for the Security Council to adopt an arbitrary limit of $4 billion per year that will guarantee continued deprivation throughout the population; and

2. Adopt alternatives to comprehensive sanctions on Iraq and in future cases. The international community should not impose massive and collective suffering on innocent civilians for the sins of their government.

BE IT FURTHER RESOLVED, that the City Manager is directed to send letters and this Resolution to the United States President, United Nations Secretary General Kofi Annan, and President and Members of the Security Council, calling for the immediate lifting of those sanctions or other obstructions that hurt the civilian population of Iraq from reconstructing their country and their lives, especially the children.

BE IT FURTHER RESOLVED, that the City Manager is directed to send communications to all Bay Area City Councils encouraging them to take similar actions.

The foregoing Resolution was adopted by the Berkeley City Council on November 18, 1997, by the following vote:

Ayes: Councilmembers Breland, Maio, Shirek, Spring, Woolley, Worthington and Mayor Dean.

Noes: None.

Abstain: Councilmembers Armstrong and Olds.

Absent: None.

Signed by Shirley Dean, Mayor. Attested by Sherry M. Kelly, City Clerk.

San Francisco Labor Council, AFL-CIO

Resolution opposing the bombing of Iraq.

WHEREAS, the United States government and military have made extensive preparations to attack and bomb Iraq, and even after the agreement brokered by UN Secretary-General Kofi Annan, not only is the "vast array of U.S. and British high-tech weaponry being kept in place in the Gulf, it is being increased" (BBC, 2-23-98); and

WHEREAS, Secretary of State Madeleine Albright issued a statement on 2-23-98 that the U.S. continued to "reserve the unilateral right to strike militarily against Iraq at any time we feel our interests are threatened," highlighting that the danger of war remains high; and

WHEREAS, union members and working people do not endorse the bombing of the Iraqi people and the unnecessary killing and maiming of innocent people that this would mean; and

WHEREAS, the Iraqi people have already suffered incomparably from seven years of U.S./UN blockade, which according to United Nations figures has caused dire shortages of food and medicine and contributed to the deaths of 1,500,000 Iraqis including over 700,000 children since the end of the Gulf War; and

WHEREAS, the International Confederation of Free Trade Unions issued a statement in Brussels on February 12, 1998, opposing the bombing of Iraq, stating the ICFTU's belief, "that the current crisis can only be resolved through diplomatic means ... that another armed conflict leading to further loss of civilian lives and suffering of the Iraqi people cannot be regarded as a valid and lasting alternative," and further that, "the ICFTU calls on the UN member countries concerned to show maximum restraint and to use all the appropriate channels to find a negotiated solution ..."; and

WHEREAS, wasting billions of dollars on the Gulf War buildup translates into cutbacks of essential and job-producing social programs at home, resulting in a loss of jobs;

NOW, THEREFORE BE IT RESOLVED, that the San Francisco Labor Council call on the AFL-CIO and all local unions, international unions, state federations of labor, and central labor bodies to publicly oppose the bombing of Iraq, and demand an immediate halt to the U.S. military buildup in the Gulf, and the lifting of the deadly sanctions against Iraq; and

BE IT FURTHER RESOLVED, that the San Francisco Labor Council encourage the trade union movement at all levels to urgently contact congressional representatives and the Clinton administration to bring this military madness to a halt; and

BE IT FURTHER RESOLVED, that the San Francisco Labor Council endorse the "Stop the War" demonstrations being held on Saturday, February 28, 1998, in San Francisco and New York and ensure broad labor participation in this national effort to prevent the bombing of Iraq; and

BE IT FINALLY RESOLVED, a copy of this Resolution be forwarded to the President of the United States and other appropriate officials.

Adopted this 23d Day of February 1998, by the delegates of the San Francisco Labor Council, AFL-CIO.

Walter L. Johnson, Secretary-Treasurer

1199 Health & Human Services Employees Union

After submission by 1199 delegates from Einstein College in the Bronx, New York, the following resolution was passed by the Delegates' Council of 1199 National Health & Human Services Employees Union, SEIU, AFL-CIO on April 15, 1998.

The 1199 Delegates' Council endorses the Iraq Sanctions Challenge, and calls for medical aid to Iraq and an end to the sanctions, and recommends to the 1199 Executive Council the following measures:

a) endorse the Iraq Sanctions Challenge;

b) contribute money towards medical aid;

c) sponsor an 1199 representative to go on the delegation delivering medical aid;

d) provide information to 1199 members about the delegation and the union's support, and how international solidarity is linked to our struggle for racial and economic justice and health care for all.

The executive council is taking up this measure and the union is considering other actions it can take.

* * * * *

To motivate the above resolution, the following was distributed to the several hundred delegates:

1.5 Million People Have Died (half of them children)
from Economic Sanctions on Iraq
1199 can help prevent more senseless deaths
A call for international solidarity

One and a half million people in Iraq (half of them children) have died from U.S./UN economic sanctions enforced by the Pentagon since 1990. Many more have died from sanctions than from the bombs dropped during the Gulf War. Most have died from preventable diseases, due to a lack of clean water, malnutrition, and a lack of medicines. The sanctions are a "quiet" way to continue the war.

Thirty years ago this month, Dr. Martin Luther King was shot down for leading the struggle for freedom and justice for all people. The day he was shot, Dr. King was working on three campaigns: racial equality, union rights and economic justice for working people, and an end to the Vietnam War— the war the government was carrying on at the time.

In thirty years, the names and places have changed, but all three struggles are still with us. Our union has the opportunity to continue our tradition of linking these three campaigns and to be in the front lines of the struggle.

In May, a delegation led by former Attorney General Ramsey Clark, Reverend Lucius Walker (Pastors for Peace) and Bishop Thomas Gumbleton (Catholic Diocese of Detroit) will bring tons of medical aid for the people of Iraq, and will challenge the sanctions. The delegation has called on unions, community organizations, and health care professionals to give support to this Iraq Sanctions Challenge. With this in mind, several 1199 delegates have introduced the following proposal to the Executive Council, and ask the 1199 Delegates' Council for support.

Executive Board, UAW Local 2334, Detroit

The following resolution was passed by the UAW Local 2334 Executive Board:

Whereas the United States/United Nations economic sanctions against Iraq have continued for eight years, killing 1,500,000 people, mainly children (ten times the number of people killed in the actual Gulf War); and

Whereas the U.S. military presence in the Persian Gulf is costing over $50 billion each year, money which could better be spent for jobs, education, health care, and housing here at home; and

Whereas the United Nations Children's Fund (UNICEF) reported about Iraq in November 1997 that "food rationing provides less than 60 percent of the required daily calorie intake, the water and sanitation systems are in a state of collapse, and there is a critical shortage of life-saving drugs"; and

Whereas Michigan Members of Congress John Conyers Jr., David Bonior, and Carolyn C. Kilpatrick wrote to President Clinton in May 1998 urging that "The time has come to re-examine the intended goals and the actual effects of these sanctions ... [which] now serve only to extend the human suffering of the population." They cite for the president the United Nations Food and Agriculture Organization report that with "the continuation of the economic embargo ... the situation will progressively deteriorate with grave consequences to the health and life of the Iraqi people"; and

Whereas the Detroit City Council passed a resolution April 14, 1998, stating that "The policy of sanctions unjustly victimizes the population of an entire country, especially the children and the elderly," and goes on to urge the "immediate end" to the "genocidal policy of sanctions" against Iraq; and

Whereas Bishop Thomas Gumbleton, former U.S. Attorney General Ramsey Clark, Rev. Lucius Walker, and eighty other religious, community, and labor leaders from across the United States recently defied U.S. law and UN sanctions by delivering over $4 million worth of medicine to the hospitals in Iraq, thus risking twelve years imprisonment for this humanitarian gesture; and

Whereas the UAW International Executive Board recently voted for an end to the U.S. economic blockade against Cuba;

Therefore be it RESOLVED that the UAW 32nd Constitutional Convention goes on record condemning economic sanctions as a form of genocide and demands the immediate lifting of the economic sanctions against Iraq.

For more information about the above resolution, contact David Sole, President UAW Local 2334, at sole@dwsd.org.

Model Resolution: End the Sanctions War on Iraq

Whereas United Nations sanctions against Iraq, which originated in Security Council Resolution 661 (August 6, 1990), were imposed to demand that Iraq withdraw all its forces to the points in which they were located on August 1, 1990, and to "restore the authority of the legitimate government of Kuwait," and these objectives have been fulfilled;

Whereas given the realization of the specific objectives for which the original sanctions were imposed, no legal ground can be claimed for the continuing enforcement of the sanctions called for in United Nations Resolution 687, nor has the Security Council cited any legal ground for the continuation of the sanctions;

Whereas the sanctions against the people of Iraq are in strict violation of Protocol I of the Geneva Convention (1977), which prohibits starvation of civilians as a method of warfare and the denial of sustenance to the civilian population whatever the motive;

Whereas the sanctions against the people of Iraq are in violation of United Nations General Assembly Resolution 44/215 of December 22, 1989, which prohibits developed countries from "applying trade and financial restrictions, blockades, embargoes, and other economic sanctions, incompatible with the provisions of the Charter of the United Nations, against developing countries as a form of political and economic coercion that affects their political, economic, and social development";

Whereas the sanctions against the people of Iraq are in violation of the legally-binding Charter of Economic Rights and Duties of States, adopted by the UN General Assembly (1974), which states that "no State may use or encourage the use of economic, political or any other type of measures to coerce another State in order to obtain from it the subordination of the exercise of its sovereign rights or to secure from it advantages of any kind";

Whereas, the sanctions against the people of Iraq constitute an act of International Terrorism, defined by the U.S. legal code {Title 18 § 2331}as acts appearing to be intended "(a) to coerce a civilian population; (b) to influence the policy of a government by intimidation or coercion";

Whereas the Nürnberg Charter, which has been incorporated into international law by a universal consensus, established that individuals should refuse to obey illegal orders, especially when such orders violate international humanitarian law;

Whereas various reports from the United Nations, including the Food and Agricultural Organization and UNICEF, have documented that over 1.2 million people, most of whom are children under the age of five, have died in Iraq due to the scarcity of food and medicine resulting from the sanctions;

Whereas, in November 1997, UNICEF stated that 960,000 children—32 percent of all children under five—are chronically malnourished. This represents an increase of 72 percent from 1991. Chronic malnourishment will likely result in permanent stunting of physical, emotional and mental growth;

Whereas CARE reported in September 1997 that "children, mothers, the aged and sick were all cared for before 1990, but are now dying while the outside world mistakenly believes it has solved Iraq's problems with the much-delayed oil-for-food shipments." The deal "will barely keep the strongest of the population of Iraq on their feet";

Whereas the sanctions against the people of Iraq, in direct violation of the Geneva Convention's prohibition of collective punishment, ban the importation of supplies needed for the sustenance of the country, including medical equipment, machine and tools for industry and agriculture, chlorine for water purification, fertilizers and pesticides for agricultural production, and educational workbooks;

Whereas United Nations Security Council Resolution 986 allows for less than 50 percent of the proceeds from the Oil for Food deal to be used to purchase needed foods and medicine, does not practically provide means by which the Iraqi people can rebuild the infrastructure of their country, and fails to recognize the illegality of the sanctions. The relief afforded under the newly proposed Oil for Food deal ($3.1 billion every six months for a population of 23 million) will provide, at best, only 60 percent of the minimum caloric needs of the Iraqi people. This small amount of money will not cover the reconstruction of the water sanitation systems that were destroyed by U.S. bombs. Polluted water has been the primary cause of disease and death for the population. (Before the 1990 sanctions, Iraq used to spend $20 billion a year on imports of civilian commodities and social development projects.);

Whereas while the United States maintains Iraq has violated parts of United Nations Security Council Resolution 687, the U.S. has not called for the complete enforcement of UNSCR 687—namely the establishment in the Middle East of a zone free of mass destruction weapons and nuclear weapons—thus ignoring Turkey's mass arsenal of weaponry and Israel's hundreds of nuclear weapons;

Whereas the U.S. has also failed to call for the enforcement of hundreds of UN resolutions that Israel, Indonesia and other countries have violated with impunity;

Therefore, Be It Resolved that [name of your organization] calls for: a) immediately and unconditionally ending the illegal and immoral sanctions against the Iraqi population; b) the formation of an independent, impartial judicial body to determine the civil and criminal responsibilities of states and individuals in causing injury to millions of civilians in Iraq through military aggression and non-military acts of hostility; c) the establishment of an ad hoc international criminal tribunal for the trial of all individuals responsible for international crimes committed against the civilian population in Iraq, regardless of rank, status, and nationality; d) the establishment of an international compensation and reconstruction fund to provide material relief to all Iraqi victims of international crimes;

Be It Further Resolved that [name of your organization] calls for: e) the abolition of economic sanctions as weapons of mass destruction; f) the United States to end its double standards on the enforcement of all United Nations resolutions.

Copies of this resolution will be sent to the President of the United States, the Secretary of State, the U.S. Ambassador to the UN, the UN Secretary-General, and the media.

Submitted by Rania Masri of the Iraq Action Coalition.

A Call for Emergency Chlorine Shipments to Iraq

From David Sole, President of the Sanitary Chemists & Technicians Association, UAW Local 2334 at the Detroit Water & Sewerage Department

U.S./UN Sanctions Crippling Iraq's Water System

Economic sanctions imposed on Iraq by the United States and the United Nations have created a crisis in fresh water and waste water treatment. Sanctions have kept Iraq from rebuilding a system severely damaged in the 1991 Gulf War. Sanctions forbid Iraq from maintaining and repairing the system in a timely manner. And sanctions make it impossible for Iraq to expand the system for increased population and industrial demands. The population, unable to get safe drinking water, is suffering widespread diarrhea and dysentery. The most vulnerable victims, the children, are dying. Unable to properly treat waste water, the country is facing even more extensive medical and ecological problems in the future.

Chlorine Needed Immediately to Alleviate Crisis

The most immediate need is for liquid chlorine to treat the fresh water and provide the entire population with safe, drinkable water. Adequate chlorination alone could eliminate a large percentage of medical cases, especially of babies and children who now fill emergency rooms at every hospital. The need for costly medical treatment (often unavailable due to sanctions for thousands with diarrhea and dysentery) could disappear. Scarce medicines could go to others with non-water-borne infections. Increased chlorination can save thousands of children's lives almost immediately.

Restrictions on Fresh Water and Waste Water Treatment
Endanger Entire Population

Chlorine is cheap and readily available for shipment. Chlorine supplies can be tracked and its use easily monitored at the various water plants. UNSCOM inspectors already monitor the limited amount of chlorine now entering Iraq from UNICEF. No reasonable or legitimate objection can be put forward to the importation of essential amounts of chlorine to Iraq. This could end a great part of the enormous suffering and needless deaths of children who have no part in political disputes among nations.

We must begin an international campaign to immediately provide adequate amounts of liquid chlorine for Iraq's water purification plants.

In discussions with various officials of Baghdad's Water Department and a visit to the "April 7" Water Purification Plant, a delegation from the United States "Iraq Sanctions Challenge" group (May 6-May 13, 1998) obtained the following picture.

Baghdad had a population of 2.5 million before the Gulf War. This has grown to 5.5 million today. Of the four water purification plants serving Baghdad in 1990, the two smaller plants are not operational due to shortages of parts and supplies caused by the sanctions. The two larger plants are running, but at reduced capacity. No upgrading or expansion has been permitted, due to the sanctions, to meet the doubled demand for water. Before the war the city was providing 132 gallons per day per capita. Now less than 42 gallons per day per capita is available, including water for industry. The United Nations 661 Committee (U.N Resolution 661 established sanctions against Iraq) either prohibits importation of certain items it has declared having potential military use ("dual-use") or stalls contracts that have been approved under the Oil for Food Memorandum of Understanding between Iraq and the UN. The Baghdad water department was only allowed a budget of $8 million for a recent six-month period under the Oil for Food program. Of nine contracts approved one and one half years ago by the 661 Committee (really the U.S. and Britain), only two contracts have been filled.

The "April 7" Plant, north of Baghdad, takes water from the Tigris River. Only seven of the fourteen pumps are working, pumping 174 million gallons per day. Standard procedures call for pre-chlorination of the incoming water. Pre-war pre-chlorination was done at 2.5 parts per million (ppm). Today, because chlorine is declared a potential military item, manufacture of chlorine is prohibited in Iraq (three chlorine plants were destroyed during the Gulf War). Importation of chlorine has been severely restricted by the U.S.-UN sanctions. Only one year ago UNICEF was permitted to provide some liquid chlorine but this is not enough for even the limited amount of water being treated. Pre-chlorination has been eliminated.

The water from the Tigris has a high turbidity. Settling tanks eliminate some of the solids. Additional precipitation of suspended solids calls for addition of alum. Prior to the war 99 percent pure alum was available. Today's sanctions make pure alum unavailable. The plant is adding a domestically mined alum ore that has about 50 percent impurities. This makes it impossible to control the alum dose and properly eliminate suspended solids. Every day the alum treatment tank has to be scraped out with a mechanical shovel. Testing of the plant's water is normally done every two hours, but because of a lack of chemical reagents, simple chemical tests to monitor the water quality are being done only once or twice a day.

The "April 7" Plant is fitted with twelve Portacel chlorinators. Six are not operational. Chlorine is supplied from 1000-kg tanks. Only three tanks were in a storage bay designed to hold at least forty tanks. Another twenty tanks were in an adjacent yard, but this is used to supply the other plants as well. UNSCOM weapons inspectors regularly visit the water treatment plants to monitor the use and location of chlorine tanks. The only chlorination of the water is just before it leaves the plant. The chlorine residual (the amount of chlorine left in the water after it reacts with any pollutants or reactive particles) is between 1.0 and 1.5 ppm. Officials want to have a residual of 2.5 ppm, but are unable to secure enough chlorine to reach this target.

The chlorine residual of 1.0-1.5 ppm is remarkably high compared to water leaving a Detroit water plant (0.15 ppm). The reason appears to be in the problem of widespread damage to the water delivery pipes under the streets of Baghdad from the massive bombing sustained in the Gulf War. Cracks and breaks in the pipes now result in a 40 percent rate for unaccounted water (compared to a 15 percent rate before the war). Pipes to repair the system are barred by UNSCOM. Low pressure from a lack of pumps and water loss leads to an influx of contaminated ground water into the system. Baghdad engineers apparently are trying to send the water from the treatment plant with enough chlorine to destroy contaminants coming into the pipes far from the plant itself. Even with a 1.0-1.5 ppm residual, some areas are receiving water at the tap with no chlorine left in it. Testing of tap water has revealed that 11 percent of the test sites are failing World Health Organization standards for water quality (before the war failure to meet WHO standards never exceeded 1.8 percent).

The result of this combination of problems, shortages, and restrictions inflicted by the Gulf War and war by economic sanctions is massive outbreaks of diarrhea and dysentery. Especially hard hit are the poor who cannot afford bottled water or the fuel to boil tap water. The hospital emergency rooms are filled with children suffering intestinal disorders. Most go untreated due to a lack of antibiotics, anti-parasite medicine, and a lack of IV fluids. Even if the doctors can treat some cases, the patients are sent back home where they will drink the water again. According to all sources, Baghdad's situation is MUCH BETTER than the rest of the country.

Baghdad's waste-water treatment now consists of primary and secondary treatment and aeration. No chlorine is available for waste-water treatment. An estimated sixty-six billion gallons a year of untreated waste water is also being returned to the Tigris River due to shortages caused by the sanctions. Industrial waste is largely going untreated into the river. Most alarming are reports that hospital incinerators are not functioning and that medical waste is going untreated into the system. The ecological long-term effects are incalculable.

About one metric ton of liquid chlorine is being used at each of two fresh-water plants in Baghdad per day. Another one to two metric tons per day would allow Baghdad to increase the chlorine residual leaving the plants to the target of 2.5 ppm. Waste-water treatment could use an additional 3.5 metric tons per day. The rest of the country has the need for five to six metric tons per day.

APPENDIX 3

UN Food and Agriculture Organization Report

Briefing Notes for TCOR Mission, Baghdad, May 1998

SOCIO-ECONOMIC SITUATION—ECONOMY

The Iraqi economy has been dominated by the oil sector, which in 1989 comprised 61% of the Gross Domestic Product (GDP). Services come second (22% of GDP), then industry (12%) with a mere 5% from agriculture. The substantial oil revenues brought prosperity for most Iraqis and high government expenditures in the public sector.

The latest national census, conducted on 16/10/1997, revealed that the total population of Iraq is 22,017,983. The total male population is 10,940,764 (49.7%) and the total female population is 11,077,219 (50.2%). The urban population is 14,994,208 (68%) and the rural population is 7,023,775 (32%).

The embargo resulted in rapid economic decline. By 1991, it is estimated that the GDP had dropped by about three-quarters of its 1990 level. By September 1995, the UN Department of Humanitarian Affairs estimated that about 4 million Iraqis (about 20%) lived in extreme poverty. These are mainly Iraqis living in areas with underdeveloped infrastructure and limited economic opportunities.

Underemployment is widely spread and many employed people look for other work to supplement their income. Iraqi families are often forced to sell their household and personal effects while borrowing money is not an option.

Productive economic activities have stagnated due to lack of investment, acute shortage of supplies, spare parts, unreliable fuel and power supplies. There has been a sharp decease in the standard of living and employment opportunities. The northern governorates are also subjected to continuing political instability. For the Autonomous Region, the 1994 ODA Household Expenditure Survey reports that the poorest 10% of households earned only 3% of the average household expenditure.

The purchasing power of the local currency has greatly reduced, with the precipitous depreciation in the value of the Iraqi Dinar (ID). Its exchange rate dropped from the equivalent of US$1/3 in 1990 to US$1/3,000 by the end of 1995, although has managed to be more stable at an average about US$1/1,500.

Iraq has a significant brain drain and professionals now accept less skilled employment. It is not clear how the erosion of professional groups has affected their gender composition.

The decline in public education is reinforced by the increased responsibility for normal family welfare and income on children.

In the health sector, the combination of severe compromises in the country's food security profile, economic decline, and destruction of Iraq's infrastructure particularly in relation to the supply of safe water, had major consequences for public health and specifically of child health.

Land mines are great risk to health and life in the northern governorates of Iraq; the region is considered to be one of the most mine-ridden areas in the world. Mines exacerbate the problems and compromises food production by blocking access and consequent household food security.

NUTRITION SITUATION

The total dietary energy supply for the Iraqi's declined from an average of 3,372 Kcal/cap/day between 1984 and 1989, to 3,150 Kcal in 1990 and then dramatically fell to 2,268 Kcal/cap/day in 1993-95.

The fall in the availability of dietary energy supplies was accompanied by declines in protein availability from 67.7 g/cap/day to 43.3 g/cap/day. Calculations of the lysine content of the Iraqi diet show simultaneous declines from 47 mg/g protein to 32 mg/g protein over the same period, indicating that protein quality as well as quantity was also affected.

In spite of some improvement made by the Oil-for-Food deal, malnutrition remains a serious problem throughout the whole country. Severe undernutrition is widespread in pediatric hospitals reflecting its presence in the general population. Both marasmus and kwashiorkor were widely observed in pediatric wards.

A population-based nutrition survey, was conducted by the FAO/WFP team[*] from June 21 to July 3, 1997, in Baghdad (900 children) and in the town of Kerbala (158 children). The results obtained indicate that, although the situation shows some signs of improvement since the 1995 survey, there was still a considerable degree of malnutrition in the population.

Adult nutritional status was also investigated by determining Body Mass Index (BMI = weight/height) on 1,278 adults: 870 females and 408 males in Baghdad and Kerbala. When compared to BMI reference population data tabulated by FAO (1994), for instance for Tunisia, the number of those with low BMI in Iraq was considerably greater than in the reference population, illustrating the considerable presence of under-nutrition in this sample of the Iraqi adult population.

Lack of good-quality proteins and minerals in the diet of children remains a problem especially for children of weaning age. Under the MOU [Memorandum of Understanding] a family with an infant could choose whether to take either the baby milk formula or an adult ration.

---

[*] Special Report, FAO/WFP Food Supply and Nutrition Assessment Mission to Iraq, 3 October 1997.

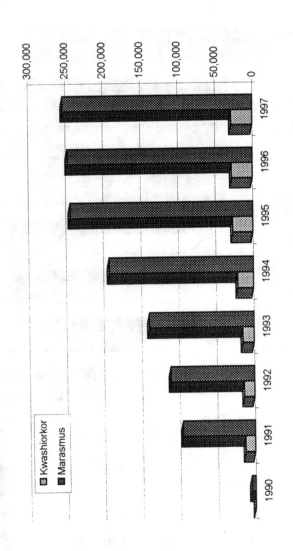

INCREASE IN CASES OF
NUTRITION-RELATED ILLNESSES
1990-1997

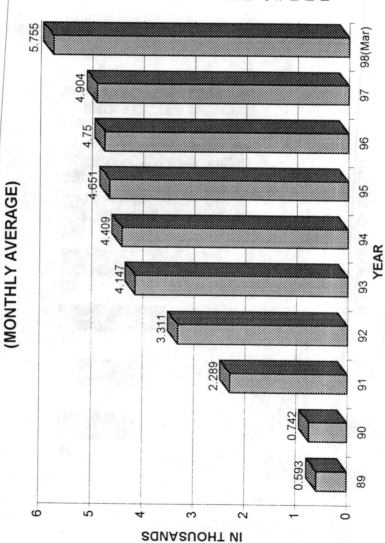

UNDER (5) MORTALITY RATE DUE TO EMBARGO (MONTHLY AVERAGE)

IN THOUSANDS

YEAR

FIGURES FROM VITAL AND HEALTH STATISTICS DEPT., IRAQI MINISTRY OF HEALTH

Year	Value
89	0.593
90	0.742
91	2.289
92	3.311
93	4.147
94	4.409
95	4.651
96	4.75
97	4.904
98(Mar)	5.755

Summary of UNICEF Report of 30 April 1998[*]

"Situation Analysis of Children and Women in Iraq"[†]
Direct quotations and summary information:
Health—increase of approximately 90,000 deaths yearly due to the sanctions (more than 250 people a day). (p. 42)
"The increase in mortality reported in public hospitals for children under five years of age (an excess of some 40,000 deaths yearly compared with 1989) is mainly due to diarrhea, pneumonia and malnutrition. In those over five years of age, the increase (an excess of some 50,000 deaths yearly compared with 1989) is associated with heart disease, hypertension, diabetes, cancer, liver or kidney diseases. ... With the substantial increase in mortality, under-registration of deaths is a growing problem." (p. 42)

"Malnutrition was not a public health problem in Iraq prior to the embargo. Its extent became apparent during 1991 and the prevalence has increased greatly since then: 18% in 1991 to 31% in 1996 of [children] under five with chronic malnutrition (stunting); 9% to 26% with underweight malnutrition; 3% to 11% with wasting (acute malnutrition), an increase in over 200%. By 1997, it was estimated about one million children under five were [chronically] malnourished." (pp. 23, 63)

"[Before the 1990 sanctions] primary medical care reached about 97% of the urban population, and 78% of rural residents. ... [Now] the health system is affected by lack of even basic hospital and health centre equipment and supplies for medical, surgical and diagnostic services. ... In 1989, the [Iraqi] Ministry of Health spent more than US$500 million for drugs and supplies; the budget is [now] reduced by 90-95%." (pp. 7, 40)

Oil for Food plan—not reduced widespread suffering nor provided supplies in full in a timely manner. (p. 2) "The Oil-for-Food plan has not yet resulted in adequate protection of Iraq's children from malnutrition/ disease. Those children spared from death continue to remain deprived of essential rights addressed in the Convention of Rights of the Child." (p. 3)

"Although SCR 986 [the Oil for Food program] is meant to provide US$210 million for each six month period of Phase I and II, only US$80 million (i.e., 20%) had been received as of November 15, 1997." (p. 40)

"As of March 15, 1988, of the allocations [from the Oil for Food plan] for medicines/health, about 75% has arrived in-country for the South/Center

---

[*] Summarized by Rania Masri, Michelle Kimball, and Mary Bernier. This summary and the more extensive 20-page summary report are available on the Iraq Action Coalition website.

[†] For copies of the full report, contact UNICEF reference librarian at 212 326 7065.

and 50% of the North; for water/sanitation, 59% and 27%; education 37% and 45%; and for electricity/power 48% and 10% each respectively for South Center and North." (p. 18)

(Lack of) Water Sanitation—resulting in increases in diarrhea, typhoid, cholera, and viral hepatitis. (p. 52)

"It is likely that lack of safe water and sanitation has contributed greatly to the steep rise in malnutrition rates and mortality. In accordance with [Convention on the Rights of the Child], the goal for the year 2000 for universal access to safe drinking water and sanitary means of excreta disposal is unlikely to be achieved with the continuation of the embargo." (p. 31)

"Water treatment plants lack spare parts, equipment, treatment chemicals, proper maintenance and adequate qualified staff. ... Plants often act solely as pumping stations without any treatment... The distribution network, on which most of the population relies, has destroyed, blocked, or leaky pipes." (p. 32)

Economy—breakdown of socio-cultural fabric of the society, due to economic collapse. (p. i) "By September 1995, the UN's Department of Humanitarian Affairs estimated about 4 million Iraqis (about 20%) lived in extreme poverty. ... The purchasing power of the local currency has been greatly reduced, ... from US$3 = 1 Iraqi Dinar (ID) in 1990 ... to about US $1 = ID1,500 in 1997." (p. 9)

"Basic causes of malnutrition are dominated by the economic situation where the GDP per capita has [been] reduced from $3,500 to $600 and the current salary of public workers now averages about $3 to $5 per month, compared with $50-100 prior to 1990. ... Accessibility to food beyond the amounts provided through public rations is limited by soaring food prices. ... At least 80% of a family's income is spent on food." (pp. 27, 29)

Education—Gulf War and sanctions resulting in limited access to and poor quality of education. (p. i)

"Historically, Iraq has given education a high priority. However, the protracted economic hardship on Iraqi population has seriously affected every level of formal and informal education." (p. 80)

"The unprecedented trend of declining school enrollment continues unabated ... [yet] does not indicate the quality of education, nor the decline in school facilities. These include lack of the most basic school supplies such as blackboards, chalks, pencils, notebooks, and paper (designated as "nonessential" by the Sanctions Committee), inaccessibility to any water, and absent or defunct sanitation." (pp. 87-88)

"84% of all schools need rehabilitation. ... The Oil for Food program is providing a rather limited contribution to the improvement of [these] conditions." (pp. 88, 96)

Over a Century of U.S. Military Interventions

The following is a partial list of U.S. military interventions from 1890 to 1994 compiled by Zoltan Grossman and revised on 1 January 1995. This guide does not include demonstration duty by military police, mobilizations of the National Guard, offshore shows of naval strength, reinforcements of embassy personnel, the use of non-Defense Department personnel (such as the Drug Enforcement Agency), military exercises, noncombat mobilizations (such as replacing postal strikers), the permanent stationing of armed forces, covert actions where the U.S. did not play a command and control role, the use of small hostage rescue units, most uses of proxy troops, U.S. piloting of foreign warplanes, foreign disaster assistance, military training and advisory programs not involving direct combat, civic action programs, and many other military activities. Among sources used, besides news reports, are the *Congressional Record* (23 June 1969), *180 Landings* by the U.S. Marine Corps History Division, Ege & Makhijani in *Counterspy* (July-Aug. 1982), and Ellsberg in *Protest & Survive*.

LOCATION/Period/Type of Force/Comments on U.S. role

SOUTH DAKOTA/1890 (-?)/Troops/300 Lakota Indians massacred at Wounded Knee.
ARGENTINA/1890/Troops/Buenos Aires interests protected.
CHILE/1891/Troops/Marines clash with nationalist rebels.
HAITI/1891/Troops/Black workers' revolt on U.S.-claimed Navassa Island defeated.
IDAHO/1892/Troops/Army suppresses silver miners' strike.
HAWAII/1893 (-?)/Naval, troops/Independent kingdom overthrown, annexed.
CHICAGO/1894/Troops/Breaking of rail strike, 34 killed.
NICARAGUA/1894/Troops/Month-long occupation of Bluefields.
CHINA/1894-95/Naval, troops/Marines land in Sino-Japanese War.
KOREA/1894-96/Troops/Marines kept in Seoul during war.
PANAMA/1895/Troops, naval/Marines land in Colombian province.
NICARAGUA/1896/Troops/Marines land in port of Corinto.
CHINA/1898-1900/Troops/Boxer Rebellion fought by foreign armies.
PHILIPPINES/1898-1910(-?)/Naval, troops/Seized from Spain, killed 600,000 Filipinos.
CUBA/1898-1902(-?)/Naval, troops/Seized from Spain, still hold Navy base.
PUERTO RICO/1898(-?)/Naval, troops/Seized from Spain, occupation continues.
GUAM/1898(-?)/Naval, troops/Seized from Spain, still use as base.
MINNESOTA/1898(-?)/Troops/Army battles Chippewa at Leech Lake.

NICARAGUA/1898/Troops/Marines land at port of San Juan del Sur.
SAMOA/1899(-?)/Troops/Battle over succession to throne.
NICARAGUA/1899/Troops/Marines land at port of Bluefields.
IDAHO/1899-1901/Troops/Army occupies Coeur d'Alene mining region.
OKLAHOMA/1901/Troops/Army battles Creek Indian revolt.
PANAMA/1901-03(-?)/Naval, troops/Broke off from Colombia, annexed Canal Zone.
HONDURAS/1903/Troops/Marines intervene in revolution.
DOMINICAN REPUBLIC/1903-04/Troops/U.S. interests protected in Revolution.
KOREA/1904-05/Troops/Marines land in Russo-Japanese War.
CUBA/1906-09/Troops/Marines land in democratic election.
NICARAGUA/1907/Troops/"Dollar Diplomacy" protectorate set up.
HONDURAS/1907/Troops/Marines land during war with Nicaragua.
PANAMA/1908/Troops/Marines intervene in election contest.
NICARAGUA/1910/Troops/Marines land in Bluefields and Corinto.
HONDURAS/1911/Troops/U.S. interests protected in civil war.
CHINA/1911-41/Naval, troops/Continuous occupation with flare-ups.
CUBA/1912/Troops/U.S. interests protected in Havana.
PANAMA/1912/Troops/Marines land during heated election.
HONDURAS/1912/Troops/Marines protect U.S. economic interests.
NICARAGUA/1912-33/Troops, bombing/20-year occupation, fought guerrillas.
MEXICO/1913/Naval/Americans evacuated during revolution.
DOMINICAN REPUBLIC/1914/Naval/Fight with rebels over Santo Domingo.
COLORADO/1914/Troops/Breaking of miners' strike by Army.
MEXICO/1914-18/Naval, troops/Series of interventions against nationalists.
HAITI/1914-34/Troops, bombing/19-year occupation after revolts.
DOMINICAN REPUBLIC/1916-24/Troops/8-year Marine occupation.
CUBA/1917-33/Troops/Military occupation, economic protectorate.
WORLD WAR I/1917-18/Naval, troops/Ships sunk, fought Germany for 1½ years.
RUSSIA/1918-22/Naval, troops/Five landings to fight Bolsheviks.
PANAMA/1918-20/Troops/"Police duty" during unrest after elections.
HONDURAS/1919/Troops/Marines land during election campaign.
GUATEMALA/1920/Troops/2-week intervention against unionists.
WEST VIRGINIA/1920-21/Troops, bombing/Army intervenes against miners.
TURKEY/1922/Troops/Fought nationalists in Smyrna (Izmir).
CHINA/1922-27/Naval, troops/Deployment during nationalist revolt.
HONDURAS/1924-25/Troops/Landed twice during election strife.
PANAMA/1925/Troops/Marines suppress general strike.
CHINA/1928-34/Troops/Marines stationed throughout the country.
EL SALVADOR/1932/Naval/Warships sent during Faribundo Marti revolt.

WASHINGTON, D.C./1932/Troops/Army stops WWI vet bonus protest.

WORLD WAR II/1941-45/Naval,troops, bombing, nuclear/Hawaii bombed, fought Japan, Italy and Germany for 3 years; first nuclear war.

DETROIT/1943/Troops/Army puts down Black rebellion.

IRAN/1946/Nuclear threat/Soviet troops told to leave north (Iranian Azerbaijan).

YUGOSLAVIA/1946/Nuclear threat/Response to shooting-down of U.S. plane.

URUGUAY/1947/Nuclear threat/Bombers deployed as show of strength.

GREECE/1947-49/Command operation/U.S. directs extreme-right in civil war.

GERMANY/1948/Nuclear threat/Atomic-capable bombers guard Berlin Airlift.

PHILIPPINES/1948-54/Command operation/CIA directs war against Huk Rebellion.

PUERTO RICO/1950/Command operation/Independence rebellion crushed in Ponce.

KOREA/1951-53(-?)/Troops, naval, bombing, nuclear threats/U.S. and South Korea fight China and North Korea to stalemate; A-bomb threat in 1950, and against China in 1953. Still have bases.

IRAN/1953/Command operation/CIA overthrows democracy, installs Shah.

VIETNAM/1954/Nuclear threat/Bombs offered to French to use against siege.

GUATEMALA/1954/Command operation, bombing, nuclear threat/CIA directs exile invasion after new government nationalizes U.S. company lands; bombers based in Nicaragua.

EGYPT/1956/Nuclear threat/Soviets told to keep out of Suez crisis.

LEBANON/1958/Troops, naval/Marine occupation against rebels.

IRAQ/1958/Nuclear threat/Iraq warned against invading Kuwait.

CHINA/1958/Nuclear threat/China told not to move on Taiwan isles.

PANAMA/1958/Troops/Flag protests erupt into confrontation.

VIETNAM/1960-75/Troops, naval, bombing, nuclear threats/Fought South Vietnam revolt and North Vietnam; millions killed in longest U.S. war; atomic bomb threats in 1968 and 1969.

LAOS/1961/Command operation/Military buildup during guerrilla war.

CUBA/1961/Command operation/CIA-directed exile invasion fails.

GERMANY/1961/Nuclear threat/Alert during Berlin Wall crisis.

CUBA/1962/Nuclear threat, naval/Blockade during missile crisis; near-war with Soviet Union.

PANAMA/1964/Troops/Panamanians shot for urging canal's return.

INDONESIA/1965/Command operation/Million killed in CIA-assisted army coup.

DOMINICAN REPUBLIC/1965-66/Troops, bombing/Marines land during election campaign.

GUATEMALA/1966-67/Command operation/Green Berets intervene against rebels.

DETROIT/1967/Troops/Army battles Blacks, 43 killed.

UNITED STATES/1968/Troops/After King is shot; over 21,000 soldiers in cities.

CAMBODIA/1969-75/Bombing, troops, naval/Up to 2 million killed in decade of bombing, starvation, and political chaos.

OMAN/1970/Command operation/U.S. directs Iranian marine invasion.

LAOS/1971-73/Command operation, bombing/U.S. directs South Vietnamese invasion; "carpet-bombs" countryside.

SOUTH DAKOTA/1973/Command operation/Army directs Wounded Knee siege of Lakotas.

MIDEAST/1973/Nuclear threat/World-wide alert during Mideast War.

CHILE/1973/Command operation/CIA-backed coup ousts elected Marxist president.

CAMBODIA/1975/Troops, bombing/Gas captured ship, 28 die in copter crash.

ANGOLA/1976-92/Command operation/CIA assists South African-backed rebels.

IRAN/1980/Troops, nuclear threat, aborted bombing/Raid to rescue Embassy hostages; 8 troops die in copter-plane crash. Soviets warned not to get involved in revolution.

LIBYA/1981/Naval jets/Two Libyan jets shot down in maneuvers.

EL SALVADOR/1981-92/Command operation, troops/Advisors, overflights aid anti-rebel war, soldiers briefly involved in hostage clash.

NICARAGUA/1981-90/Command operation, naval/CIA directs exile (Contra) invasions, plants harbor mines against revolution.

HONDURAS/1982-90/Troops/Maneuvers help build bases near borders.

LEBANON/1982-84/Naval, bombing, troops/Marines expel PLO and back Phalangists, Navy bombs and shells Muslim positions.

GRENADA/1983-84/Troops, bombing/Invasion four years after revolution.

LIBYA/1986/Bombing, naval/Air strikes in attempt to topple nationalist government.

BOLIVIA/1987/Troops/Army assists raids on cocaine region.

IRAN/1987-88/Naval, bombing/U.S. intervenes on side of Iraq in war.

LIBYA/1989/Naval jets/Two Libyan jets shot down.

VIRGIN ISLANDS/1989/Troops/St. Croix Black unrest after storm.

PHILIPPINES/1989/Jets/Air cover provided for government against coup.

PANAMA/1989-?/Troops, bombing/Nationalist government ousted by 27,000 soldiers, leaders arrested, 2000+ killed.

LIBERIA/1990/Troops/Foreigners evacuated during civil war.

SAUDI ARABIA/1990-91/Troops, jets/Iraq countered after invading Kuwait. 540,000 troops also stationed in Oman, Qatar, Bahrain, UAE, Israel.

KUWAIT/1991/Naval, bombing, troops/Kuwait royal family returned to throne.

IRAQ/1990-?/Bombing, troops, naval/Blockade of Iraqi and Jordanian ports, air strikes; 200,000+ killed in invasion of Iraq and Kuwait; no-fly zone over Kurdish north, Shiite south, large-scale destruction of Iraqi military.

LOS ANGELES/1992/Troops/Army, Marines deployed against anti-police uprising.

SOMALIA/1992-94/Troops, naval, bombing/U.S.-led United Nations occupation during civil war; raids against one Mogadishu faction.

YUGOSLAVIA/1992-94/Naval/NATO blockade of Serbia and Montenegro.

BOSNIA/1993-?/Jets, bombing/No-fly zone patrolled in civil war; downed jets, bombed Serbs.

HAITI/1994-?/Troops, naval/Blockade against military government; troops restore President Aristide to office three years after coup.

List compiled by Zoltan Grossman, 731 State St., Madison WI 53703; phone: (608) 246-2256; e-mail: mtn@igc.apc.org; website: http:// ns1.netphoria.com/wort/shows apa.html#zoltan.

INDEX

BOOKS AND VIDEOS
to help organize opposition to sanctions on Iraq

CHALLENGE TO GENOCIDE: LET IRAQ LIVE

Essays and detailed reports on the devastating effects of economic sanctions on Iraq since the Gulf War. Features "Fire and Ice," a chapter on the history of the U.S. war against Iraq by former U.S. Attorney General Ramsey Clark. Also included are personal memoirs from many who defied the sanctions and U.S. law by taking medicines to Baghdad as part of the May 1998 Iraq Sanctions Challenge. Contributors include Ramsey Clark, Bishop Thomas Gumbleton, Rania Masri, Sara Flounders, Ahmed El-Sherif, Brian Becker, Barbara Nimri Aziz, Kathy Kelly, Monica Moorehead, and Manzoor Ghori. International Action Center, 1998, 264 pp., photos, index, resource lists. $12.95

GENOCIDE BY SANCTIONS
1998 Video

Excellent for libraries, schools, and community groups and for cable-access television programs. This powerful new video documents on a day-to-day, human level how sanctions kill. An important tool in the educational and humanitarian Medicine for Iraq campaign to collect medicine while educating people so U.S. policy will be changed. VHS, 1998, 28 minutes.

$20 individuals $50 institutions

THE CHILDREN ARE DYING
THE IMPACT OF SANCTIONS ON IRAQ
*** New Revised 1998 Edition ***

Report of the UN Food and Agriculture Organization, supporting documents, and articles by Ramsey Clark, Ahmed Ben Bella, Tony Benn, Margarita Papandreou, and other prominent international human rights figures. The human face of those targeted by the new weapon of sanctions. The UN FAO report showed with facts and statistics that over 500,000 Iraqi children under the age of five had died as a result of U.S./UN imposed sanctions. Accompanying photos and chapters define the social implications. International Action Center, 1998, 170 pp. with resource lists, photos. $10

THE CHILDREN ARE DYING
Companion video, 1996

Includes a view of Iraq's hospitals, schools, and neighborhoods. Impact of sanctions can be seen, from destroyed water purification plants to empty pharmacy shelves, enhancing the statistics and charts of UN Food and Agriculture team studies. VHS, 1996, 28 minutes.

$20 individuals $50 institutions

METAL OF DISHONOR: DEPLETED URANIUM
HOW THE PENTAGON RADIATES SOLDIERS & CIVILIANS WITH DU WEAPONS

Learn about the criminal use of depleted uranium to poison Iraq's people and U.S. soldiers. Selections by Rosalie Bertell, Helen Caldicott, Ramsey Clark, Jay M. Gould, Michio Kaku, Manuel Pino, Anna Rondon, and others. Scientists, Gulf War veterans, leaders of environmental, anti-nuclear, anti-military and community movements discuss:

*A new generation of radioactive conventional weapons.
*The connection of depleted uranium to Gulf War Syndrome.
*The Pentagon recycling of nuclear waste—a new global threat.
*An international movement to BAN all DU weapons.

International Action Center, 260 pp. with photos & index. $12.95

METAL OF DISHONOR
Companion video.

Interviews with noted scientists, doctors, and community activists explaining dangers of radioactive DU weapons. Explores consequences of DU from mining to production, testing, and combat use. Footage from Bikini and atomic war veterans. Peoples Video Network, 45 min.

VHS $20   PAL version for Europe $35

TO ORDER:

All mail orders must be pre-paid. Bulk orders of 20 or more items available at 50% off cover price.

Include $4 U.S. shipping and handling for first item, $1 each additional item. International shipping $10 for first item, $2 each additional item.

Send check or money order to: International Action Center, 39 W. 14th St., Rm. 206, New York, NY 10011; phone 212 633 6646.

To place individual CREDIT CARD orders (VISA & MC) or for bookstore and university invoice orders and discounts, call 800 247 6553 toll-free (24-hour service) or fax purchase order to 419 281 6883.